academic writing

how to read and write scholarly prose

academic writing

how to read and write scholarly prose

janet giltrow

broadview press

Cataloguing in Publication Data

Giltrow, Janet Lesley

Academic writing

ISBN   0-921149-62-X

1. Report writing.   2.   English language — Rhetoric.   3.   Exposition
(Rhetoric).   I.   Title

PE1408.G55 1990   808'.042   C90-093413-1

broadview press   in the US, broadview press
P.O. Box 1243   269 Portage Rd.
Peterborough, Ontario   Lewiston, NY
K9J 7H5   Canada   14092   USA

academic writing
acknowledges its sources

What follows is not a scholarly acknowledgement: in other words, it stakes no claim on the map of established knowledge. This book intends to provide students with useful information about the university writing situation, not to earn the author any territorial privileges. As a result, the acknowledgements below name only the principal sources which have contributed to this book's content, and they neglect many publications which were also influenced by those principal sources and which, in turn, refined my own understanding of them.

For its approach to the university writing situation, this book is deeply indebted to current ideas about the composing process. Not so long ago, these ideas were revolutionary, but, because they were such good ideas, they rapidly rooted themselves in pedagogy. In fact, these ideas rooted themselves so rapidly that they now seem to be indigenous elements of the compositionist landscape.

Nowadays, to exactly attribute such ideas requires a history of composition pedagogy—a history which I am not qualified to write. So I acknowledge generally rather than specifically the tradition represented by the researchers and teachers who contribute to College Composition and Communications, and College English and their disciplinary offspring. Among these offspring, though, I do mention one publication in particular whose application of the process paradigm sharpened up some of this book's sketches of the stalled writer: the articles collected by Mike Rose in *When a Writer Can't Write* (1985). In other areas, I can identify more specific sources.

My outlook on the structure of prose originated in the theory and research of Teun van Dijk (*Text and Context* 1977; *Macrostructures* 1980) and his collaborations with Walter Kintsch (*Strategies of Discourse Comprehension* 1983). When I read *Text and Context*, I found a way of orienting myself to the problem of how sentences get together to become texts, and in the ten years since my first reading of *Text and Context*, its analyses have remained the point of departure for much of my thinking.

Although van Dijk's early work has been superseded in some ways by his own later research, and by the work of the many scholars influenced by him, I can still locate my original and deepest inspiration in *Text and Context*. I recognize as well research in the American compositionist tradition which has paralleled van Dijk's work, and extended our understanding of the levels of information in text: in particular, the line of inquiry initiated by Frances Christensen's "Generative rhetoric of the paragraph" (1965), and carried on most prominently by Nold and Davis' "The discourse matrix" (1980) and Richard Coe's *Toward a Grammar of Passages* (1988).

By itself, van Dijk's work could lead to applications which risk the product-centredness that process pedagogy warns against. But it can evade these risks when it merges with text theories which suggest the ways readers and writers negotiate meaningfulness: among such theories at work in this book are Wolfgang Iser's account of indeterminacies (*The Act of Reading* 1980); de Beaugrande and Dressler's account of processing efficiencies (*Introduction to Textlinguistics* 1981); Brown and Yule's account of topic (*Discourse Analysis* 1983). And from pragmatics I have seized research and theory which focus on the role of "mutual knowledge" or "common ground" in communication: in particular, I have been influenced by Clark and Marshall's "Definite reference and mutual knowledge" (1981) and, especially, Dan Sperber and Diedre Wilson's *Relevance* (1986) and "Inference and implicature in utterance interpretation" (1986).

In my attempts to explain text-level structures, I have tried to fuse the fact of the text with the occasion of its reception: texts are the way they are because people reason the way they do. Britton, Glynn, and Smith's "Cognitive demands of processing expository text" (1985) provided the blueprint for the reader's mental desktop, which in its actual construction owes a lot to van Dijk's "macro-rules." Similarly, in advising writers on style, I have tried to evaluate stylistic choices on the basis of predictions about the reader's experience. In making these predictions, I have relied in part on Halliday and Hasan's description of cohesion (*Cohesion in English* 1976) and Halliday's account of thematization (*Introduction to Functional Grammar* 1985), and combined these and other linguistic re-searches with the cognitive implications of Britton, Glynn, and Smith's model and earlier A-I-based descriptions of text processing, such as the ATN model (Wanner and Maratos (1981), "An ATN approach to comprehension"). For my "challenge to established knowledge" about the fundamentalness of the active voice, I am indebted to Suzanne Romaine (*The Language of Children and Adolescents* 1984).

An earlier version of *Academic Writing*, in use for four years before this version's appearance, relied more heavily on heuristics than this one does. These heuristics were predictable applications of (1) Aristotelian definition; (2) Pike, Becker, and Young's tagmemics (*Rhetoric: Discovery and Change* 1978); and James Kinneavy's description of "exploratory discourse" (*A Theory of Discourse* 1971).

In the interval between the two versions of this book, I found myself reconsidering the role of heuristics in academic writing: although students often produced impressive texts for their composition class by operating a heuristic mechanism, I was sceptical about the validity of heuristics in real scholarly practice. (And some recent research suggests that the heuristic itself may impose a handicapping load on reasoning: e.g., John Sweller (1988), "Cognitive load during problem solving.")

So, in this version of *Academic Writing*, I have redesigned the heuristic component. Blending definition and tagmemic description, I have tried to position the heuristic more realistically in the midst of the reasoning by which thinkers handle data and construct them into a product they can offer to a reader. Umberto Eco's *Semiotics and the Philosophy of Language* (1984) provided important clues as to the proper positioning of this redesigned heuristic.

In reconsidering the heuristic I had developed from Kinneavy's "exploratory discourse," I found that the intervening years had shifted my point of view away from the structures Kinneavy described to the social context in which these structures arise. In particular, Clifford Geertz's *The Interpretation of Cultures* (1973), Bruno Latour and Steve Woolgar's *Laboratory Life* (1979; 1986), and research in applied linguistics [e.g., Jon Shwales' *Citation Analysis and Discourse Analysis* (1983 vol. 7 no. 1); Greg Meyers' "The pragmatics of politeness" (1989)] have contributed to my analysis and interpretation of the scholarly argument. In addition, Foucault's analysis of disciplinary formations themselves (*The Archeology of Knowledge* 1972; *Discipline and Punish* 1979) has hovered in the background of my thinking, urging me to reflect on every claim about knowledge and its expression.

Roughly, then, the sources identified above are those which have most directly informed me, always close to the heart of my reasoning. But, certainly, they should not be seen as responsible for the warping and distortions that have no doubt occurred as I forced these sources into alliance with one another or shoved them up against my own observations of reading, writing, and scholarship.

Even closer to the heart of my reasoning are other sources: colleagues and students. While *Academic Writing* lived its life in an earlier form, its approach to writing was entertained in other teachers' classrooms. These teachers' responses were both encouraging and sobering. Especially, the thoughtful advice and wise commentary of Michelle Valiquette, David Stouck, and Roslyn Dixon were priceless to me. And so was what I learned from the students who visited the Simon Fraser University English Department's Writing Centre during the six years that I have worked there. Face-to-face with these writers, I learned about the details of their struggles and achievements in making sense of the academic community and its intricate ways of communicating with itself.

CONTENTS

INTRODUCTION

0.1 The goals of **Academic Writing**

Academic Writing is designed to help you do the writing assignments associated with your university or college studies. Because so much of academic writing is based on reading, this book concentrates on the processes by which you turn your reading into writing. Not all writing, of course, is reading-based. Writing often comes about from firsthand experience, or from the need to express your convictions or feelings, or from the need to direct other people's actions and attitudes. Other composition textbooks are available to help you with these other kinds of expression. *Academic Writing* is specifically concerned with helping you do writing tasks that depend on written sources of information presented in academic settings.

But this is not to say that what you learn from *Academic Writing* will not help you in other writing situations. On the contrary, what you learn about the structures of prose, about readers' needs, about clarity and coherence, will be pertinent in many other writing tasks that you will face in other areas of your life. Your experience with the assignments and activities in *Academic Writing* will prepare you to write more confidently and convincingly in any situation.

Academic Writing explores the kind of writing and reading that goes on in universities. It is designed for students who want to improve their abilitiy to express complex ideas and intricate information; for students who feel uneasy about the capacity of their writing skills to accommodate the crowd of concepts and data they meet at university or college; and for students who have felt frustrated because their writing has seemed to be an obstacle to success rather than a vehicle for it.

The course of studies presented in this book is not easy—because, while academic writing is certainly do-able, it isn't exactly easy. In learning about scholarly prose, you will be introduced to some complicated principles that inform serious writing. And the readings on which you base your writing will be a long way from informal descriptions of someone's summer holidays. And the assignments you will be doing will be more onerous that a description of your pet. Over-simplified accounts of how prose works, or readings about holidays and writings about pets would not prepare you for the kind of exertion entailed in academic writing.

0.2 Becoming familiar with the structure of academic prose

Academic Writing presents ideas about the structure of prose. Some of these ideas originate in classical times and have stood the test of centuries. Other ideas come from current theory about and research into the way writers and readers work. I offer you these ideas to help you master your university reading and writing assignments: on the one hand, you will be better able to manage the difficult readings you will face in your studies; on the other hand, you will be better able to express in writing the complicated concepts and information you have learned and the ideas you have developed.

The first four chapters concentrate on the way writers of scholarly prose organize proof and develop topics. As you work through these chapters, you will write summaries of assigned readings. The summarizing activity will give you close-up experience of the structure of proof and topic in prose at the same time as it gives you practice in putting your reading to use in your own writing.

To provide you with ways of organizing the results of your reading and research, the next four chapters present types of argument characteristic of scholarly prose. One type of argument isolates a phenomenon—*retirement*, for example—through definition and description and then re-connects the phenomenon with the world-at-large. The second type of argument challenges a common assumption, thereby constructing a revised picture of reality. Each of these modes of argument can structure a whole essay, helping you to manage the results of your research. The units that introduce these typical forms of argument help you do something with what you've found out from your reading.

The last chapter of the book offers advice on making oral presentations and writing examinations. It outlines some differences between these two uses of language and the use of language in the formal essay.

0.3 Getting to know the academic reader

Throughout these chapters, *Academic Writing* will be sketching a portrait of the academic reader. Some characteristics of this reader are common to all readers: readers' expectations about coherence and relevance, for example; readers' limited short-term memory capacity, for another example. The portrait will include these features, and *Academic Writing* will suggest techniques which will help you satisfy readers.

But academic readers have some characteristics they don't share with all readers. Academic readers have, for example, certain ideas about what constitutes a proper introduction or conclusion. And they have, for another example, some rather precise ideas about documentation: they like to see footnotes and bibliographies or their equivalent.

Academic Writing will introduce you to these readers and to the values of the academic community as they are revealed in the styles and practices of scholarly prose. You could say that *Academic Writing* lets you set out to do field research, stationing yourself among the artefacts of the academic micro-culture, helping you make inferences about the attitudes and beliefs of that culture.

0.4 Getting to know yourself as a writer

Academic Writing will try to make you familiar with the territory of scholarly prose, so you can feel more at home as you make your way through that territory. But *Academic Writing* will also try to help you discover that the scholarly product is the result of a variety of reading/reasoning/writing processes. Long before the reader steps into the picture to get hold of the text, the academic writer reads, reasons, and speculates; starts, stops, erases false starts; develops, reduces, re-orders good starts; goes back to the beginning and reads, reasons, and speculates some more. Experienced writers know about themselves and the way they typically go through these stages. From this self-knowledge, they know what they can expect of themselves. They get the confidence to push on—or relax—when the going gets tough; the confidence to start all over again when their own judgement tells them things will only get worse if they continue with things as they are; the confidence to know when it's time to call the reader in. I hope you will get this kind of confidence from *Academic Writing*. This textbook doesn't tell you exactly how to conduct yourself; that would be, in my view, too great an intervention in the private space of composing. But this book will give you experience of a wide variety of processes and activities that contribute to a final product. From these experiences, you can learn about your own writing behavior—learn, for example, that you have a real knack for looking at a draft and discovering opportunities for emphatic connectives that clarify your message not only for your reader but for you, too; learn that you do your most constructive thinking in the planning stages—or, alternatively, that it's not until you start writing sentences that you discover the connections between your ideas; learn that your brain works best when you adopt a constructive or critical attitude early in your reading/research, writing brief commentaries on the material you're reading as you read. From the reading and writing experiences offered in this book, you can make a self-portrait—a picture of yourself as a writer. That self-portrait will help you manage your own writing behavior efficiently.

0.5 Writing across academic disciplines

This book offers you samples of academic prose. These writings have been selected with the real conditions of scholarly writing in mind: at university or college, you have to read academic prose, and you have to produce writing that at least partly follows the academic style. The selections in this book are not all what you'd call easy reading. You may even dislike some of them: you may say that they are too complicated, too difficult and obscure. You may even suspect that they are élitist in their complexity, shunning the ordinary reader, inviting only specialists with peculiar tastes.

In fact, these features—complexity and obscurity that can seem élitist—are genuine characteristics of academic writing. At first, they can be off-putting. But most students eventually get used to the scholarly style: either they resign themselves to this style, and put up with it, or they come to see it as a legitimate offspring of scholarly practice and scholarly reasoning.

So you can expect to see some complexity and some aloof forms of expression. Take heart in the fact that this book is designed to help you master complexity and get used to aloofness. You can also expect to see, within what we generally call "scholarly style," a group of sub-styles, or sub-sets of scholarly style; different disciplines value slightly different forms of expression, different ways of presenting an argument. Moreover, each discipline has its own preoccupations— its own themes, major assumptions, current trends. This book attempts to put you in contact with scholarly styles and preoccupations across the disciplines. At the same time as it introduces you to all-purpose principles that should work in any academic writing situation, it exposes you to reasoning and argument specific to certain areas of scholarly activity. In this book you will be asked to work with concepts from a wide range of subjects: portrait art, health-care architecture, Japanese retirement, education in seventeenth-century France, land-use economics, civil dissent, and many other topics. You may feel like resisting some of these topics.

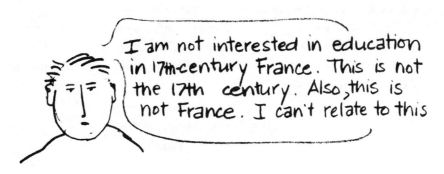

Try to overcome this resistance. It may very well be that you can't "relate" on the level of firsthand, personal experience. But one of the features of academic reading and writing is its appeal to intellectual experience and broad inquiry beyond our own backyards. If you try to answer this appeal openly and without prejudice, you may find—paradoxically—that it's finally your own backyard that you've come to know better.

0.6 Finding out that academic writing is feasible

Early on in your university or college career, you may discover that some published academic writing is not very good: it's stiff, stilted, stuffy; it's more complicated that it needs to be. From this discovery, you can learn that many academics are not gifted writers. They may be gifted researchers, thinkers, and teachers—but they are not gifted writers. Yet they nevertheless manage to communicate their ideas and their findings to their colleagues. This communication is possible because, over time, academic disciplines have developed *conventions*—standard, widely accepted, recognized ways of expression—which contribute to communicative efficiency. These conventions make things easier for both readers and writers: they select and organize information in practical ways for delivery to readers; they guide the writer in practical ways, directing him in his composing decisions. With these conventions in hand, the writer doesn't have to wait to be inspired with a shining vision of his article or paper; and he doesn't have to abandon his academic career just because he has no literary genius. Anyone capable of the reasoning associated with academic courses can do academic writing.

The best academic writing, of course, is not stuffy, stilted, and stiff, and it's not unnecessarily complicated. This book will show you ways of expression which enable you to address your reader clearly and directly, without needless and obscuring complications. But you should keep in mind nevertheless that the scholarly style designed itself not to be used by literary geniuses, but to be used by ordinary people like us—ordinary workers in the academic community.

CHAPTER ONE

summarizing what you've read
(part 1)

1.1 The qualities of summary

Summarizing something you have read may seem like a humble activity—neither a very creative thing to do nor one where you can show your independent thinking. And it's true that summary is one of the most straightforward connections between reading and writing: you read, and then you report—*accurately and economically*—what you have read. The summary repeats someone else's ideas in a shorter form.

But summary deserves respect because those goals of *accuracy* and *economy* are important. Your readers will appreciate writing that achieves them.

- The *accuracy* of your summary is a sign that you have learned from your reading, and that's an accomplishment.

    Research in reading comprehension shows that, when subjects have trouble recalling the contents of a passage they have read, they resort to previous knowledge or habitual beliefs or prejudices to fill in the gaps. As a result, they produce inaccurate summaries. These inaccurate summaries based on habitual notions show that the readers are really back where they started—no further ahead for having done some reading. Your aims are different: you want your university reading to help you move forward. An accurate summary is a sign that you are getting somewhere.

- The goal of *economy* is not to be despised either. For one thing, it's not easy to achieve. The original writer had ten times or maybe twenty times as much space to explain himself. You have only the small space of your summary to get the same points across. Summaries can be hard work, and they can take longer to produce than you'd expect.

But economy is important not just because it's a challenge. It's also essential to the *usefulness* of your reading and writing. The economy of your summary—its brevity and clarity—enables you to *put your reading to use*. If, in order to report expert views, you have to ramble on and on, long-windedly reproducing your reading, then your own argument will be engulfed. Your own work, the ideas you make from your reading, will be smothered rather than supported and strengthened. You'll end up submitting a 15- page paper when an eight-page paper was assigned. And what your reader will remember is your essay's bulky, droning repetition of what other writers say.

Instead, you want a summary that is compact and useful. You want summary that is productive, summary that substantiates your argument and enables you to put your reading to use.

This chapter and the next one focus on summarizing activities. They examine typical structures of the kind of reading you will put to use in your own writing. Especially, these chapters examine levels of prose: the arrangement of ideas from the *highest* level of generality to the *lowest* level of specificity. Insight into this arrangement will give you more control over the summarizing activity. You'll have means of judging what material from the original text can be left out and what must be retained for the summary to be true, concise, and useful.

1.2 Where have I heard this before? You and the reader of your summary

One of the most paralyzing circumstances of university writing is the fact that your readers are also your instructors. They not only mark the essay, but also assign the reading preliminary to it. And, worse, they make a career of giving lectures and seminars on the subject, and writing about it. They've heard it all before, haven't they?

It's true that your readers "already know" much of what you're saying. Your economics instructor knows all about the Canadian banking system; your philosophy teacher is thoroughly familiar with British Idealism. And it's certainly true that your readers' greater familiarity with the subject makes them difficult readers to address. Your essay might seem to you about as useful and pertinent as last week's newspaper.

Nevertheless, we know that instructors can and do respond cheerfully and positively to many essays on subjects with which they are very familiar.

Instructors find some essays lively and interesting; they find others lacklustre and uninteresting. Yet both types of essays rely on the same readings and sources; both draw heavily on established ideas and information. What distinguishes the successful essay from the lacklustre one? A big part of the distinction lies in the way the essay-writer handles his sources of information: the way he summarizes.

1.3 You and your sources

Your instructor asks you to write about economic nationalism in Canada, or about class consciousness among turn-of-the-century British workers. Moreover, she tells you what sources to consult. Clearly, summary will have to be a major part of your paper. You will have to repeat what someone else has said. The most extreme form of this repetition is *copying.* And probably the most conspicous instances of this copying appear early in our schooling: in the elementary-school classroom. Perhaps you remember being asked to do a "report" on South America, or the animals of Africa. You didn't know anything about either of these subjects. So you consulted the encylopedia. And you copied out parts of it—but only parts, because you couldn't fit a 10,000-word encyclopedia article into your ten-page report.

Jason writes a report on South America

The copied parts sounded very good. After all, they were written by grown-up experts. But, put together in this new document, they made a kind of gibberish. On one page you would be discussing, very learnedly, the productive organization of an interior region of Bolivia, while the next page would fling the reader into a surprisingly detailed description of the topography of Tierra del Fuego. Next, maybe even on the same page, you might offer a neatly copied account of a harvest festival. Although the ten-page "report" was accurate (after all, it was copied, word-for-word, from authoritative sources), and it was economical (it was shorter than the encyclopedia), it was not useful. It didn't really make sense.

Writing reports on South America or on African animals was an innocent but childish activity, and it was liable to produce a childish text, despite the authority and elegance of the copied passages. But the same kind of gibberish can show up in university essays. *Copying* is not only likely to bore your readers (they've read this before), but also likely to create an incoherent text, full of odd leaps and jumps.

1.4 Your own words

From time to time in your schooling, you've probably been told to "use your own words" to express information you have gathered from written sources. Sometimes your teacher may have told you this so he could distinguish between rote learning and real understanding; or maybe he wanted to prevent that terrible *copying*. But, whatever its motivation, this turns out to have been very good advice, supported by experts' understanding of how language works.

Sometimes, when you are immersed in the reasoning of another writer's argument, copying may seem a very practical solution to the problems presented by the process of putting reading to use. The original author's sentences which express the point so well are very tempting: why not just repeat them?

There's a good reason for not just repeating them. They are convincing and impressive *in context*, supported, explained, modified and extended by all the material that surrounds them. *Out of context*, they are not nearly so powerful. Figure (1) shows important sentences (******) occurring in the context of supporting ideas (~ ~ ~ ~ ~ ~). The arrow (—>) yields a summary that copies the important ideas.

Figure (1)

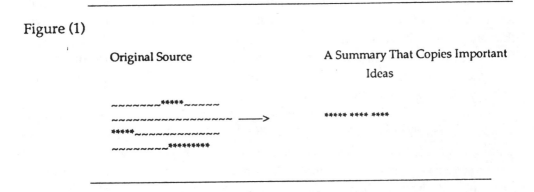

You have read all the ~ ~ ~ ~ ~ ~ ~. But your reader doesn't have that material in mind. Consequently, the ***** nuggets you've saved are stranded. Like a marooned sailor, they can seem quite eccentric. Just as a Grade-Six explanation of the topography of Tierra del Fuego sent a sudden and erratic message to the reader, who had no sense of the context it came from, these stranded sentences can be odd things, difficult to understand.

It's very important to get a sense of this situation from the reader's point of view. So we're going to set ourselves up as readers of copied-out points. Sample (2), below, presents key sentences, just about word-for-word, from a 700-word passage which analyzes the nature of TV violence. (The original passage occurs in *Reading Television*, by John Fiske and John Hartley; it appears as a whole in Chapter 2, where it is the basis for a summary exercise.) Sample (2) copies the key sentences in the order in which they appear; they occur at roughly equivalent intervals in the original passage. *In context*, they express important ideas—or parts of important ideas—that Fiske and Hartley want to get across. But *out of context* they are uncooperative entities, making a disjointed, very difficult text. As readers of Sample (2), we face a text that only copies important points from the original:

(2) Violent figures are the most masculine, and the victims the least masculine and the oldest. The television message system is a system of "cultural indicators" by which the value structure of society is symbolically represented. Violence on television is not a direct representlation of real-life violence. The criminal is distinguished from the hero primarily by his efficiency and his social group.

The copying has taken Fiske and Harley's words out of their habitat—out of the environment of repetition, explanation, examples, and logical connectives that made them intelligible and convincing to the reader of the whole passage. Stranded outside this habitat, the sentences are confusing rather than convincing: what's the connection between age and value structure? Between age and efficiency? Between efficiency and TV not being "real"?

As a copier, the writer/summarizer may still have that connective, supportive material in mind, so he may not notice the discontinuities and gaps in what he offers his reader. But, as readers, we do notice the gaps. At best, we just skim over the passage as not worth the trouble. At worst, we strongly object to its lurching from one notion to another. (In Chapter 2, we do a better job of summarizing the original, taking account of our readers' needs.)

We know, then, that the copying respresented by Figure (1) doesn't work. In carrying forward material from another source, using *your own words* instead of the words you've highlighted or underlined in the original is much more than a politeness to please your teachers. It's actually a matter of making yourself intelligible to your readers, even when you are summarizing someone else's ideas. Summary makes *something new*. The material from the original text takes on a *new form to fit a new context*. Whereas copying can be represented by Figure (1), Figure (3) schematizes the activity of summary. The material yielded by the arrow

(—>) is no longer just a repetition (****) of important sentences (****), but a new form (●●●●) of the original ideas.

Figure (3)

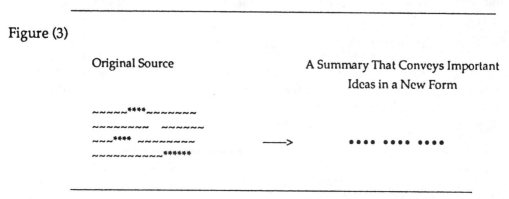

Original Source

A Summary That Conveys Important Ideas in a New Form

The rest of this chapter introduces some ideas about prose structure that will help you make accurate, readable summaries. The next chapter offers a formal method for summary that will help you avoid copying and help you find your own words.

1.5 Up and down: levels in prose

To summarize effectively, you have to recover and express the essential elements of what you've read, and get rid of the rest. So it's comforting to know that coherent texts (a category to which your university reading normally belongs) are already structured according to principles that present some information as dominant and other material as subordinate. Some material occurs at a conceptually higher level, dominating or generalizing from lower level material.

This system of levels in prose is a crucial condition of reading and writing, and we will be pursuing it relentlessly in later chapters. In the meantime, we will approach it as a characteristic of prose that is important in thinking about summary. If you can recognize the levels of information in your reading, and if you can discover the level of expression that dominates, you will have found a guide to making a summary. You will have found a means of conserving essential material and trimming away less essential material, producing a summary that is both accurate and economical. Sample (2), which only copied from the TV violence passage, shows that this conserving and trimming is not simply a matter of keeping some things intact and throwing away other things. Instead, it's a matter of *construction*: making a text that conserves essentials in a new form.

1.5.1 What the levels look like

To put it simply, the highest level is the *most general*. It accommodates all the lower levels. Here is a brief passage with prominent levels of generalization. It begins at a high level of generality—ideas about individuals and institutions—and descends to a much lower level: reference to a particular clinic in London.

(4) Institutional buildings rise in people's neighbourhoods, marking the connection between public and private domains. The architecture of community hospitals expresses institutional health strategies addressed to individual patients. Like a family caring for its members, the hospital cares for members of the community. But the scale of care is not domestic and private, like family care, but civic and public. This conflict in scale can disorient and alienate the patient, confusing or coercing him, adding to his distress. The hospital building itself focusses these conflicts in scale at the interface between public presence and private life, and some hospital design now tries to rationalize the interface, making it readable and clear rather than confusing and imposing. At the Bethnal Green Health Centre in London, architectural design tries to harmonize institutional prominence with personal outlook.

The passage begins by introducing its "highest" concepts: the connections between *private* and *public* domains, between *individuals* and *institutions*. These highest concepts generalize what comes next: hospitals (one kind of *institution*); patients (one form that *individuals* take); conflicts of scale (one kind of *connection*) and rationalized interface (another form of *connection*). Some of these second-level generalities are further specified before the passage descends to its lowest level: conflicts of scale are narrowed to disorientation, alienation, coercion, while rationalized interfaces narrow to clarity and readability. Finally, at the lowest level of generality, the passage reaches its greatest specificity, mentioning one health-care building in particular: Bethnal Green Health Centre.

We can roughly diagram this descent through levels of generalization, constructing a picture of the up-and-down relationships among ideas and mentions:

Figure 5

connections		public presence		private life
conflicts in scale	rationalized interface	institutional buildings	people's	neighbourhoods
		hospital		patient
		Bethnal Green Health Centre		

This diagram only sketches the structure of the passage: it's not technically valid, for other analysts might have found fewer levels or more levels, or used other words to identify the levels. But constructing and examining such diagrams can give us a feel for the patterns that underlie our experience as readers, as we make our way from general claims to specific references and back again.

This passage about hospitals and patients might have extended itself even further through the range of generalization. The version which follows rises one level higher at the beginning, and descends to even more specificity at the end, mentioning site dimensions, holes in the wall, waiting rooms, and examination rooms.

(6)   In the landscapes of modern urban communities, public systems connect with private lives; individual roles intersect civic institutions. Institutional buildings rise in people's neighbourhoods, marking the connection between public and private domains. A school's facade, for example, expresses large-scale social priorities; its interior interprets those priorities in light of the needs of individual students. Similarly, the community hospital's architecture expresses institutional health strategies addressed to the individual patient. Like a family caring for its members, the hospital cares for members of the community. But the scale of care is not domestic and private, like family care, but civic and public. This conflict in scale can disorient and alienate the patient, confusing or coercing him, adding to his distress. The hospital building itself focusses these conflicts in scale at the interface between public presence and private life, and some hospital design now tries to rationalize the interface, making it readable and clear rather than confusing and imposing. At the Bethnal Green Health Centre in London, architectural design seeks to harmonize institutional prominence with personal outlook. The Centre's site itself blends domestic and public scale: while the site's depth is 14 m — only a

domestic expanse—its length is 60 m, and the building spans this frontage with civic mass. To orient visitors to the arrangement of the building, circular holes in wing walls allow people to approach from the rear (actually on the main street) and see through to the building's front. In effect, the holes say, "Come around to the other side and you'll see the main entrance." Inside, three separate waiting rooms provide immediate and recognizable access to nurses' and specialists' examination rooms. From the waiting room, clients can see where they will be going, and, when they emerge from their consultation, they can quickly orient themselves and recognize the route back to the waiting room and exit.

A revision of the first diagram illustrates the reader's encounter with this stretched-out range of generality.

Figure (7)

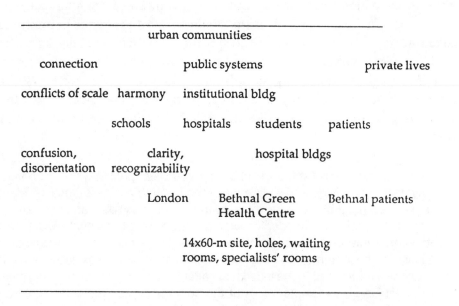

This diagram represents the passage's development: the system of assertions which support and develop one another. When your instructors ask that you "develop" your ideas further, they are reacting to the absence of such a pattern of levels in your writing. Sometimes they will be looking for more specific assertions to support high-level claims; other times they will be looking for more high-level claims to explain specific mentions.

Moreover, this stretch across the range of generalization is characteristic of scholarly discourse. While you will rarely encounter it in the compact form of Sample (6), which is an example made up from a series of articles, you will often find yourself reading in the midst of this kind of movement through levels of generality.

Samples (5) and (6) are about how people feel when they go to a clinic or hospital—how a sick person feels about approaching a reception desk in a public building full of corridors and medical technology. There are many ways to talk about feelings like that: a cartoon's black humour might capture feelings of anxiety and alienation; a personal conversation might express the patient's distress or confusion; a letter to the editor might complain about the way patients are treated. Each of these modes has its own characteristics, and so does the scholarly mode have its own characteristics. Especially, the scholarly mode stretches across the range of generalization, reaching high levels of conceptualization (concepts of public and private) and touching low levels of specificity (the position of a particular clinic's waiting rooms in relation to its examination rooms). This stretching is something you will get used to in your university reading, and something you will develop in your own university writing. To help you acclimatize yourself to these conditions, we'll reflect on what this system of levels means to us as *readers*, and then as *writers* of summary.

1.5.2 Reading through the levels

Inspecting Figure (7), we notice that the descent in the centre of the diagram—from *urban communities* through *public systems* to *specialists' rooms* and *waiting rooms*—is deeper than elsewhere, dropping through seven levels of generality. If we diagram the same information another way, we can get an idea of what such a descent feels like in the reading process. Taking into account the reading process, where things happen one after another, this diagram will show us making our way through the text, going from one level the next.

Figure (8) shows what we could call the *landscape* or *topography* of the text, revealing the reader's experience of its ups and downs. Figure (8) traces the *reader's path*. While the first kind of diagram showed the conceptual organization of the text as it exists *all at once*, the topography diagram shows that conceptual organization as the reader experiences it *over time*.

Figure (8)

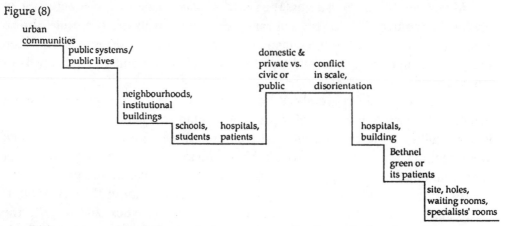

This topography of the text gives us some feeling of what happens to us as readers as we travel through a text's landscape. A fully developed passage will lead us up and down through several levels. And if we are going to get the whole picture, we're certainly better off if we have some sense of where we are—at a summit, deep in a valley, lingering briefly on a plateau—as we make our way through our reading.

1.5.3 Summarizing the levels

Both kinds of diagram help us understand what happens to us as readers; both help us understand the kind of work the text makes us do. But both kinds of diagram also help us understand our role as summarizers. Figure (7) shows how material *spreads* at the bottom, at the lowest levels of generalization. Figure (8) shows us that getting down to and up from the lower levels is *time-consuming*. Summary, in its brevity, cannot accommodate this spreading, time-consuming material. To summarize, we will have to get rid of *waiting rooms, site dimensions*, and *holes* in the wall. Common sense will support what the diagrams tell us: a reader who came away from the health-care architecture passage saying that the crucial issue was about going from the waiting room to the examination room would have missed the point.

Yet so too would the reader who clung only to the highest level of generality have missed the point. The reader who claimed that the gist of the passage was the notion that there are connections in urban landscapes would not be summarizing accurately. That reader would have missed the point *this* passage makes about connections in the urban landscape. There are many things somebody could say about public and private meeting points in the urban scene: the reader who got the point would be able to say what *this* writer claimed about such connections and meeting points. Since we can't simply repeat all the assertions this writer makes about urban connections (we would not achieve summary's goal of *economy*), we have to *reconstruct* this material into a *new form*, using our own words.

Exercise

Write one sentence of 50-60 words which summarizes passage (6). Compose your sentence in such a way as to answer this kind of question:

A sample one-sentence summary appears at the end of this chapter, along with an explanation of its features and their relationship to the original.

1.5.4 Selecting to communicate: between triviality and platitude

The concept of levels of generality tells us something about the selective nature of communication. At the lowest and most specific level, we could present *total information*: for example, an exhaustive description of every corridor, doorway, and examination room in the Bethnal Green hospital. Or a complete report of every visit made by every patient. But those kinds of description would not communicate. Readers can't tolerate such completeness, except under very rare and specialized circumstances. When these rare conditions are not in effect, expression that dwells endlessly on specifics run the risk of being *trivial*.

Working at the other end of the scale from triviality, we could go higher than the general claim that "[in] the landscapes of modern urban communities, public systems connect with private lives." We could top that by saying, "In life there are many connections"—an idea with which few people would disagree. But this kind of saying does not communicate information. Just as a description of every corridor and doorway and examination room in Bethnal Green can't get through to the reader, neither can the big, floppy claim about connections in life. It's a *platitude*.

Platitudes express what everybody already "knows"—or at least would not bother to actively dispute. Platitudes have no information value, although they can stimulate feelings of unanimity and rapport among members of social groups seeking to reaffirm their connections with one another. A participant in an informal conversation, for example, might express his acceptance of another speaker's anecdote by uttering a platitude: "Well, isn't life funny!" Or a valedictory speaker may utter platitudes about the future to arouse confidence-inspiring feelings of connectedness among members of the audience. We have all encountered conversationalists who resort too much to platitude and triviality.

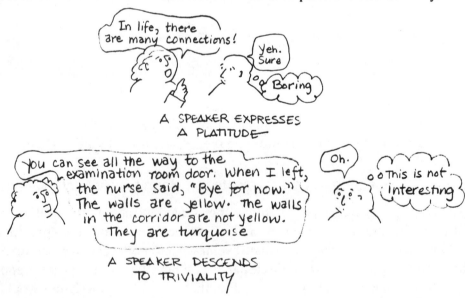

In life, there are many connections!

Yeh. Sure

Boring

A SPEAKER EXPRESSES A PLATITUDE

You can see all the way to the examination room door. When I left, the nurse said, "Bye for now." The walls are yellow. The walls in the corridor are not yellow. They are turquoise

Oh.

This is not interesting

A SPEAKER DESCENDS TO TRIVIALITY

Academic writers avoid both platitudes and triviality. To communicate, they work in the range between these two extremes of *no information* (platitudes) and *total information* (triviality). Effective scholarly writing ranges between these extremes, moving up and down through the levels of generality.

In writing summary, the challenge is to preserve the logic of the original text's ups and downs even when you don't have room to represent its full range of levels of generality.

Exercise

The following five passages give you an opportunity to practise investigating the levels of prose and to practise writing summaries. For each passage,

1. construct a diagram like those in Figures (5) and (7), to show the arrangement of concepts from the highest level of generality to the lowest level.
2. construct a map like that in Figure (8), to show the reader's experience of the levels of generality.
3. write a summary.

On the correctness of diagrams

Sketching the diagrams and maps is only a means of discovering certain characteristics of writing which we can benefit from thinking about from time to time. Practice in the diagramming and mapping techniques is not meant to train you as analysts, but only to make you aware of the sources of your experience as a reader. At the same time as you become more aware of your own reading experience, you can become more aware of the structure of information in written texts. This will help you *locate the essentials* that are the target of your own writing and summarizing.

Now, your trees and maps may differ from those your classmates construct. Maybe they did a better job; maybe you did a better job, noticing things they missed. But it's also very possible that the differences come from differences in your reading experiences. There's no reason to try to erase these differences as long as you can justify them with evidence from the original.

You will find Passage (a) the easiest: it's one I wrote to demonstrate a very orderly case of the descent from high-level concepts to low-level details. (A possible tree and map for this passage appear at the end of the chapter.) The other passages come from published sources, mainly scholarly, and you may find them a little more difficult.

On the length of summaries

There is no single correct ratio between original and summary. In your reading, you may come across a single sentence that summarizes a whole book. Or, in your own writing tasks, you might fulfill an assignment by using 1000 words to summarize a 15-page article.

In this exercise, try to reduce the passages to 15%-25% of their original length.

Passage (a) "City"

The city-dweller's environment is not a fixed or static setting, and our own urban neighbourhoods are changing. In areas of small shops some merchants are increasingly focussing on particular socio- economic markets, while others are abandoning storefront merchandising in favour of relocation to large malls that aim at broader market segments. Narrowed market focus has shown up in northside districts of the City which have witnessed a notable tendency among merchants to specialize in goods addressing specific high-income groups. Members of these groups are attracted by imported kitchenware, exotic foods, and costly footware and athletic equipment. One block in Harrisdale, for example, offers the upper middle-class consumer espresso machines from "Mr. Gourmet," rabbit paté at "Le Fromage," and rain-proof jogging suits that "breathe" from "Brinkley's." In central districts, merchants specializing in apparel and foods appealing to ethnic groups have established themselves. In the meantime, residential areas traditionally devoted to single-family dwellings on large lots are experiencing economic and zoning pressure to re-develop to higher density. The spacious front and back yards that have characterized our city neighbourhoods are vanishing and, with them, conventional notions of privacy and property.

Passage (b) "Educational television"

Some of the best educational television, and indeed some of the best general television, has altered some of our concepts of teaching and learning. There is, as we noted, a good deal of transmitted teaching and demonstration. But there are many examples of what can best be called educational practice: the language "lesson" which is simply half an hour in a foreign town, listening to people speak while we watch them doing things and meeting each other, in a whole social context; the natural history or geography "lesson" which is in effect a televisual visit to some place where we can see as if for ourselves; the presentation of some other way of life, or some work process, or some social condition. These kinds of practice, which television makes possible by its range and scope, are directly related to some of the most encouraging methods within formal education itself, trying to experience a process rather than being taught "about" it. They do not replace other kinds of education, but they add to them, and in some cases change them qualitatively, in what is clearly an innovating way.

From Raymond Williams, *Television: Technology and Cultural Form* New York: Schocken, 1975, p. 74.

Passage (c) "Taiwan"

Although there are exceptions, the small-to-medium size, single- unit firm is so much the rule in Taiwan that when a family business becomes successful the pattern of investment is not to attempt vertical integration in order to control the marketplace, but rather is to diversify by starting a series of unrelated firms that share neither account books nor management. From a detailed survey of the 96 largest business groups (jituanqiye) in Taiwan, we find that 59% of them are owned and controlled by family groups (Zhonghua Zhengxinso 1985). Partnerships among unrelated individuals, which, as Wong Sui-lun (1985) points out, will likely turn into family-based business organizations in the next generation, account for 38%. An example of such a family-controlled business group is the Cai family enterprise, until recently the second largest private holding in Taiwan.[1] The family business included over 100 separate firms, the management of which was divided into eight groupings of unrelated businesses run by different family members, each of whom kept a separate account book (Chen 1985, pp. 13-17.)

1   The family enterprise was rocked by scandals in the early months of 1985. The scandal forced
     the family to open their books and to account for their economic success. For one of the better
     descriptions of the Cai family enterprise, see Chen (1985).

From Gary G. Hamilton and Nicole Woolsey Biggart, "Market, Culture, and Authority: A Comparative Analysis of Management and Organization in the Far East." *American Journal of Sociology.* 1988 Vol 94 Supplement S52-294.

Passage (d) "Finsbury"

Democracy...is surely to do with freedom of information, or, architecturally speaking, abut legibility of organisation, explictness of intention, in short, about the admission of causality. Finsbury Health Care Centre is saturated with such ideals. The entrance is unmistakable, surmounted by its municipal crest like a seal of guarantee — pro bono publico — and approached by a comfortable ramp that conveys you directly to reception, minimising the distance from the front door to a smiling face. The waiting area is self-evident, the lavatories at once visible but discreet. The circulation allows for easy mental mapping wherever you are in the building, so providng a simple reference system back to one's point of departure. The causal chain of interconnected decisions leads on and on, through the structure, the servicing strategy, the curtain walling, providing a sort of continuous running commentary — "This is so because this is so...." Even otherwise bare plaster is recruited to the cause, being originally adorned with murals by Gordon Cullen proclaiming such truths as "Chest Diseases are Preventable and Curable" as if to eradicate any lingering supersition that the cause of such afflictions was a divine mystery.

From John Allan (1988), "Finsbury at 50: Caring and Causality." *Architectural Record.*

Passage (e) "Vocal music"

"Humanization" was a pedagogical device which involved the development of the capacities for feeling and moral behaviour. While these capacities were ethically and aesthetically pleasing to school reformers, they were also political instruments for the development of new modes of self-regulation. The "moral" attitude which this pedagogy sought was a way of relating to others and also an ethically-founded acceptance of and affection for existing political forms. The "humanist" pedagogy contains, to a large degree, the key to the explanation of Ryerson's curricular reforms — especially his adamant opposition to that instrument of rote learning par excellence, the spelling book. The thrust of pedagogy upon curriculum is perhaps nowhere more evident than in the matter of vocal music. "All men," Ryerson quoted in his argument for teaching vocal music in all the elementary schools, "have been endowed with a susceptibility to the influence of music."[1] Vocal music was an important and intrinsically pleasing avenue to the faculties. Teaching children moral songs could displace the ribald and frivolous amusements they pursued, while turning their recreation into a means of instruction. "Music," if correctly used, could "refine and humanize the pupils." Ryerson approvingly quoted the English Privy Council Committee on Education which claimed that since the common schools of Germany had begun to teach workers to sing, "the 'degrading habits of intoxication' so common there had been much reduced."

Ryerson's humanistic and inductive pedagogy was an instrument and tactic aimed at developing the senses so they could be enlisted to make contact with human energy. Humanistic education was not a form of social control in any simple sense. It sought not to repress workers or students by feeding them doses of propaganda or ideology, but rather to develop their capacities for feeling and moral behaviour. Students were to become self-disciplining individuals who behaved not out of fear or because their experience at school had created in them certain moral forms for which they had a positive affection. In Ryerson's pedagogy, the student would have no desire to oppose the process of education and no grounds upon which to do so. Education would be intrinsically pleasing to the student and in consequence he or she would become the character sought by pedagogy. Education would produce in the population habits, dispositions and loyalties of a sort congenial to the state and to representative government. The problem of governance faced by generations of conservative educational critics would vanish: political rule would no longer by dependent upon "social control," coercion, terror, or bribery. One would be able to appeal to the "higher sentiments" of the subject formed by education; the state would rule by appeals to the emotions and intellect of the educated population.

1   Egerton Ryerson, Report on a System of Public Elementary Instruction for Upper Canada . 1847. All other quotations in the passage are also from this source.

From Bruce Curtis (1987), "Preconditions of the Canadian State: Education Reform and the Construction of a Public in Upper Canada, 1837-1846." In *The "Benevolent" State: The Growth of Welfare in Canada* , ed. Allan Muscovitch and Jim Albert. Toronto: Garamond, 57-58.

1.5.5 Styles of levels

Analyzing and summarizing the passages above will have given you a feel for how academic prose moves through the levels of generality. Perhaps you noticed as well that not all the passages made exactly the same kinds of moves. Passage (d) "Finsbury," for example, drops quite abruptly from very high conceptual levels—

democracy—to very low levels—lavatories and bare plaster. The deepest descent to specifics in Passage (c) "Taiwan" occurs in a footnote. Passage (a) "City" moves methodically lower, but also sideways, coming up with residential districts near the end, after having already descended right down to jogging suits under the concept of commercial districts. These slight differences contribute to the particular style of each passage.

Despite these differences, however, the passages nevertheless resemble one another in their routine descent through levels of generality. That resemblance constitutes one of the criteria of their shared membership in the academic genre. Other genres—that is, other types of writing—don't necessarily behave this way. Their pattern of levels—their conceptual style—can differ noticeably from those you have just investigated.

The following exercise gives you a chance to explore other possible patterns of levels: non-academic ones. Knowing about these other possibilities can improve your sense of what scholarly style is—and isn't.

Exercise

Select one short article from each of the following:
- a tabloid daily or weekly newspaper
- a more conventional daily newspaper
- a news magazine

(1) *Construct a tree diagram and a map of each article.*
(2) *Compare these diagrams to each other and to those of the "academic" passages you worked on in the previous exercise. What system of differences and similarities can you describe?*
(3) *Write a one- or two-sentence summary of each of these articles. How does this writing experience resemble or differ from your summarizing of the "academic" passages?*

1.6 A special case of summaries: stories

Some of the information in your university reading will arrive in narrative form: that is, in story form. The life of Trotsky, the events leading up to the War of 1812, the actions of the International Monetary Fund in 1982—such information presents itself according to how it occurred in time. These stories are organized chronologically: Event 1, Event 2, Event 3....

Writers sometimes find such material very difficult to summarize, and nowhere is the difficulty more severe than in literature courses. On the one hand, your instructor insists, "Don't tell me the story!" And, on the other hand, he complains that you haven't provided enough "context" or "proof" for your claims. These may seem like contradictory directions, but they're not. Both can be satisfied by accurate and economical summary.

It could be that the most likely source of difficulty in summarizing stories is the fact that narratives often don't carry those higher levels of generality which explained, for instance, the *significance* of data about a London hospital or a family business in Taiwan. With no access to higher levels of generality, we are apt to get stuck at the lower levels of happenings. We have no easy means of levering ourselves up to broader, more economical levels where details can be collapsed into briefer statements. Once we get on the track of a series of happenings, we stay on it, and the track becomes a rut. This condition seems to be a natural feature of the story-telling humans do.

The way out of the rut is to supply the higher-level concepts that the original text doesn't provide—that is, to *give names* to the story's episodes. This *naming* can turn plot summary (and other types of narrative summary) from dull writing with no end in sight into writing that's intellectually creative and useful in support of larger arguments.

1.6.1 Finding high-level names for events

Passage (9) which follows is an imitation of a common kind of beginning to a certain type of French Canadian tale. Its level of detail is a little uncharacteristic, but it will do for our present purposes. (As in most stories of this kind, there's no messing around with evocative settings and pschological inquiries into mood or character: things get off to a pretty fast start.) Next to the narrative, I have given names to its elements, generalizing its details , finding a more compact and abstract expression of them.

(9)   Ti-Jean and his mother lived in the midst of a forest, vast and dark. Their cottage was little more than a shed — its floor only earth, its walls pierced by the weather. Once each day they sat down to their bowls of thin soup, in which they dipped hard bread to soften it. Ti-Jean and his mother became ill. They suffered days and nights of wretched fever. One dawn, before the stars faded, Ti-Jean's mother died. But the boy recovered, although in a weakened condition.

ISOLATION

POVERTY

LOSS
WEAKNESS

I have condensed the 84-word fragment to four words, each of which gives a *general name* to the specific circumstances mentioned in the tale. I might have used other words instead of or in addition to the ones I chose: "misery," "affliction," or "hardship," for example. You can no doubt think of some that haven't occurred to me. This range of possibilities suggests that this stage of the summarizing process—this discovery of general names which will condense details— is not a routine, mechanical activity but, instead, one that challenges the summarizer's insight, ingenuity, and individual perceptions.

There is no one set of "right" names that will stand for this passage. The most we can say is that some names will work very well as respresentatives of the story's details: these names will be plausible and reasonable *interpretations* of the conditions and events reported in the narrative. Other names will be less effective, less convincing and useful.

1.6.2 Summarizing with the help of the high-level names

Once you've found those names, you can go on to put your reading to use, without getting stuck in the rut that makes you re-tell the whole story. Passage (10) uses the names I found for the Ti-Jean fragment, summarizing the fragment in one sentence.

(10) Ti-Jean's career begins in conditions of poverty and isolation, suddenly intensified by his own physical weakness and the loss that makes him an orphan.

The *naming* has not only economized, reducing the original substantially, but it has also made *something new*. Instead of re- telling the story, the summary has recreated the text in a new version for new purposes. And that is the goal of summary: to *make use* of your reading. The names you put to narrative episodes like the Ti-Jean one can enable you to approach serious issues efficiently, without having to drag the whole story along behind you. In this case, we might now be prepared to talk more directly about some elements of the world view suggested by Québecois Ti-Jean tales: the way the stories are generated from conditions not simply of materail deficit but social deficit as well. The one-sentence summary provides a basis for an argument about the story—an interpretation, a claim about its significance.

Exercise

Below are two more narrative fragments. One of them you may recognize: it's the beginning of "Little Thumb," a well known folk tale. The second is an excerpt from an account of conditions in Alert Bay, a small community on Vancouver Island.

Summarize each of the two fragments, reducing the original to 15%-25% of its original length. Begin by finding names which conceptualize the conditions described in the narrative. Use these high-level names to compose your summary. Both passages are narrative—that is, they are both arranged according to order of events. But you will find that they are very different kinds of narrative. The second proceeds at a much higher level of generality, and at its highest levels you may find some of the generalizing and abstracting expressions you will need in your summary.

Passage (a) "Little Thumb"

There was once upon a time, a man and his wife, fagot-makers by trade, who had seven children, all boys. The eldest was but ten years old, and the youngest only seven.

They were very poor, and their seven children incommoded them greatly, because not one of them was able to earn his bread. That which gave them yet more uneasiness was that the youngest was of a very puny constitution, and scarce ever spake a word, which made them take that for stupidity which was sign of good sense. He was very little, and when born no bigger than one's thumb, which made him be called *Little Thumb*.

The poor child bore the blame of whatsoever was done amiss in the house, and, guilty or not, was always in the wrong; he was, not withstanding, more cunning and had a far greater share of wisdom than all his brothers put together; and, if he spake little, he heard and thought the more.

There happened now to come a very bad year, and the famine was so great that these poor people resolved to rid themselves of their children. One evening, when they were all in bed, and the fagot-maker was sitting with his wife at the fire, he said to her, with his heart ready to burst with grief:

"Thou seest plainly that we are not able to keep our children, and I cannot see them starve to death before my face; I am resolved to lose them in the wood tomorrow, which may very easily be done; for, while they are busy in tying up the fagots, we may run away, and leave them, without their taking any notice."

"Ah!" cried his wife; "and canst thou thyself have the heart to take thy children out along with thee on purpose to lose them?"

In vain did her husband represent to her their extreme poverty: she would not consent to it; she was indeed poor, but she was their mother. However, having considered what a grief it would be to her to see them perish with hunger, she at last consented, and went to bed all in tears.

From *The Blue Fairy Book* (1969), ed. Andrew Lang. New York: Airmont, 232-233.

Passage (b)

The first recorded European contact with the Kwakwaka'wakw was the arrival of Captain George Vancouver in 1792, who described his visit to a village at the mouth of the Nimpkish River, located directly across Johnstone Strait from Alert Bay....

The Kwakwaka'wakw became actively involved in the fur trade during the first half of the nineteenth century and in 1849, the Hudson's Bay Company established Fort Rupert in the central Kwakwaka'wakw area. To the Kwakwaka'wakw, the new opportunities for trade and the increasing availability of European manufactured goods provided an opportunity for the elaboration of the central institution of aboriginal society: the potlatch. Potlatches became more frequent and access to, and the ability to accumulate, large amounts of European goods became a determining factor in achieving rank. During the fur trade era, such an elaboration of the potlatch did not directly conflict with the objectives of the Europeans, who were clearly interested in trade rather than settlement. Ships' logs and journals kept by traders testify to the fact that Native peoples on the Northwest Coast exercised significant control over the trade by such means as withholding furs to drive up prices, placing "advance orders" for specific trade goods, and refusing to trade unless satisfied with the good being offered in exchange.

The latter half of the nineteenth century brought with it the collapse of the European and Asian fur markets and, consequently, the decline of the fur trade. This corresponded to the advent of the Gold Rush and the beginning of intensive and permanent European settlement on the B.C. coast. These years mark the period during which basic colonial structures that continue to shape the relationship between Euro-Canadians and Native peoples came into being. On the B.C. coast, as elsewhere, the decimation of the aboriginal population by epidemic diseases brought by Europeans played a major role in establishing the foundations of this relationship. Indigenous peoples found themselves rapidly becoming minorities in their own lands, and while a certain degree of economic independence could be maintained by continuing to live off the land, social demoralization, sickness, and dependence on European medical care to cure European diseases began to take their toll.

As early as 1787 epidemics of smallpox, influenza and measles had been recorded among the Native populations of B.C. However, with more and more Indians travelling to trading forts and camping around new cities like Victoria, these contagious diseases, against which the Indians had neither natural immunity nor effective medicine, began to threaten their very existence. [In 1862, a white man with smallpox arrived in Victoria from San Francisco. The disease reached the Native camps around the city, killing many people. The survivors returned to their coastal communities, taking the disease with them. The only medical aid available was provided by missionaries.]

* * *

The first census of the Kwakwaka'wakw was conducted by John Work around 1835 and he estimated the total population to be around 10,700. Fifty years later, in 1885, this figure had dropped by approximately 72 per cent, to around 3000.

From Dara Culhane Speck (1987), *An Error in Judgement:The Politics of Medical Care in an Indian/White Community*. 70-72.

One-sentence summary of the Bethnal Green passage:

In health care, we find one of modern life's connections between the public domain and the private – a connection with potential conflicts of scale. Trends in hospital architecture suggest that these conflicts can be resolved by design that familiarizes patients with the institutional environment, arranging settings in recognizable rather than disorienting ways.

The summary takes account of the fact that "school" as institution is not a well developed point: whereas the "hospital" theme is developed right down to the details of design, schools are only mentioned as an example. This structural descent also justifies the summary's whole focus on health care and its elimination of higher level ideas about institutions and individuals in general. Bethnal Green itself, however, had to go: there wasn't room to introduce it and, at the same time, inform the reader of the point about Bethnal Green's particular characteristics.

Sample diagram and map of Passage (a) "City"

city environments

our urban neighbourhoods

areas of small shops   residential areas

merchants specialize   merchants   redevelopment
                            move to malls   pressures

high-income   ethnic   yards and privacy
target market   target market   change

espresso, rabbit,
  jogging suits

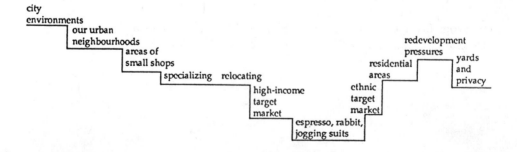

CHAPTER TWO

summarizing what you've read (part 2)

2.1 Abstract and concrete words

At the end of the last chapter, we looked at *naming* activities that can generalize circumstances or episodes, condensing them into concepts that represent or interpret their details. *Isolation*, for example, gathers up the circumstances of living in the middle of a forest and at the same time leads into the event of Ti-Jean losing his mother. *Poverty* and *weakness* were other names for occurrences and attributes reported in the story fragment. We might find other words to name and interpret the sequence of happenings and conditions in Ti-Jean's life: *deficit, powerlessness, hardship, survival.*

All these words occur at a higher level of generality than the narrative itself. And they *condense* the original. But, besides their appearance at a high level of generality, and their ability to condense text, they also share another feature: they are all abstract words. *Poverty*, for example, is an abstract word that gathers up soup, bread, earth floor and thin walls. All those latter items are represented by concrete words.

Abstract words refer to concepts, ideas, entities which could be said to have essentially mental existence: *hope, freedom, power, unfairness, change, authority* are such entities, and the words which express them are abstract words.

Concrete words refer to objects, phenomena and beings which exist physically: *bread, stapler, fire, car, daffodil, day-care worker.*

Daffodil can be touched; *unfairness* cannot. "Wait a minute," you say. "*Poverty* is an abstraction, and it can be experienced, felt." Quite true, and so can *hope* and *unfairness* be known. But their expression in language occurs in two ways, and the distinction between abstract and concrete words accounts for the differences between these two ways of expression.

> *Poverty* (not touchable) names *thin soup and hard bread* (touchable).
> *Thin soup and hard bread* demonstrate *poverty*.

> *Isolation* (not touchable) names *the cottage* (touchable) surrounded by *trees* (touchable).
> *The cottage* surrounded by *trees* demonstrates *isolation*.

The relations between abstract and concrete expression are extremely complex—much more complex than these examples suggest. They are standard examples which avoid the foggy zones between abstract and concrete reference, areas where the distinction is not quite so clear. These zones are more the business of semanticists and philosophers than they are our business, but we should make a quick reconnassance of these areas just so we're not taken by surprise when abstract and concrete references don't behave according to text book examples.

In (1), *an undergraduate* refers to an entity which exists physically.

(1) An undergraduate presented his grievance to the committee.

Presumably, this presenter existed physcially and could be touched, if necessary to verify his existence: *undergraduate* is, in (1), a concrete noun. But let's change the indefinite article to the definite article (*an* becomes *the*) and at the same time change the sentence's predicate (the verb and its aftermath):

(2) The undergraduate in Canada cannot expect to forecast accurately the character of the job market he or she will encounter at graduation.

Can we "touch" the undergraduate referred to in this sentence? I don't think so: *undergraduate* seems to be becoming a concept or an idea. But if we change *undergraduate* to *the undergraduates in Canada* we could conceivably manage to touch all the entities referred to. However, the difficult of this undertaking—verifying all those undergraduates—suggests that we can resolve, practically if not philosophically, the foggy boundaries between abstract and concrete reference by resorting to ideas about levels of generality: *undergraduates in Canada* is an expression at a high level of generality—far above *an undergraduate* before the committee.

2.2 Abstraction and generalization as products of reasoning

The examples in Section 2.1 above present abstraction and generalization as types of reference in writing or speech. But both abstraction and generalization are also products of *reasoning*. When we generalize, we reason by interpreting specifics to identify common features: having noticed similar behaviour in many individuals, we might say "Baby-boomers are the most relentless consumers the marketplace has ever seen." When we express an abstraction, we reason by giving a name to the identifed feature: "The values and behaviors of baby-boomers are characterized by *materialism*." When we write down these generalizations and abstractions, we offer our readers the products of our reasoning. When in our reading we encounter generalizations and abstractions, we are meeting the products of the writer's reasoning.

The following exercises ask you to develop abstractions from concrete data. They will help you focus on the abstraction *process*, letting you experience the fact that abstraction is not just a type of reference. Abstraction is also something we *do* when we reason. Having made yourself aware of the *process* of abstraction, you can overlook the technicalities of philosophical accounts of reference.

Exercise

1. *Write a passage which describes a room in your home, using concrete words to account for its physical components — its furniture, surfaces, dimensions, occupants, and so on. Continue your description by using abstract words to interpret the specifics you have written about. (Remember how the abstractions "poverty" and "isolation" were able to gather up and interpret details about Ti-Jean's house — walls, food, floor, trees outside.)*
2. *When you've written this passage, take a look at it. Underline the words that refer concretely; circle those that express abstractions. Consider the pattern these words make, the experience they construct for the reader. Would the passage make a different impres-*

sion on the reader if the abstract expressions preceded rather than followed the concrete expressions? If the reader encountered only abstract claims? Or only concerete description?

Exercise

Finding the general and abstract words which interpret details is important to producing a well-developed discussion relevant to the reader. But it's not that easy to find these words that express larger meanings. This exercise gives you some practice in coming up with these words and using them in sentences that generalize and interpret specifics.

Read each of the following paragraphs, and then develop a statement of these facts' general significance:

1. *What abstract word or words name the conditions described in the passage? In other words, what is the passage about?*
2. *What do we learn from the specifics in the passage? In replying to this question, write a sentence or two using the abstract word or words which answer Question 1. Use that sentence (or two) to introduce these facts to a reader.*

(a) "Baboons"

Among communities of olive baboons of the Serengeti savanna, some male individuals get the shady spots for midday rests and use the highest branches, safest from predators, as perches. Females groom these males, keeping them free of parasites. These males get the most food, and they have easy access to sexual partners. Other males in the group have what food they dig up stolen from them and have their sexual liaisons interrupted by sexually privileged males. And they are overrun with parasites.

   Adapted from Robert M. Sapolsky (1988), Lessons of the Serengeti, *The Sciences*, May/June. 38-42.

(b) "Brian"

(Brian is 14; his behaviour at school troubles staff and other students; he has become aggressive at home and at school; he sniffs glue; he is referred to a counselling clinic.)

Brian was escorted each day to and from school either by family or by social services personnel. At school he was given "jobs" in the classroom during breaks. Two evenings weekly he was taken to a voluntary youth club run by some police officers in their spare time, and at weekends he joined a church youth centre for youngsters like himself, for outings and organized games. Once a week he also went to an intermediate treatment centre, and one morning weekly he attended the clinic for group counselling and activities like painting and building models.

Adapted from Denis O'Connor (1987), Glue sniffers with special needs, *British Journal of Education*. 14, 3, 94-97.

2.3 Abstraction and the levels of generality

In prose, the levels of generality enable both writers and readers to manage complex information. And *abstract words* build a very important, very high-level platform in that system. Abstractions enable writers to name and manage otherwise unruly details, pinning them down and respresenting them compactly and meaningfully.

Abstractions cooperate with generalizations, which also condense and manage spreading details.

You have now had some direct writing experience in consciously using abstract words to *condense* detail in summary, and to *interpret* detail in your description of a room in your house, and to interpret the facts about baboons and about Brian. The passage that follows will give you direct experience of the role of abstraction in your *reading*. Without its stages of abstraction, you could say that the passage is just a description of a picture of woman in a white dress. But you'll find that, because the passage does express abstractions, it's more than that. The high-level abstractions explain what's significant or important about this picture of a woman in a white dress.

(3) "White dress"

Art can directly challenge popular ideas abut power and status. But it can also appear to reiterate and display those ideas – at the same time exposing some instabilities in popular ideologies. Royal portraiture, for example, in nineteenth-century Europe, displays notions of imperial and economic power intersecting with ideas of status expressed in images of female sexuality which conflict with measures of social standing. Portraits of the period show royal women in gorgeous, costly clothes, the latest in Parisian styles. Franz Xavier Winterhalter (1805-1873), the most popular portrait painter of his time, painted women of the court in sensuous, luxurious outfits, and ravishing poses. In his Pauline

Sandor, Princess Metternich (1860), the princess' white dress—designed by the foremost couturier of the time—slips from her side-lit shoulder into high-lighted ripples and folds. Wrapped in a diaphanous gauze shawl, the princess wears five strands of pearls at her neck, and five strands on each wrist—her jewels and skin sensually brilliant against a dark, wooded background. She is imperial—but also sexual, dressed as seductively, as some contemporary critics complained, as a café habitué occupying the lowest rung of the social ladder.

Adapted from Carol Ockman (1988), "Prince of Portraitists," *Art in America*. November, 45-59.

Abstractions—*art, ideas, ideologies, power, status, female sexuality*—explain what is significant about a particular picture of a woman in a white dress. The tree diagram which follows shows how these abstractions occupy the highest levels of generality, and how the descent to detail is managed at intermediate stages by generalization: a mention of "portraits of royal women" is more general than mention of one picture in particular, *Pauline Sandor, Princess Metternich* . In the analysis, ABSTRACT references appear in capitals, generalizations are underlined, and specific references get neither underlining nor capitals.

---

(4)   IDEAS/IDEOLOGIES

                        ART   SOCIAL STATUS, IMPERIAL POWER

              ROYAL PORTRAITURE   FEMALE SEXUALITY

              portraits of royal women   19th-century women

                  costly, stylish clothes   ravishing poses

      women of the court in gorgeous clothes

          Pauline Sandor, Princess Metternich

          highlighted white dress, 5 strands of pearls, shoulder, jewels, skin

                      café habitué

These levels—stretching from the highest abstraction about art and ideology to the lowest detail that counts the strands of pearls—cooperate with each other. The lower levels depend on the higher ones for significance, and the higher levels depend on the lower ones for proof.

2.2.1 Descending to prove

In the Princess Metternich passage, the lowest levels *develop* the ideas expressed at the highest levels. Details about Winterhalter's picture of this woman *prove* that art can express conflicts in ideologies of power and status. That's how writers prove their claims: they descend to lower levels of generality. Readers expect such descents. For example, if you have written that your living room possesses the abstract quality of *comfort* or *austerity*, your reader would want to know what made you say this: what do you have in your living room that you interpret as austere? Your reader would expect that you can show how this abstract concept satisfies concrete conditions.

In scholarly writing, abstract claims arouse the same expectations in readers—expectations, that is, that you can show how this abstract idea works at concrete levels. We could say that this demonstration constitutes *proof*. Proof in writing has a lot to do with demonstrating abstractions and generalities at a lower level, thereby making them acceptable and knowable to the reader. When your instructors ask you to prove your assertions, they are asking for this kind of descent to specifics.

2.2.2 Ascending to establish relevance

Many composition textbooks warn against the overuse of abstractions. This is good advice. Writing that stays up there at the highest levels of information is hard to read, and often unconvincing.

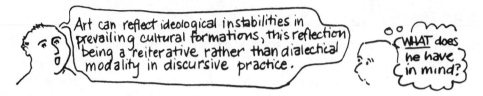

Had the "White dress" passage, for example, clung to "ideology," "art," "power," "status," and lingered in the rarefied atmosphere surrounding such notions, the reader would soon be out of breath— desperate for descent to detail, desperate for proof. The reader has to get to know your reasoning on familiar, close-up grounds.

But writing *without* abstraction can seem only local and trivial, drawing attention to things without explaining why they're worth the reader's attention.

Abstractions *interpret* details, claiming their *relevance*. Academic writing relies heavily on abstractions because it addresses issues wider than individual experience. Academic writing goes ahead on the assumptions that there are general patterns and principles that can be learned, discussed, overturned, renewed, qualified—and applied to individual cases.

To participate in these activities, you need to be able to use abstract words capable of naming the principles that interpret specifics. At the same time, however, you need to be able to manage the descent to proof and specifics that substantiates abstraction and generalization.

Exercise

1. Write a sentence expressing the gist of the "White dress" passage. Remember the lessons you learned from summarizing passages in Chapter 1: because the summary is shorter than the original, it cannot afford to retain much material from the lowest level. At the same time, however, the summary that only repeats the original's highest level will not accurately represent its focus and development.

2. Below is another passage from Raymond Williams' Televison: Technology and Cultural Form (1975). Williams has something general to say about a specific feature of televison. He says that broad principles are at stake. (One of the abstractions he uses to name the principles is "sympathetic curiosity.") Analyze this passage and identify its highs and lows. Look for abstractions, generalizations and specifics. Use a tree diagram

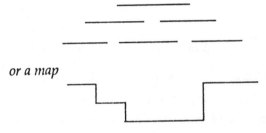

or a map

or both to help you discover the structure of Williams' argument. From your analysis, answer these questions:

(a) *What is Williams' most general and abstract claim about TV? In other words, how does he interpret facts about TV programs?*
(b) *What is Williams' lowest, most specific level of reference?*
(c) *How could Williams have been even more specific in proving his main claims about TV?*

Write a one-sentence summary of the passage.

> Certain forms have evolved within the conventions of current televison programming. In American television, with its extraordinarily short units and as it were involuntary sequences, mainly determined by commercials, there have been such interesting innovations as *Laugh In*, *Sesame Street*, and *The Electric*

Company. The comic effects of the local techniques of commercials and trailers made *Laugh In* in its early years a fascinating example of an effective form created out of a deformation. In Britain, in a different way, *Monty Python's Flying Circus* developed new kinds of visual joke out of standard television conventions, by simply altering the tone and perspective. *Sesame Street* is perhaps a different case. It has been said that it uses the techniques of commercials for education. Yet this is a doubtful description. Many of the technical possibilities for mobility of every kind were first exploited, at a popular level, for commercials, and have no necessary connection with that kind of simplified selling. Some of the best mobility of *Sesame Street* and *The Electric Company* is a way not only of responding to a highly mobile society but of responding in some depth, since the central continuities, within the fast-moving sequences, relate not only to planned teaching but to a kind of eager openness, a sympathetic curiosity, which is perhaps a truer social use of some of the intrinsic properties of television than any of the more fixed and confirming social forms.

2.3 Travelling companions in the scholarly landscape

As a *writer*, you lead your reader up and down the levels of generalization, demonstrating high-level statements with detail and explaining the general principles at work in specific phenomena. You offer evidence of particular cases, and interpret these cases for your reader, showing their relevance.

As a *reader*, you track other writers' movements up and down the ladder of generalization. Some readers do a better job of this than others. Those who are consciously or unconsciously aware of the levels of information in what they are reading are more likely to remember what they have read—and more likely to be able to summarize it accurately and economically.

Being aware of the ups and downs of what we read may be part of a natural or early-learned capacity we all have as receivers of messages. In conversation, for example, we are acutely aware of the pointlessness of utterances that linger at a very low level of reference: we get restless when a speaker just strings details together without ascending to higher levels to explain the relevance of such material. As experienced conversationalists, we are skilled judges of the organization of messages.

The materials of conversation, however, are usually more accessible and familiar that those of scholarly writing. Our day-to-day talk hovers around familiar ideas or matters of immediate, specific concern: doctors earn high incomes; you have to get your sweater from the dry cleaners. The printed versions of our informal talk—articles in newspapers and popular magazines—also treat generally familiar or immediate matters: dissent from the Opposition; someone's experience in a highway accident. When these printed versions of informal talk do introduce unfamiliar concepts (turmoil in Hyderabad) or new concepts (measures of toxicity in landfill), they do so without much explanaltion or proof. In their efforts to simplify, these sources of public information are often accused of *distortion* , and failing to tell the whole story.

Unlike the materials of conversation and the news media, the materials of scholarly writing are often quite unfamiliar to the reader. Moreover, scholarly writers, in their efforts to *not distort* through oversimplification, present long and exhaustive arguments whose movements up and down the levels of generality are very elaborate indeed, and difficult to follow.

So, as readers of scholarly material, we face two obstacles to understanding.

2.3.1 Unfamiliar territory

The content of scholarly writing is often remote from our immediate, daily interests and habitual beliefs. As readers, we are under great pressure to absorb new information and to abandon comfortingly familiar domains.

"Add 250 ml milk. Mix well."

"Unlike regular jurisdiction, summary jurisdiction ... originally indictable offence ... statutory powers ...,"

2.3.2 Precipitous terrain

At the same time as we struggle with the burden of new information, we are faced with arrangements of the levels of generality which are far more elaborate than those we encounter elsewhere. Dragging this burdensome new information with us, we have to make our way across a precipitous landscape that's rugged with hills and valleys.

If you find academic reading difficult, don't be discouraged: we all find it difficult because of its very nature. Scholarly discourse overlooks the boundaries with which we surround ourselves to make comfortable, familiar places. And the structures of scholarly prose—steep ascents to abstract, airless summits, treacherous descents to unheard-of valleys of detail from which it seems there can be no exit—are hard going for all of us. And we all feel some alarm at the idea of not only having to understand what we read but also having to be able to summarize it to put it to use in our own writing.

Be assured: this is difficult terrain, and any problems you have in traversing it are not unique. But be assured as well that are useful techniques for getting around in this territory.

2.4 Note-taking

Experienced readers have ways of coping with difficult texts and managing new ideas and information in such a way as to be able to use them in their own writing. Nearly all these techniques are forms of *note-taking*.

Note-taking functions at the boundary between reading and writing. On the one hand, it secures new information, in effect making a record of reading for re-reading. On the other hand, it *transforms* the text that has been read into a form that is eligible for a new life in a new text. With efficient note-taking, the reader is becoming a writer.

Inefficient note-taking gets stuck in record-keeping. It leaves material *untransformed*, only making way for re-reading. Such note-taking gets stranded on the airless summits, having secured only the highest level assertions without accounting for their origins and proof.

Or inefficient note-taking gets stuck in those valleys of detail without exit. Often, hard-working students make pages and pages of notes that painstakingly

record the details of their reading—details without overview. They find themselves with a massive amount of material on hand.

Or these hard-working students may do their note-taking right in the original, using a yellow marker to "highlight" important passages. Unfortunately, it's often the whole the whole text that is "highlighted" in a blaze of yellow that obliterates the distinction between levels of information and suggests that every assertion is equally important.

With "notes" like these, students are understandably frantic at the prospect of beginning to write—and they may find themselves delaying their start on the essay itself. Their notes are so bulky and comprehensive as to be unmanageable. Their notes provide no overview of the original, no perspective, no leverage. These are inefficient methods of note-taking, time-consuming and unproductive.

Efficient note-taking does give the reader/note-taker an overview of the text. It does provide a perspective on the original. And it prepares the reader to write. Efficient note-taking tracks the structure of information, revealing the ups and downs of the path of argument. It makes a map, locating the high points and situating detail. It identifies *gist* and traces *proof*. Once the argument is mapped, even the most exotic, far-fetched or unfamiliar terrain becomes a more hospitable place.

Knowing the structure of a text, you can command its content.

2.4.1 A strategy for efficient note-taking

The method of note-taking proposed here will provide you with a perspective on the structure of the original. This method may seem rather laborious and mechanical. Nevertheless, I recommend it for several reasons:

(a) It provides an *overview* of the landscape of the text. This overview will help you absorb new information, and it will help you distinguish between crucial high-level material that your summary must retain and low-level material that your summary can omit.

(b) It goes towards ensuring *accuracy*. Readers tend to respond to texts on the basis of personal and therefore idiosyncratic experience. Even capable readers are liable to find what they expect to find, and, in representing material they have read, are liable to distort information. This method prevents such distortions by forcing the reader to recognize *all* connections and emphases in the original – not just the ones the reader grasps most readily.

(c) It makes reading an *active process*. It puts readers to work, preventing them from being just bystanders or spectators. Having already warmed up during the reading process, readers are ready for the exertions of writing.

(d) It avoids the pitfalls of copying.

This strategy for note-taking is a very *self-conscious* form of reading. So it may seem artificial. However, it is only a more methodical version of what capable readers do anyway when they encounter a difficult text that they want to put to use in their own writing. They scribble in the margins; they gloss passages; they write summarizing statements and commentaries in their notebooks. They do all this to get hold of the text firmly so they can use it in their own thinking and writing.

Our reading/note-taking/summarizing will be very methodical—more laborious than real-life practices. But we undertake it in this laborious form to discover the structure of information and to learn that, whatever the difficulty of the text and the writing assignment connected with it, we have *a strategy for handling difficulty.*

2.4.2 Collapsing a passage

We'll call this reading/note-taking/summarizing strategy "collapsing" because that's what we're going to do: we're going to "collapse" a text into a portable unit that can be carried off for other occasions (your essays and writing assignments). And we're going to collapse it without destroying or disfiguring it.

Our first sample text is a five-paragraph passage from a book called *Reading Television* (1982), by John Fiske and John Hartley. The passage comes from a chapter in which the authors review the results of various "content analyses" of television—results from studies conducted as early as 1954 and from more recent studies. The overall aim of this chapter, which appears early in the book, is to show that simple quantitative surveys which "count" the incidence of certain types of televised images and episodes cannot fully explain the meaning of a sequence of TV transmissions, or of TV as a phenomenon. They argue instead for a more sophisticated approach which would account not just for the parts (and their frequency or infrequency), but also for the *relationships among the parts*. The number of white female nurses who show up on TV, for example, is not an informative figure in itself: we must know what other ideas and images these characters are associated with when they do show up.

In the selected passage, Fiske and Hartley analyze the results of inquiries into violence on televison. (You will find them referring to "violents": by this they mean figures or characters who perform violent actions.) We aim to *collapse* this passage into a 70-90 word summary—a summary which accurately represents the content and logic of the original. Our aim can be graphically demonstrated the way shown in figure (5).

Column 1 is the text we are reading. At the first stage of note-taking, we transform it into the nuggets of information presented in Column 2: these are the *main points* of each paragraph. They are the *gist* of each section. They answer a question you ask yourself as you leave each paragraph: "What do I predict to be necessary in the paragraph for understanding the rest of the passage? That is, what should be kept in mind from this?" *To make sure that your note-taking will liberate you from the original, freeing you to use your own words when you actually come to write the summary, make every effort to compose these answers in fragments and phrases. Make every effort to avoid simply copying out clumps of the original.*

To compose Column 3, a further reduction and transformation, we assess each of the Column 2 items: if they operate at too low a level of detail (remember

↓ text   ↓ main pts of each para   ↓ further reduction
          gist   + transfordion

Figure (5)

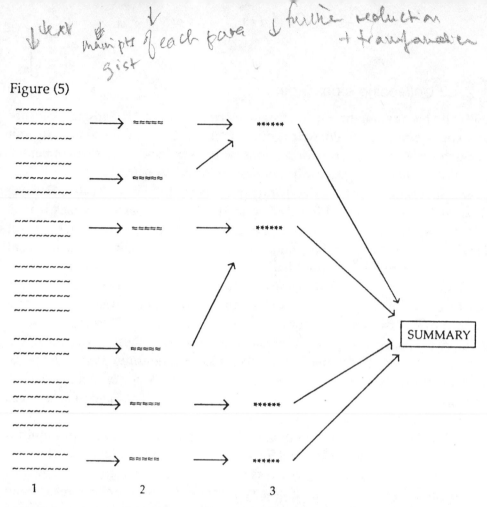

1   2   3

how texts spread out at the lowest level of generality, too space- and time-con-
sumingly for summary), we delete them, crossing them out. If they are only
repetitions of earlier items, we arrange for them to be absorbed into the other
items. If items are two elements of the same point, we rewrite to incorporate them
with one another, making just one item. If they can be neither deleted, absorbed
nor incorporated, we simply carry them forward. The contents of Column 3, the
products of this evaluation process, are what we must present in our summary.
These are the essentials which the summary must find a way of representing.

Here is the passage about TV violence. You should try summarizing it on
your own first. But, for your guidance, we also provide a sample of the collapsing
technique applied to this passage, as well as a sample summary. Notice that, just
as everybody's diagrams of levels of information in the Chapter 1 exercises would

not be the same, so too the results of the reading/note-taking/summarizing technique will not be the same.

(6) "TV violence"

In general, all violents are more logical than non-violents; the key to violence with a happy fate is efficiency; unhappy-fated killers and victims are presented as bunglers. Violents are also the most masculine, and the victims the least masculine.

The attractiveness of the hero correlates with his happy fate and efficiency; 'violence does not mar, nor non-violence improve, the attractiveness of the hero,' comments Gerbner, who goes on the sum up the implications of his findings thus: 'Cool efficiency, and, to a lesser extent, manliness and youth, appear to be the chief correlates of success and virtue in a fairly impersonal, self-seeking, and specialized structure of violent action.' (1970, p. 78.) He concludes that violence is not a matter of simple behaviour, and that television portrayals of it mirror rather than illuminate our society's prejudices. The television message system is, he suggests, a system of 'cultural indicators' by which the value-structure of society is symbolically represented.

Violence, then, is used in the pursuit of the socially validated end of power, money, and duty, and is *inter*personal although *im*personal: that is, takes place between strangers. So, despite its obvious connection with power or dominance over others, it is not the dominance of one personality over another, but of one social role over another social role. It is linked to socio-centrality, in that the victims are likely to belong to less esteemed groups, defined in terms of age, sex, class, and race, and the successful aggressors are likely to be young, white, male, and middle-class or unclassifiable. Violence is not in itself seen as good or evil, but when correlated with efficiency it is esteemed, for efficiency is a key socio-central value in a competitive society. Violence on television, then, is not a direct representation of real-life violence. Unlike real violence, its internal rules and constraints govern what it 'means' in any particular context to the observer, rather than the combatants themselves. Its significance in a television fiction is that it externalizes people's motives and status, makes visible their unstated relationships, and personalizes impersonal social conflicts between, for example, dominant and subordinate groups, law and anarchy, youth and age. It is never a mere imitation of real behaviour.

In other words, all the evidence of content analysis points us to a crucial distinction between violence in televised drama and real violence, and should make us aware of the inaccuracy of the commonly held belief that these are similar in performance and effect. Television violence is encoded and structured into a governed relationship with the other elements of the drama; this

(7)

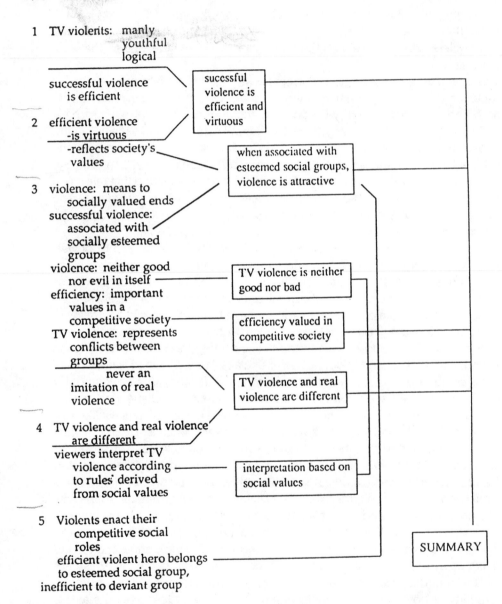

1   TV violents: manly
                   youthful
                   logical

successful violence
    is efficient

    ┌─────────────┐
    │ successful   │
    │ violence is │
    │ efficient and│
    │ virtuous   │
    └─────────────┘

2   efficient violence
        -is virtuous
        -reflects society's
            values

        ┌──────────────────────┐
        │ when associated with │
        │ esteemed social groups,│
        │ violence is attractive │
        └──────────────────────┘

3   violence: means to
        socially valued ends
    successful violence:
        associated with
        socially esteemed
        groups
    violence: neither good
        nor evil in itself
    efficiency: important
        values in a
        competitive society
    TV violence: represents
        conflicts between
        groups

        ┌──────────────────────┐
        │ TV violence is neither│
        │ good nor bad   │
        └──────────────────────┘

        ┌──────────────────────┐
        │ efficiency valued in │
        │ competitive society   │
        └──────────────────────┘

            never an
        imitation of real
        violence

        ┌──────────────────────┐
        │ TV violence and real │
        │ violence are different │
        └──────────────────────┘

4   TV violence and real violence
        are different
    viewers interpret TV
        violence according
        to rules derived
        from social values

        ┌──────────────────────┐
        │ interpretation based on│
        │ social values   │
        └──────────────────────┘

5   Violents enact their
        competitive social
        roles
    efficient violent hero belongs
    to esteemed social group,
    inefficient to deviant group

        ┌──────────────┐
        │ SUMMARY   │
        └──────────────┘

relationship is controlled by rules that are themselves derived from social values, and which are common to all television texts in their particular genre. Our familiarity with the genre makes us react to violence according to its own internal rules, and not as we would to real violence. We know, as we approve of the death of the socially deviant criminal under the hail of socio-central police bullets, that we would not approve in the same way if the equivalent real-life villain were gunned down in front of us. The difference in our reaction is not explained by saying that a death on television is weaker, less perceptually imperative, for the difference is one of kind, not of degree.

It is at this level that violence is seen as a complex system of signs of behaviour, more or less efficient, by which the socio-central hero and deviant villain enact the competitive relationship of their roles. The policeman/detective hero is a sign of socio-centrality; the criminal/victim becomes, then, the social deviant, not only because criminal behaviour is by definition deviant, nor because criminal/victim status correlates with deviant groups – the wrong sex, class, race, or age – but also because, in a competitive society, inefficiency or bungling is deviant. The criminal is distinguished from the hero primarily by his inefficiency and his social group; his morals, methods, and aims are the same.

(8) *Sample Summary*

Fiske and Hartley argue that television violence – unlike real-life violence – is neither good nor bad; its interpretation depends on what it is associated with. When good actions are efficient and successful, and associated with esteemed social groups, they are virtuous. When they are performed inefficiently, by members of socially subordinate or deviant groups, they are interpreted as unattractive. Fiske and Hartley note that efficiency is a crucial value in a competitive society: televison violence is one means of expressing this social value.

2.4.3 Repetition: making do with less

In transforming the original into a summary, we notice that, as the authors develop their ideas, they repeat themselves—especially in confirming their main points about the interpretive connection between social values and the difference between TV violence and real-life violence. They even signal to the reader that they are repeating themselves: as they begin to restate their argument and insist on its implications at the beginning of the fourth paragraph, they say "In other words...."

The summary's economy requires that we reduce this repetition. We can't repeat these main ideas as often as the authors of the original do. But we do recognize this repetition as an important signal: the repeated points are crucial, and they must show up in the condensed version of the authors' longer argument.

2.4.4 Word choice: translating for the reader

"Socio-centrality" appears to be an important term for Fiske and Hartley: they use it in different forms three times, and they situate it in opposition to the more familiar term "deviance." But I decided not to use it in my summary. I made this decision in the interests of economy and clarity, suspecting that to many readers "socio-centrality" might be an unfamiliar term liable to be interpreted vaguely or improperly. Had I taken time to explain it, I would have sacrificed economy; had I used it without explanation, I would have sacrificed clarity. Instead, I used the idea of "esteemed social groups"—one which Fiske and Hartley use too in connection with the idea of socio-centrality.

My decision about word choice takes into account features of what some people call "jargon." I hope my account of this decision will help you understand a common experience among student writers. These writers read a scholarly, highly specialized book or article—one which uses some highly specialized terms. Taking their cue from the original, these writers go ahead and use the specialized terms. And then their readers complain about jargon. "Well," says the student writer, "these words were in the original. Why can't I use them in my writing?"

The answer lies in the nature of "jargon" itself. Specialized words aren't very hardy: they flourish only in refined, hothouse environments. In these environments, all conditions are managed for their use: their exact meanings and application are specified; the evidence and arguments which justify and limit their use are minutely presented or reviewed. In the summary, these supportive conditions are missing. The specialized word seems unhealthy and not very useful.

It's better to find words that are closer to garden variety if you don't have room to prepare the nourishing conditions that specialized words require.

2.4.5 How the note-taking strategy helps us monitor and manage the summarizing process

Constructing the gist of each paragraph allows us to check our own summarizing (reading-into-writing) process.

(a) We can verify that we *really understand* the *connections* between each part of the argument (between, for example, the idea that violence in itself is neutral and the idea that efficiency is a positive value in a competitive society). If we haven't really grasped these connections, we're going to have trouble writing a coherent summary.

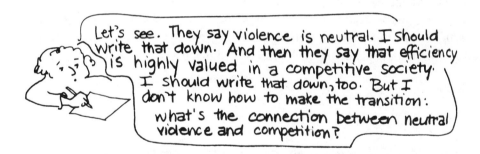

(b) We can verify that we really have accounted for *all parts* of the passage. We can make sure that we have not been waylaid by some part of it that is conspicuous to us because of our own particular preoccupations.

(c) By collapsing the passage to short fragments expressing *gist*, we ensure that we will be free to express the argument in our own words, and avoid incoherent copying. (In Chapter 1, we looked at an example of the incoherence that copying can bring about.)

(d) Collapsing the passage helps us see the argument as a whole and at a glance. This means that we can manipulate and arrange the parts to satisfy the new requirements (mainly brevity) of the new text we are making. For example, in my summary, I abandoned Fiske and Hartley's arrangement of assertions and chose to begin the summary with elements that actually occur in the middle of the original passage: the assertions that TV violence is not like real-life violence, and that TV violence in itself is neutral, neither good nor bad.

2.4.6 Working with longer texts

In the "TV violence" example, we are working with a very short text. With such a short text, it's practical to account for the gist of each paragraph. When you are working with longer passages—articles, chapters, even whole books—this thoroughness may not be so practical. Then you may want to define your targets differently—not by paragraphs, but perhaps by half pages or by stages of discussion. Often the writer will help you with this, dividing her text into labelled sections. Then, you can track the argument by constructing the gist of each section. If you find yourself getting lost, however, you can always shift down to paragraph level, registering each step of the discussion.

Exercise

Using the note-taking and summarizing strategies suggested above, write a summary of the following passage. The summary should be 15%-20% of the length of the original.

Universal free public school systems had been established in the majority of the states and in Upper Canada by 1860. In the United States, over half of the nation's children were receiving formal education, and more students than ever before now had access to levels of schooling previously restricted to an elite few (Cremin, 1961; p.16). In Canada, under the direction of Egerton Ryerson, the Ontario Schools Act of 1841 had subsidized the existing common school system; by 1872, British Columbia had legislated a public school system modeled on that of Ontario.

Late-19th-century literacy instruction in Canada differed in one crucial respect from its American counterpart. For whereas Canadian schools imported curricula from England, teachers in America were by this time provided with locally developed textbooks, in the tradition of the McGuffey readers. Noah Webster's *American Spelling Book* (1873), the most widely used textbook in United States history, not only promoted American history, geography, and morals, but was itself a model for an indigenous vocabulary and spelling. Textbooks and dictionaries of this period attempted to engender a national literacy and literature free of European "folly, corruption and tyranny," in Webster's words. In Canada, by contrast, classrooms featured icons of colonialism: British flags and pictures of royalty adorned the walls, younger students were initiated to print via the Irish readers, and literature texts opened with Wordsworth's and Tennyson's panegyrics to the Crown. In Canada, the reduction in pauperism and crime associated with illiteracy was seen as requiring the preservation of British culture and a colonial sensibility; in the United States, "custodians of culture" (May, 1959; p.30) sought to assure economic independence and political participation. The match between these differing societal and educational ideologies and the "civilizing" effects of traditional three Rs and classical education was near-perfect.

The model for this classical education was found in the philosophy, psychology, and social theory of Plato's educational treatise *The Republic*. Platonic psychology subdivided the mind into three faculties: reason, will, and emotion. The child, a "barbarian at the gates of civilization" (Peters, 1965; p.197) was regarded as a bundle of unruly impulses needing to be brought under the control of the faculty of "right reason"—that is, morally informed rational judgment. Paraphrasing a speech of Ryerson's, the *Journal of Education* declared in 1860 that "a sensual man is a mere animal. Sensuality is the greatest enemy of all human progress" (in Prentice, 1977; p.29). To that end, rigid discipline and rigorous mental training characterized classical instruction.

Adopting Plato's stress on mimesis and imitation as the basis for the development of mind, classical pedagogy stressed rote learning, repetition, drill, copying, and memorization of lengthy passages of poetry and prose. Mental, moral, and spiritual edification were to be had through exposure to, in the words of Matthew Arnold (1864), the "best that has been thought and said in the world." Accordingly, the intermediate and secondary grades adopted a "great books" literacy curriculum which featured the Bible, Greek and Roman classics, and after some debate, acknowledged works of English and American literature; "far more time [was] spent...on ancient history and dead languages than upon the affairs of the present or even recent past" (Joncich, 1968; p.48). In the United States, public high schools retained a modified clasical curriculum, sans Greek, as a 'uniform program'. This universal implementation of a classical curriculum in secondary schools forced practical studies of law, bookkeeping, and vocational skills outside the public system. In Canada, it was left to industry to initiate vocational education (Johnson, 1964; p.65).

Curricular material did not vary from grade to grade according to controlled level of difficulty. In practice, this meant that the same literary texts, particularly the Bible, would be studied in greater and greater detail and depth; underlying "truths" were explicated in terms of grammatical rules, rhetorical strategies, moral content, and aesthetic worth. In the elementary grades, students copied passages for "finger-style" penmanship exercise, in preparation for advanced composition study. Thus, stylistic imitation and repetition, guided by explicit rules, dominated writing instruction; students at all levels undertook précis and recitation of exemplary texts.

Following the European model, reading took the form of oral performance to an audience. Individual reading time was limited, and all students progressed at a fixed rate through the text. Both in grade and secondary schools, each student, in turn, would read passages aloud; those not reading were expected to listen attentively to the reader, since the intent of oral reading instruction was not merely to ascertain the reader's ability to decode the text, but to develop powers of effective public oration. Pronunciation, modulation, and clarity of diction were stressed. In the 19th-century classroom, reading was neither a private nor a reflective act, but a rule-bound public performance.

Although texts were meticulously dissected and analyzed, and block parsing was a daily routine, the emphasis was not on mere grammatical correctness. In theory, analysis and repetition subserved the development of sensitivity to the aesthetic and didactic features of the text. Thus, the student's encounter with the text, whether fairy tales or Shakespeare, was to be both aesthetically pleasing and morally instructive — in accordance with the Horation edict that literature should be "dulce at utile."

In the same way, vocabulary study subserved the ends of moral and literary education. Spelling lists often featured poetic language and Biblical and literary terminology. Precision of meaning and rhetorical effectiveness were to be achieved through the apt selection of words from this cultural lexicon — the range of vocabulary legitimated by "literati" as appropriate for each generic form of literate expression. The overriding serie of conformity and decorum was reflected in the rules that constrainted classroom discourse and behavior. Corresponding to each literate act was a correct bodily "habitus" (see Bourdieu, 1977); reading, writing, and speaking were performed in prescribed physical postures. Moreover, "provincial" speech codes were frowned upon as evidence of rudeness or ignorance; textbooks of this period advised students to cultivate the friendship of children of higher station, so that they might assimilate more cultured and aristocratic speech habits.

Suzanne de Castell and Allan Luke (1986), "Models of literacy in North American schools: social and historical conditions and consequences." In *Literacy, society, and schooling*, ed. S. de Castell, A. Luke, K. Egan, Cambridge: Cambridge University Press, 87-109, 92-94.

2.5 Frames for summary

Most academic essays depend on outside sources of information. Everybody knows this. Various practices have arisen to account for this dependency: the most conspicuous and familiar of these practices are probably the *documentation* techniques of footnoting and reference-listing. Even elementary-school writers know about these practices.

Equally important, although less rule-governed, are some other practices that account for sources. These are perhaps less conspicuous to outsiders, but, to members of the academic community, they are crucial. These practices *introduce the source* of information in the body of the essay. These practices *mark the boundary* between the writer's own argument and her summary of another writer's argument. As well, they mark the boundaries between contributions from one source and contributions from another source. These practices *frame* summary.

Often, student writers submit papers with only the first kind of acknowledgement showing: footnotes and/or bibliography are the only sign that the content of the paper depends on outside sources. In these essays, unseen authorities and experts haunt the margins, directing the course of the argument but never themselves materializing. Only the bibliography offers a fleeting glimpse of these disembodied speakers as they scurry back to the library shelves.

Whatever authoritative and distinguished views these mystery papers express, they are not quite what your readers are looking for. Despite their bibliographies, or even the occasional footnote, they have not adequately acknowledged and presented their sources. Fortunately, it's easy to learn how to make up this deficit: certain conventional *frames* for summary can make these mystery papers more substantial.

These *frames* are phrases and sequences that establish your sources of information and attribute that information clearly. In effect, the frames for summary tell, in a formal way, the story of how you wrote your essay.

In your essays, the *frame for summary* is a formal answer to the "where-did-you-get-your-information?" question. In your essays, the *frame* will:

(a) introduce your sources openly and directly;
(b) establish the boundaries between diverse sources of information, signalling to the reader that you are shifting from contributions from one text to contributions from another;
(c) establish the boundaries between the material you have collected from other sources and your own commentary on or evaluation of this material.

2.5.1 Making a frame: introducing the source

Your reader is eager to meet your sources of information.

So your first step in framing your summary is to introduce your source to your reader in a straightforward way. One form of straightforwardness identifies the source by author and title, and broadly describes what the source does. The

sentence in (6), below, illustrates how you might frame a source of information that has contributed to an essay on modern advertising's images of family life.

(6)

> In his 1962 book *Communications* Raymond Williams analyzes the content of the British print and electronic media and describes the relation between content and the profit motive.

DATE: a judgement call, and not always necessary. Here, because the subject is so contemporary, and the book is nearly 30 years old, I decided that date might be interesting to the reader. In the samples which follow and in Chapter 5 on documentation you will see other ways of dealing with date of publication.

AUTHOR'S NAME: here both first and last name. Not all frame styles use the source's first name, as you will see in examples presented below and in Chapter 5 on documentation.

TITLE: Not all frame styles state the title of the source. Chapter 5 on documentation will show how and why this omission occurs.

BROAD DESCRIPTION OF THE SOURCE'S FUNCTION: what it does.

After this forthright introduction, the statement of function can be narrowed to adapt to your essay's topic. Sample (7) shows this narrowing:

(7)

> In his 1962 book *Communications* Raymond Williams analyzes the content of the content of the British print and electronic media and describes the relation between content and the profit motive. Among other things, Williams' research reveals a category of publication—mostly women's magazines—that advises readers on how to manage every detail of their domestic and working lives.

These broad, introductory statements of the source's main functions are often the part of the summary that is hardest to write. (Notice how the two sentences in (7) make use of abstraction—*profit motive*—and generalization—

readers' domestic and working lives—to condense and represent the content of Williams' work.) But these statements are very important, first in that they fully identify a major source of information, and second in that they build a wide shelter to house subsequent statements which summarize lower-level details. Following remarks about *women's magazines, advice,* or *domestic practices* can evidently be attributed to Raymond Williams' book.

2.5.2 Making a frame: keeping in touch

Broad introductory statements acquaint your readers with your sources. But they should not be left to maintain that acquaintance alone. The further your readers move from that introducing statement, the less certain they will be about the source of information. Say, for example, we keep (6) as it is, firmly introducing Williams and his book, but we rewrite (7) without mentioning Williams again, and then go on to summarize in greater detail, still keeping Williams out of the picture. Passage (8) below illustrates a frame that dissolves too soon.

(8)

> In his 1962 book *Communications* Raymond Williams analyzes the content of the British print and electronic media and describes the relation between content and profit motive. There is a category of publication – mostly women's magazines – that advises readers on how to manage every detail of their domestic and working lives. Advice is often closely related to shopping information. Readers are shown how they can adjust to problems in their lives by making certain types of purchases which advertising features associate with domestic tranquility or picturesque romance.

By now, the reader can't be sure whether the observations about shopping information and adjustment to problems come from Williams, from another source, or from the essay-writer's own reasoning. And this uncertainty comes about despite the thoroughness of the introducing statement. The introducing statement needs help from other conventional *frame* elements:

Communications	focusses on...
	inquires into...
	explores...

Williams' study shows that...
    research reveals...

goes on to describe...	notes...
maintains that...	explains...
Williams argues...	considers...
observes...	examines...
claims...	

Rarely do such *frame* elements need to appear in every sentence: too much framing can sound odd. But the appearance of frame elements at intervals throughout the summarized material will keep your reader directly in touch with your sources. Moreover, the frame helps you establish the boundary between your summary and your own reasoning, showing where summarizing ends and your own commentary begins. By marking this boundary, you will make your own original work more conspicuous and earn yourself the credit you deserve. Passage (9) below extends the topic of families and advertising, showing the writer going beyond Williams' contribution and offering something new. It also uses additional framing to keep the reader in touch with the writer's source as the discussion develops.

(9)

In his 1962 book *Communications* Raymond Williams analyzes the content of the British print and electronic media and describes the relation between content and profit motive. Among other things, Williams' research reveals a category of publication — mostly women's magazines — that advises readers on how to manage every detail of their domestic and working lives. Advice is often closely related to shopping information. According to Williams, readers of these magazines are shown how they can adjust to problems in their lives by making certain types of purchases which advertising features associate with domestic tranquility or picturesque romance. Williams limits his study of women's magazines to analyzing this link between feature-article advice and the accompanying advertisements, suggesting that editorial content and profit motive cooperate indirectly. But his findings can also help us understand the special role assigned to women in the maintenance of family norms: we can speculate that these publications deliver to readers more than just images of ideal family life. They also instruct the reader in minute behaviors, prescribing exact household practices associated with domestic ideals. The woman who takes these instructions to heart will help her family measure up to the ideal.

2.5.3 Originality and indebtedness

The academic community values originality. Academic readers want to read something that hasn't been said before. (If you don't believe this, try handing in a re-typed version of someone else's paper that the instructor has already marked as an *A* paper. You won't get *A*.)

But this valued originality is not supposed to be a bolt out of the blue, a shot in the dark. Academic readers expect this newness to be related to what *has* already been said on the subject, and they want to be shown *how* it's related. While these readers respect originality, they also respect writers' indebtedness to other sources.

Your reader expects your argument to be based on as much information as possible. So acknowledging your sources by *framing* your summaries isn't just a matter of admitting that you got some of this material from someone else. Acknowledging your sources with frame elements shows that you're engaged in scholarly activity. You're working with reliable information and respected reasoning.

Your readers will think *more* of you rather than less for openly mentioning your sources. Your readers *like* you to have sources, and they like to see you working with them in the body of your argument. Of course, they also like to see you document them formally in citations and bibliography. Chapter 5 will deal with current citation practices in the academic community.

Exercise

The summary-framing techniques suggested in this section replicate practices in scholarly publications—the kinds of publications your instructors read and write for. Below are two passage from such publications. One is from a book, the other from an article in an academic journal. They show how framing techniques work in the real world.

Underline all the frame elements you can find—that is, all wordings that remind the reader of the source of information. You will also find cases of the documentation techniques—"Ellul 1973, p. 58," for example—you will be learning about in Chapter 5. Underline these too.

(a) "Propaganda"

[The popular view of propaganda which predicts the presence of an active propagandist] is not the only one rejected in Ellul's comprehensive and pioneering *Propaganda: The Formation of Men's Attitudes*. He sees the tendency to equate propaganda with "lies" as likely to further the interest of propaganda by concealing its nature as "an enterprise for perverting the significance of events" behind a facade of inassailable "factuality" (Ellul 1973, p. 58). It is in this sense that education, despite its professed belief in the liberating effect of literacy, can be seen as a pre-propagandist process through which facts are interpreted according to the symbols which express a group's collective ideas about its past and its future (Ellul 1973, pp. 108-12). Ellul's account is disturbingly provocative, even though he occasionally slips into a mood of what has been rightly criticized as "Aristotelian Christian pessimism" (Sanzo 1978, p. 205). I shall return later to some of his arguments and examples, but would first like to summarize a section of his book in which he makes a crucial distinction between two types of propaganda, the understanding of which is essential to a discussion of propaganda in literature.
In his attempt to define categories of propaganda, Ellul (1973, pp. 61-87) makes four distinctions within the general phenomenon. Each of these distinctions embraces a pair of types, the first one of which is associated with popular views of "classic" propaganda. The four distinctions he makes are between: 1. political and sociological propaganda; 2. agitation and integration; 3. vertical and horizontal propaganda; 4. rational and irrational propaganda.

From A. P. Foulkes (1983), *Literature and Propaganda*, 10.

(b) "Market explanation"

The market explanation for organizational structure is associated most importantly with Alfred D. Chandler's analysis of the American business firm. *The Visible Hand* (1977) attempts to account for the development and rapid diffusion of the modern corporation. The invention of the corporation, what Chandler calls "multiunit" business enterprise, accelerated the rate of industrialization in the United States and, as American management ideas spread abroad, in the industrializing world generally. Although Chandler (1984) recognizes local differences in the spread of the multiunit firm to Western Europe and Japan, he attributes such differences largely to market characteristics. The United States was the "seed bed" of managerial capitalism, not Europe, because of "the size and nature of its domestic market" (1977, p. 498).

The logic of Chandler's analysis is a straightforward developmental thesis of institutional change based on changing market conditions. Chandler shows that the preindustrial American economy was dominated by small, traditional organizations: partnerships or family-owned businesses with limited outputs. The traditional business typically received its raw materials and tools from a general merchant who in turn purchased at wholesale the business's finished goods and distributed them in nearby markets at retail prices. The general merchant was the kingpin of the colonial economy (1977, p. 18). After the colonial period and until the advent of the railways, traditional businesses became more specialized, with the general merchant giving way to the commission merchant. But even with these changes, the essential organization of the traditional firm stayed the same. They "remained small and personally managed because the volume of business handled by even the largest was not yet great enough to require the services of a large permanent managerial hierarchy" (1977, p. 48).

From Gary G. Hamilton and Nicole Woolsey Biggart (1988), Market, Culture, and Authority: A Comparative Analysis of Management and Organization in the Far East, *American Journal of Sociology*, 94, S52-S94, S61-S62.

Exercise

Look at your summary of the passage on 19th-century North American education: introduce the necessary frames, if they have not already shown up of their own accord.

CHAPTER THREE

topics and readers

In the last section of Chapter Two, we looked at conventional framing techniques which establish the relationship between you and your sources. While these techniques explain your *indebtedness* to other writers, they also point to your *originality*: they show where your summary of someone else's reasoning ends and your own reasoning begins.

As long as you are summarizing from reliable sources, you can feel pretty confident that the content of your writing fulfills some of your reader's basic expectations about the kinds of focus and reasoning that are appropriate for academic writing. But what happens when you leave the summary and begin to express your own ideas? What kind of reasoning does your reader want to see? Later chapters of this book will explore some typical forms of scholarly argument that are capable of structuring a whole essay. Here, though, in the section below, we'll look at a more limited form of argument—the kind which shows up in an assignment that is chiefly summary-based but which also requires some of your own reasoning.

3.1 Beyond the frame: evaluation

Having composed an accurate, compact summary of difficult reading, you've done something important. In reconstructing a complex argument, you've created a worthwhile text. By representing the argument in your own terms, you show that you have really mastered it, not just repeated it. Your readers will appreciate your achievement.

But your readers are probably also hoping for something more.

Some readers might ask explicitly for the "something more." They will ask you to write a "critique" or a "critical summary" of assigned readings. They may go so far as to direct you towards the critical stance they want you to take: "Consider x's discussion in light of recent developments in y theory." Or your instructors may make no such explicit assignment. Only when you get your work back will you find out about these hidden expectations. For no reason you can detect, you get B instead of A: the reader has no complaints about your reconstruction of the source, but, still, something's missing. Or your B is accompaned by a comment from the reader complaining that you haven't developed a critical attitude, or you haven't said where *you* stand, or you haven't come up with any "conclusions."

In different disciplines, and even in different courses in the same discipline, this missing part, or shadowy expectation, has different manifestations. But we could say that, in general, it's a requirement for *evaluation*. Your reader would like to see you evaluate the argument you have reconstructed in your summary. This doesn't mean you have to condemn the argument as badly mistaken—or praise it as very excellent. Nor does this mean that you should burst out with an "opinion": "In my opinion, these are pretty strange ideas." After your meticulous reconstruction of complicated reasoning, praise or blame or personal opinion may very well seem anti-climactic or crude. And, after you have submitted yourself to the authority of the original, respecting every turn and station in its argument, you may feel you are in no position to criticize.

So what *is* this "evaluation"? How do you come up with it without being crude or without seeming like an up-start? Different instructors will offer you different—and sometimes rather obscure—advice on generating an evaluation, on developing a *critical stance*. They will be trying to tell you about a crucial, delicate process: detaching ourselves from our own knowledge of something in order to judge the knowledge itself.

TAKING A CRITICAL STANCE

Because this process is so delicate and difficult, it also seems to be a very private, personal, evasive process, not easily opened to public view. I know that, when reasoning processes are this private, they tend to resist method. But I will try to provide you with some materials for method—if not the method itself.

3.2 Developing a critical stance: inspecting connections and evidence

Your own experience in constructing a summary of the argument can be one of your first sources of material for developing a critical stance. An argument that looks airtight and irreproachable at first reading can show signs of weakness when you try to reconstruct it. Pieces that seem to slide together so easily in the original suddenly won't fit together in the new version you are making. Take note of these difficulties in the summarizing process: they may be evidence of weakness in the original, evidence that some *connections* in the argument are not entirely solid. In evaluating, ask yourself

- are there faulty or weak connections in the explanation offered by the original?
- are there gaps in the reasoning of the original?

Just as connections that look sturdy in the original can become flimsy-looking in the reconstruction, so too can evidence that seems overwhelmingly convincing and abundant in the original become slight and limited-looking on further inspection. So, ask yourself

- what kinds of evidence does the source provide? does it seem to you sufficient to justify the writer's main claims?

Notice that even if you come up empty-handed when you ask yourself if the evidence is sufficient—"well, yes, it seems OK"—you have still taken a step towards a critical stance when you identify the *kind* of evidence the writer has presented. Your reader will appreciate your observation that, for example, the evidence is "mainly anecdotal," or "wholly statistical and quantitative," or "limited to one phase of the issue in question."

Moreover, you don't need to state these observations as aggressively negative: by simply expressing your awareness of *the kind of proof* the original offers, you move towards a critical stance. Similarly, your discovery of a flimsy *connection* in the original shouldn't necessarily be inflated into a savage condemnation. Maybe *you* can beef up that logic with your own reasoning, respecting the original writer's glimpse of the connection and recognizing that even some extremely valuable arguments and insights don't have their whole logic worked out in their original expression.

3.3 Developing a critical stance: the other side of the argument

Once you have become immersed in the argument you have analyzed and reassembled in summary, you may find it difficult to get free of it again, difficult to detach yourself from its explanations and arrangements of evidence. One way of keeping your distance is to see the original as *one side* of an argument by constructing the *other side*. Ask yourself

- what views does the original oppose?

Often, the original will outline the argument it opposes; other times, you will have to coax the rival argument out of the margins. In either case, to detach yourself from the domain of the original, ask yourself

- what would someone who held those opposing views say about the argument you have summarized?

For example, people who claim that televised images of violence habituate viewers to real-life brutality would oppose the views expressed in the Fiske and Hartley passage on TV violence that appears in Chapter Two. By constructing that competing interpretation of TV-watching, you can situate Fiske and Hartley's argument in relation to other views.

Notice that, by presenting the other side of the argument, you do not commit yourself to opposing the material you have summarized. You may see the original as having convincingly overcome its rival, or of having failed to do so. Or you may make no judgement either way, but simply point out what territory is contested by these competing claims. Each of these three positions can constitute a critical stance.

3.4 Developing a critical stance: generalizability

By detaching yourself from the original, you get some perspective on it: you see it as part of a larger picture. You evaluate your source's contribution to more general issues. To sketch in the larger picture, ask yourself

- what important phenomenon does the argument address? why is this an important phenomenon?

In naming the important phenomenon, you will probably resort to *abstractions* of the type we examined in Chapter Two. Calling on these abstractions, you will be constructing the highest level of generality in your critical summary, making a strong *topic* for your writing.

In evaluating the *generalizability* of the original's argument, you show how it contributes to our knowledge of the world. Or you may only speculate on what it *could* contribute to knowledge of general matters: your evaluation of the original may only suggest directions for further investigation. Ask yourself

- what still remains to be explained?

3.5 Positioning the evaluation: writing beyond the frame

Now that you've developed material that extends beyond the frame and provides you with a critical stance, you may wonder where you should put this material.

The rest of this chapter and the chapter which follows introduce you to principles that will help you predict your reader's experience of your writing.

These principles will also help you make decisions about where to position your evaluation. For the time being, you might consider two simple patterns for arranging a critical summary.

(a) Offer your reader your well-framed summary, and then present your evaluation of the material you have summarized. That is, let your source have the floor first, and then state your position.
(b) Compose a beginning paragraph that broadly introduces the content of the material to be summarized, and also introduces the reader to the main thrust of your evaluation. Then present the summary with commentary following.

These are the simplest patterns for critical summary—not the only ones, and not always the best ones. As you get more experience in academic writing, you will find yourself able to make more discriminating judgements that lead to more complex structures, custom-made for each writing situation.

3.6 Sample evaluation

Below is an evaluation of a passage you have already read and summarized. It expresses one possible critical stance vis-à-vis the argument in "Vocal music" (Chapter 1). In composing it, I answered some but not all of the questions suggested in Sections 3.1-3.3 above on developing a critical stance.

(1) Curtis accounts for curricular and pedagogical reform in Upper Canada by claiming that they aimed to eliminate the need for "'social control'" in the "simple sense" in political rule. It's not entirely clear in the excerpted passage how the

rejection of the spelling book contributed to this project, but Curtis' analysis of Ryerson's instructional philosophy does draw attention to the possibilities for a less blatant, less "simple" form of social control than "propaganda," "coercion, terror, or bribery." As Curtis interprets them, Ryerson's reforms manipulated individuals by reaching into the mind and personality, recruiting character to the service of the state. Some might argue, however, that the formation of moral attitudes is in fact a proper purpose of schooling, and beneficial rather than sinister. Modern educational philosophies still look for means to develop moral character, encouraging and rewarding, for example, sharing and cooperation among primary-school students. Moreover, we might question whether there is any educational system that does not try—overtly or implicitly—to recruit the child's personality to the values of the institution or the community or the state.

Nevertheless, Curtis' account of Ryerson's pedagogy does alert us to the role of reform in social control. While reforms may seem to remove forms of injustice and unrest, they may in some cases only be replacing one form of control with another that is less conspicous and less open to dissent and resistance.

Exercise

Take a critical stance in relation to two passages you have already read and one of which you have already summarized: write an evaluation of the argument Fiske and Hartley present in the TV violence passage and of de Castell and Luke's analysis of North American educational practice in the nineteenth century.

3.7 Topic

In doing some of the exercises presented so far in this book, you will have been faced with decisions about how to arrange your material: how to begin, what ideas to put next to each other, how to get from one idea to another, on what point to conclude. The summarizing technique introduced in Chapter Two is meant to liberate you from the arrangement of the source, so you don't find yourself just listing main points in the order in which they appear in the original and hoping the reader won't notice insecure connections between these points. Whether you enjoy that liberty or not may depend on whether you feel you have any grounds for making decisions about arrangment.

The evaluation techniques suggested in this chapter also leave you with arrangement decisions: can the evaluation just be stuck on at the end? Or should it be integrated into the summary? What will the reader think if, all of a sudden, you start talking about the "important phenomenon"? Or, out of the blue, you start picking apart the source's evidence, finding faulty connections?

The remainder of this chapter begins to establish criteria for making arrangment decisions. You will find that some of these criteria are formal or *conventional*: that is, readers respond well to certain patterns of arrangment because they are used to seeing those patterns in certain situations: for example, introductions of a certain length with a certain kind of focus. (You may have learned how to write a five-paragraph essay in school. The five-paragraph essay is a *conventional* form, one that many schoolteachers recognize readily; they are used to seeing it in the schoolroom situation. And you may have already discovered that the five-paragraph-essay arrangement that satisfied schoolroom situations is not so satisfying to academic writing situations. Sometimes your readers will not even recognize it.) These formal features that organize prose are important, and, throughout this book, we will be looking into some of the main organization conventions of scholarly writing.

But conventional criteria are not the only ones to consult when you make decisions about how to organize your material, how to get from one point to another. Effective writers don't just fill in the slots in a predetermined form. They keep the reader in mind not just as a stickler for form but as a reasoning intelligence who works efficiently under some circumstances, and inefficiently under others. The discussion which follows begins to sketch a portrait of this reader—reckoning his capacity for remembering, concentrating, tying things together. I expect that you will recognize some of the features of this being: as readers, we all share pretty similar capacities for remembering, concentrating, and figuring things out. And you will also find that the work you have done in Chapters One and Two—analyzing levels of generality, situating abstractions, reducing passages to gist—will contribute to your portrait of the reader. Some ways of arranging levels of generality put gist within easy reach and make the reader behave very cooperatively; other arrangements are less likely to encourage cooperation.

You will discover as well that it is from the organization of prose, its arrangment, that *topic* emerges. The reader we are sketching is able to *negotiate topic* with the writer. Under certain conditions, the reader is a willing and clever collaborator with the writer in these negotiations. Under other conditions, he is resistant and stupid. It is the writer who is responsible for these conditions.

Rather than define the auspicious conditions for establishing *topic*, and rather than define *topic* itself right now, we will start by looking at situations marked by the absence of those good conditions, and by the absence of topic.

3.7.1 Conditions for *topic*: meaning and recall

There used to be a party game—a test of memory—played at bridal showers and birthdays. In this game, the hostess brought in a tray covered with a cloth. Under this cloth were twenty commonplace items: a safety pin, a pencil, a measuring spoon, a packet of matches, or other small articles like these. In turn, each player was permitted a ten- or 15-second glimpse under the cloth. After this quick look, contestants had to write down as many of the items as they could remember: the player who remembered the most won the game.

A PARTY-GOER REMEMBERS ONLY SIX ITEMS

Despite the commonness and familiarity of the items—everybody recognizes a safety pin or a spoon—*recall* was very difficult (that's why it was a game). Recall was difficult because the selection and arrangment of the items was *random* and, hence, *not memorable*. Had the items been all cooking utensils or all articles stocked by, say, a stationery store, the task would have been easier. In that case, the collection would have been arranged according to some higher organizing principle, and that principle would have made recall easier.

We could say that the collection on the tray had no *title* or no *topic*: nothing to correspond to "A Display of Items Used for Meal Preparation" or "An Arrangement of Articles Useful for Clerical Work." The tray collections weren't *about* anything. They had no meaning, and, as a result, their "nonsense" was unintelligible and not memorable.

Meaning and *intelligiblity* depend on a dominating organizing principle. This is true not only in party games but also in communication. High level concepts like "Meal Preparation Items" and "Clerical Articles" dominate lower level assertions, and they make utterances *intelligible*. They make texts *readable*. They help us understand what we read, and they help others understand what we have written. They are the text's *topic*. Topic emerges from the reader's experience of the levels of generality in what he's reading.

3.7.2 Aboutness

For a communication to be acceptable, it has to be about something. We know this from common sense and from our ordinary experience as senders and receivers of messages. When aboutness is missing, we are acutely aware of its absence.

In this speech at the bus stop, reference is clear but meaning is unclear. The listener can easily understand what kinds of things the speaker is referring to and would not deny the truth of any of the speaker's claims: he knows best about his sister's teeth; that article about insulation could very well have appeared in the paper; there's nothing much to question in someone feeling an obligation to mow his lawn. But the utterance as a whole, as a text, is unclear and unacceptable. It is not *about* anything; it has no *meaning*. A test for this is that there is no conceivable *title* for this outburst: no answer to the question "what is this all about?"

The speaker's message is obscure. There is no more *reason for these sentences to appear together* than for the items on the tray to appear together.

3.7.3 Coherence and the effort after meaning

The bus-stop speech illustrates in an exaggerated way a fundamental feature of human communication: the need for *coherence*. Despite the acceptability of the man's sentences (they are grammatical; they combine familiar words in a plausible way), the speech as a whole is *not coherent*. So important is this feature of human communication that some linguists specialize in studying coherence: the phenomenon that makes a groups of sentences a text and, hence, acceptable and meaningful.

The exaggerated nature of the bus-stop man's incoherence makes that case a simple one: there's no conceivable title for his utterance, no plausible answer to the "what's-this-about?" question. His listener dismisses his speech as nonsense. We usually avoid conversations with people like the bus-stop man, mostly because we don't know what to say in reply. Not knowing what the topic is, we don't know what kinds of comments would count as appropriate.

But other cases, where incoherence is less conspicuous or obvious, cause far more problems. And they cause problems because of another feature of human communication long recognized by linguists. This phenomenon has been called the *effort after meaning*. In *Cohesion in English* (1976), M.A.K. Halliday and Ruqaiya Hasa describe the *effort after meaning* (although they do not use that term). They call it the "very general human tendency to assume in the other person an intention to communicate, an assumption which is no doubt of very great value for survival"(54). In other words, listeners and readers will give speakers and writers the benefit of the doubt, and, even when meaning is not at all clear, they will do their best to make sense out of a text.

Making the *effort after meaning*, listeners or readers try to supply the *topic* for themselves when the text does not make the topic clear. Listeners and readers will try to answer the *aboutness* question for themselves from the materials available, however scant or confusing.

Listeners and readers make the effort after meaning facing any text. They soon abandon the effort in the most extreme cases of incoherence—like the bus-stop man's speech. But even the slightest hint of *aboutness* or connectedness will encourage the listener or reader to keep trying to discover meaning. The listener or reader will keep trying to figure out the connection between sentences.

Is this principle of *effort after meaning* a consolation for essay writers? Does it mean they can relax, knowing that their readers will go to great lengths to figure out what they mean? Not really. As we will find out, the effort after meaning is not always a friendly principle.

3.7.4 Ambiguity and the effort after meaning

Here we will observe the effort after meaning in operation. We can see this "very general human tendency" at work in our own reactions to pairs of sentences.

(1) Mountain climbing is a costly and time-consuming sport. My neighbour plays hockey at 5 a.m. two mornings a week.

We respond to the fact that these sentences occur next to each other: *proximity* signals that they have something to do with each other, and we make an effort to find out what they have to do with each other—an effort after meaning. In effect, we try to discover what the writer had in mind that made her put these two sentences one after the other.

In this case, our effort after meaning is likely to be more sustained than that of the bus-stop listener, who would quickly abandon the effort in the face of such irreconcilable concepts as tooth extraction and home insulation. Here, at least, we can detect a hint of aboutness and connectedness. We can make out a *higher level of generality* to which both assertions belong: "sport." The utterance is *about* "sport," but aboutness is still a feeble structure here: we ask "*what* about sport?"

Although we have something to go on here—the two sentences can share the abstraction "sport"—we don't have much. The writer hasn't given us much guidance. So we speculate. We hypothesize and try to supply a full *topic* in our effort after meaning. "Costliness" and "5 a.m." may have something in common: does the writer mean to say that some sports are simply too difficult to pursue, too inconvenient? Or does she mean to say that hockey, in contrast to climbing, is not costly? Or that hockey players can get their playing over with early in the morning, while mountain-climbers are still out scaling peaks? Which message does the writer mean to convey by putting these two sentences together?

Because we are left to *speculate*—left on our own with this—we are likely to say that the passage is ambiguous. It lacks a strong topic despite the shared dimension of "sport." In making their effort after meaning, different readers are liable to come up with different conclusions about the utterance's *meaning*, and it's more than possible that none of these conclusions will match the writer's intention. If the writer assumes that the reader got what she intended when, in fact, the reader has constructed a different topic, and the writer goes ahead on this mistaken assumption, soon reader and writer will be miles apart in their negotiation of meaning, and hard feelings could set in. The effort after meaning can be quite unfriendly to the writer's goals.

The kind of ambiguity evident in Passage (1) is often acceptable in conversation, where we are likely to communicate with those who are aware of our attitudes and outlook, and can make fairly reliable guesses about our intended meaning. (This fact of common ground can explain why friends and relatives who read your essays may find them more intelligible than your instructors do.) And such ambiguity is often a compelling feature of literary utterance. In literary texts, the effort after meaning is intended to be strenuous and exhilarating and even inconclusive. After centuries, readers are still asking, "What is *Hamlet* really about?" It seems that the answers are as numerous as the play's readers.

But such ambiguity is unacceptable in your essays: for one thing, the conventions of scholarly writing are opposed to ambiguity, and, for another thing, ambiguity just won't work very well for you in the academic writing situation. Your readers should never be left to wonder what your writing is *about*, or left to speculate on your reasons for putting sentences together. Nor should you expect your readers to read your essay more than once to get your point.

Part of the effort of composing is estimating the point at which what is clear to you is also clear and unambiguous to your reader. The mountain-climbing example gives us one basis for making these estimates: implying or even showing a general category to which two or three lower level claims can all belong is not enough to get the reader's effort after meaning working in the right direction and on your behalf. Despite the fact that both sentences in Passage (1) are about "sport," the passage is nevertheless ambiguous. The following exercise gives you further experience of the reader's predicament when she finds herself facing sentences whose connections with one another are not secured more precisely.

Exercise

Read the following groups of sentences. Monitor your own effort after meaning by asking, for each group, "what is this about?" In each case, you will find one or more very high-level answers—like the abstraction "sport" in the mountain-climbing passage. Then go further by constructing plausible answers to the question "Why has the writer put these sentences together?"—that is, construct plausible topics for each passage. Compare the results of your effort after meaning with those of your classmates. These comparisons will reveal the range of ambiguity in each passage. Fix the passages by controlling the reader's effort after meaning: make topic clear.

(a) In seventeenth-century France, the vast majority of girls who attended school stayed there for two or three years at the most, leaving when they had made their first communion, somewhere between the ages of ten and twelve. They then moved back into a world which was still largely illiterate.

   Adapted from Elizabeth Rapley (1987), "Fénelon Revisited: A Review of Girls' Education in Seventeenth Century France," *Histoire Sociale – Social History* 20, 40: 299-318.

(b) Humans have a biological attachment to land, and this may explain their emotional attachment to it. Energy flows through the ecosystem, and ultimately it is the means by which physical life (whether of peasant or urban dweller) is sustained. Generally, private owners make decisions about how land will be used, but their control is limited by cultural and legal constraints.

   Adapted from A.S. Mather (1986), *Land Use* London: Longman.

(c) In the 1780s in New England, women began binding shoes in their homes to increase the earnings of their families. They sewed shoe uppers alone in their own kitchens. These shoe binders had no craft status. They did not organize to demand higher wages.

   Adapted from Mary Blewett (1983), "Work, Gender, and the Artisan Tradition in New England Shoemaking, 1780-1860," *Journal of Social History*, 17, 221-48, cited in Ruth M. Alexander (1988), "'We Are Engaged as a Band of Sisters': Class and Domesticity in the Washingtonian Temperance Movement, 1840-1850," *The Journal of American History* 763-85, p.769.

(d) In 1912, one-third of recruits to the Toronto police force were former policemen, half of them Irish. In 1920, 1930 and 1940 roughly one-quarter of policemen born in Britain had served on Old Country constabularies. Many Toronto policemen had spent several years in the British or Canadian armed forces, a trend that was most pronounced in the decade after World War I when the public setor was under pressure from the Great War Veterans' Association to hire veterans. The architects of the early twentieth- century Toronto police department, Magistrate Col. George T. Denison and Chief Constable Col. Henry Grasett, had served in their younger days in units mustered against the Fenians. Dension was an ardent imperialist, a recognized expert on cavalry tactics and an advocate of preparedness and cadet training. The first-class constable of 1921 earned roughly $1800 a year following pension deductions. According to Michael Piva's study of real wages and the cost of living in early twentieth-century Toronto, this did not leave the average family man with much of a monthly surplus after paying rent and grocery and fuel bills. During the 1920s, policemen were denied salary increases. In relation to many skilled and most public sector workers, policement were well paid.

Adapted from M. Greg Marquis (1987), "Working Men in Uniforms: The Early Twentieth-century Toronto Police," *Histoire Sociale — Social History*, 20, 40, 259-277.

3.8 Sources of incoherence and ambiguity

The kind of incoherence that leads to amiguity can easily creep into essays. That ambiguity-producing incoherence is a hazard of the writing process itself—a solitary business that soon tempts us to forget our readers. And the *essay*-writing process presents its own special invitations to incoherence, in both the drafting process and the planning process. On the one hand, in the process of writing out the results of your extensive research, you may find yourself constructing an essay which, in its efforts to provide complete information, creates huge pockets of detail that begin to take on a life of their own, regardless of the topic you started out with. We'll call this condition *disproportion*, and in 3.8.1 we'll look at its probable effect on the reader, and at ways of correcting it. On the other hand, before you even begin writing, you may be committing yourself in the planning process to a scheme that will make the reader undertake exhausting *efforts after meaning* which, in turn, lead to the ambiguity you want to avoid. We'll identify this planning problem as originating in *list-like outlines*, and in 3.8.2 we'll look at ways of avoiding it, and making the plan a constructive instrument that helps you ward off incoherence and ambiguity when you start writing.

3.8.2 Disproportion

Sometimes those areas of your writing which do not convey a strong sense of *topic* to the reader come about because of *disproportion* in your essay. In developing an idea, you descend to lower levels of generality, and you find yourself pursuing details that require a lot of explanation and verification. They take a lot of space. Although you may feel yourself securely on track, your readers may feel no such confidence. They may feel abandoned in this long valley of explanation, and begin to look for their own way up and out, having given up the hope that you will rescue them and return them to a higher level of generality.

Stranded in the valley of detail, the reader responds to ambiguity by trying to make his own hypotheses about meaning. Constructing topic without direct guidance from the writer, he is liable to make faulty decisions that lead him far away from the essay's intended destination. Or he may simply stop concentrating—the effort after meaning is too much.

Passage (3) below illustrates the conditions which trigger these undesirable reactions in the reader. (We'll identify this passage "Asian corporations," but later discussions in Chapter 8 of *titles* in academic writing will reveal that this is not a proper title.)

(3) "Asian corporations"

Corporate growth—the development of multiunit firms—can be explained in terms of business response to the conditions of industrialized markets. According to Chandler (1977), when markets grow, businesses need to develop efficient systems of management to handle increased volume and coordinate multiple activities. Another theory also explains corporate development in industrial economies in terms of the market: as the number of transactions increases in the process of transforming raw materials into market goods, uncertainty increases (Williamson 1977, 1981, 1983, 1985). To reduce uncertainty, businesses grow, internalizing transactions and thereby governing them more reliably. These explanations of corporate development, however, do not fully account for corporate growth in Japan and South Korea, where prevailing organizational structures predate industrialization.

The Japanese economy is dominated by large, powerful, and relatively stable enterpise groups. One type of enterprise group consists of horizontal linkages among a range of large firms; these are intermarket groupings spread through different industrial sectors. A second type of enterprise group connects small- and medium-sized firms to a large firm. These networks are normally groups of firms in unrelated businesses that are joined together by central banks or by trading companies. In prewar Japan, these groups were linked by powerful holding companies that were each under the control of a family. The zaibatsu families exerted strict control over the individual firms in their group through a variety of fiscal and managerial methods. During the U.S. occupation, the largest of these holding companies were dissolved, with the member firms of each group becoming independent. After the occupation, however, firms (e.g., Mitsui, Mitsubishi, and Sumitomo) regrouped themselves.

In Japan in the Tokugawa era, from 1603 to 1867, a rising merchant class developed a place for itself in the feudal shogunate. Merchant houses did not challenge the traditional authority structure but subordinated themselves to whatever powers existed. Indeed, a few houses survived the Meiji Restoration smoothly, and one in particular (Mitsui) became a prototype for the zaibatsu. Other zaibatsu arose early in the Meiji era from enterprises that had been previously run for the benefit of the feudal overlords, the daimyo. In the Meiji era, the control of such han enterprises moved to the private sphere where, in the case of Mitsubishi, former samurai became the owners and managers. In all cases of the zaibatsu that began early in the Meiji era, the overall structure was an intermarket group. The member firms were legal corporations, were large multiunit enterprises, and could accumulate capital through corporate means.

In South Korea, the chaebol — large, hierarchically arranged sets of firms — are the dominant business networks. In 1980-81, the government recognized 26 chaebol, which controlled 456 firms. In 1985, there were 50 chaebol that controlled 552 firms. Their rate of growth has been extraordinary. In 1973, the top five chaebol controlled 8.8% of the GNP, but by 1985 the top four chaebol controlled 45% of the GNP. In 1984, the top 50 chaebol controlled about 80% of the GNP. The chaebol are similar to the pre-war zaibatsu in size and organizational structure. Their structure can be traced to premodern political practices and to pre-World War II Japanese industrial policy: Japan colonized Korea in 1910.

Adapted from Gary G. Hamilton and Nicole Woolsey Biggart (1988), "Market, Culture, and Authority: A Comparative Analysis of Management and Organization in the Far East," *American Journal of Sociology*. 94. 552-594.

The writer of (3) states her topic in the first paragraph. This is what the reader expects, and it's good to fulfill that expectation. But we soon find that this statement does not hold up over the long stretches of text which follow. Right after the first paragraph, where the writer has made her high-level claims about corporate organization and Asian firms, she plunges into explanations of Japanese corporate linkages, merchant houses in feudal Japan, (relatively) low-level detail about Mitsubishi, samurai owners, statistics on growth among the chaebol in South Korea. These explanations and clusters of detail are *huge* compared to the modest size of the high-level claims in the first paragraph.

Despite a clear topic statement at the beginning, the writer of an essay with a disproportionate shape like this is letting ambiguity seep in. The reader may or may not interpret the explanatory details as the writer intended.

Maybe this seems unreasonable. After all, the writer *told* her reader what her topic or "thesis" was: why can't he just keep that in mind? Well, he simply *can't*. He's got too much on his mind already, what with central banks, trading companies, samurai, the U.S. occupation, 80% of the South Korean GNP. We have to face the fact that, by the end of the second paragraph, or maybe even sooner, the reader has *forgotten* the topical claims about the industrial-market *vs.* cultural explanations for corporate organization. These claims having slipped his mind, the reader now makes the effort after meaning on his own, in the midst of what he experiences as incoherence.

The very process of writing itself can distort our judgements of the apparent coherence of our own writing. Single-mindedly tracking a subject, we are liable to forget that not everyone else is similarly preoccupied with the notions that interest us so deeply at the moment. Think of the reader making his way through the description of Japanese firms' linkages. All this fits loosely within the high-level categories of "corporate structure" and "Japan," but its exact connection with the topic of alternative explanations for corporate structure is not secured. This is not to say that it *isn't* connected, but that the reader needs to be shown *how* it is connected, or he will soon abandon the initially-stated topic and look for other ones that explain why the writer is saying these things. (Think of the reader with a perpetual question in mind: "Why is she telling me this now?")

Left to make their own way through true but not tightly relevant material, readers are liable to hypothesize new topics—answers to the "what-is-this-about?" question. These hypotheses *may* be correct, but it's more likely that they won't be. The material you have so painstakingly gathered to develop and support your main point will have been wasted. It will be used by the reader to support some other purpose altogether. For example, the reader of the second paragraph in (3) may begin to get ideas about the failure of U.S. influence, or about the irresistible domination of powerfully linked firms. Remember that texts which generate competing ideas of *aboutness*—like the pair of sentences which mention mountain- climbing and hockey—are ambiguous texts.

We could say that the ambiguity of (3) is structural: it has to do with the arrangement and organization of the text. Taking this structural perspective, we can illustrate ambiguity-producing disproportion spatially.

Figure (4)

●●●●●●●●●●●●	**topic** (or "thesis")
●●●～～～～～～～～ ～～～～～～～～～～～ ～～～～～～～～～～～	partial renewal of **topic** (Japan & enterprise)
～～～～～～～～～～～ ～～～～～～～～～～～ ～～～～～～～～～～～ ～～～～～～～～～～～	all about 20th-c Japanese firms
●～～～～～～～～～～ ～～～～～～～～～～～ ～～～～～～～～～～～	little bit of **topic** (Japan)
～～～～～～～～～～～ ～～～～～～～～～～～ ～～～～～～～～～～～	all about pre-industrial Japan
●●●～～～～～～～～ ～～～～～～～～～～～ ～～～～～～～～～～～ ～～～～～～～～～～～	partial renewal of **topic** (Japan and Korea)
～～～～～～～～～～～ ～～～～～～～～～～～ ～～～～～～～～～～～	all about size & growth of chaebol

Supporting material—explanation and detail—is massed in such a way as to overshadow by its uninterrupted volume the high-level claims that are intended to establish and confirm *topic*. We'll use this spatial interpretation of disproportion to demonstrate an improved structure. This improved structure insures that the reader interprets supporting detail in light of the intended topic.

Figure (5)

••••••••••••	topic
•••••••••••	supporting paraphrase of topic
•••••••••••	**renewal of topic** (corporate structure
••••••••••••	Japan, enterprise) with narrowing of
••••••~~~~	**topic** (Japan in this century)
~~	
~~	
~~	all about 20th-c Japanese firms
~~	
~~	
••••••••••••	**renewal of topic** (explanations of
•••	corporate structure)
•••••••••••	**partial renewal of topic** (commerce
••~~~~~~~~~	in Japan, cultural influence)
~~	
~~	all about pre-industrial Japan
~~	
~~	
•••••••••••	**renewal of topic** (cultural explan-
••••••••••	of corporate structure)
•••••••••••	**renewal of topic** (Japan and South
••••••••••	Korea, culture and corporate structure)
~~	
~~	all about size and growth of chaebol
~~	
~~	
•••••••••••	**renewal of topic** (Asian corporate
••••••••••	structure, preindustrial culture)

While the first structure abandoned readers to make what they could of supporting details, the revised version interrupts the imposing bulk of lower level material to *reinstate or reactivate the topic*, and *control* the reader's interpretation of this material. Passage (6) below shows how the revision reads. The reinstatements of topic are in **bold**: these are the points at which the writer steps in to manage the reader's effort after meaning.

(6) "Asian corporations"

Corporate growth – the development of multiunit firms – can be explained in terms of business response to the conditions of industrialized markets. According to Chandler (1977), when markets grow, businesses need to develop efficient systems of management to handle increased volume and coordinate multiple activities: multiumit structures coordinated by managerial linkages provide this efficiency. **Another theory also explains corporate development in industrial economies in terms of the expanding market**: as the number of transactions increases in the process of transforming raw materials into marketed goods, uncertainty increases (Williamson 1977, 1981, 1983, 1985). To reduce uncertainty, businesses grow, developing multiple units and thus internalizing transactions in order to govern them more reliably. **These explanations of corporate development, however, do not fully account for corporate growth in Japan and South Korea, where prevailing organizational structures predate industrialization. While the historical conditions of industrialization may explain why North American and European corporations operate the way they do, Japanese and South Korean corporate structure can be better explained as the result of other conditions: cultural factors which favor family links and which have all along adapted corporate management to older, pre-industrial forms of authority.**

The Japanese economy is dominated by large, powerful, and relatively stable enterprise groups of business units — groups whose structure can be traced to traditional patterns of authority and family connection. Contemporary corporate structures in Japan are distinguished by characteristic systems of family connection that have persisted throughout this century, re-emerging powerfully in the post-war period. Today in Japan, one type of enterprise group consists of horizontal linkages among a range of large firms; these are intermarket groupings spread through different industrial sectors. A second type of enterprise group connects small- and medium-sized firms to a large firm. The networks of large firms are the modern descendants of the pre-World War II zaibatsu — powerful, family-controlled holding companies. These networks are normally groups of firms in unrelated businesses that are joined together by central banks or by trading companies. In prewar Japan, these groups were linked by the powerful holding companies that were each under the control of a family. The zaibatsu families exerted strict control over the individual firms in their group through a variety of fiscal and managerial methods. During the U.S. occupation, the largest of these holding companies were dissolved, with the member firms of each group becoming independent. After the occupation, however, firms (e.g., Mitsui, Mitsubishi, and Sumitomo) regrouped themselves along traditional lines. **While market conditions can account for some features of the Japanese corporate structure, these persistent network linkages are better explained by cultural frames which influenced the organization of commerce long before industrialization reached Japan.**

Commercial growth in Japan arose amidst and adapted to traditional authority in a feudal rather than an industrial culture. In Japan in the Tokugawa era, from 1603 to 1867, a rising merchant class developed a place for itself in the feudal shogunate. Merchant houses did not challenge the traditional authority structure but subordinated themselves to whatever powers existed. Indeed, a few houses survived the Meiji Restoration smoothly, and one in particular (Mitsui) became a prototype for the zaibatsu. Other zaibatsu arose early in the Meiji era from enterprises that had been previously run for the benefit of the feudal overlords, the daimyo. In the Meiji era, the control of such han enterprises moved to the private sphere where, in the case of Mitsubishi, former samurai became the owners and managers. In all cases of the zaibatsu that began early in the Meiji era, the overall structure was an intermarket group. The member firms were legal corporations, were large multiunit enterprises, and could accumulate capital through corporate means. **In Japan, the corporate framework of industrial society preceded the appearance of expanded industrial markets, and that framework — indigenous and culturally specific — persists today.**

Like the Japanese economy, the South Korean economy depends on large groupings of firms which are the descendants of traditional forms of authority and commerical cooperation. Today in South Korea, the chaebol — large, hierarchically arranged sets of firms — are the dominant business networks, and their recent growth has been extraordinary. In 1980-81, the government recognized 26 chaebol, which controlled 456 firms. In 1985, there were 50 chaebol that controlled 552 firms. Their rate of growth has been extraordinary. In 1973, the top five chaebol controlled 8.8% of the GNP, but by 1985 the top four chaebol controlled 45% of the GNP. In 1984, the top 50 chaebol controlled about 80% of the GNP. But this surge of growth — recent and unmistakable — is nevertheless a phenomenon related to older patterns of commercial affiliation. The chaebol are similar to the pre-war zaibatsu in size and organizational structure, and, like the zaibatsu and their descendants, the chaebol are rooted in traditional cultural schemes. Their structure can be traced to premodern political practices and to pre-World War II Japanese industrial policy which directed Korean development after Japan's colonization of Korea in 1910. **Intermarket linkages among business units coordinated by family affiliation rather than managerial principle are expressions of preindustrial culture as much as they are responses to expanding markets.**

Each reinstatement returns the reader to the abstractions and high levels of generality that make up the topic, and each reinstatement of the topic wards off *ambiguity.* In the first paragraph the paraphrase of the topic (or "thesis") gives the reader a chance to think about the issue again, in slightly different terms (culture, family, authority, tradition) which anticipate the discussion which follows.

But even this doubling isn't enough to ensure that the reader is going to construct the information in the second paragraph along these lines. The restatement of the topic at the beginning of that section tells the reader not only what to keep in mind, but also how the content of the paragraph will relate to the topic. Before the reader even comes across, for example, mention of the Japanese economy's return to pre-war forms after the U.S. occupation, he is told what this return *means* in this argument: deep-rooted corporate dispositions towards traditional, family-based linkages. And, when the reader has finished with the lower level material on Japanese firms in the twentieth century, he is told how this material relates to the topic: these network linkages are persistent, and they can be traced to cultural conditions that prevailed before industrialization. If the reader has been reasoning this way, this claim will confirm his reading; if he hasn't been reasoning exactly along these lines, it will get him back on track, ready for the next stage of the discussion.

Compared to the diagram of the first version of "Asian corporations," the second diagram is heavy with topical repetition (●●●●). Correcting the disproportion between ●●●● and ~ ~ ~ ~ results in this repetition. You may think that the revised version is *too* repetitive: why is the first expression of the topic, at the beginning, not enough?

The answer lies in the way the reader's brain works—not just your instructor's brain, but everybody's. Your brain, my brain, everybody's brain can concentrate on just so much at one time. Think of the reader's attention span as a desktop that can accommodate about seven items at a time.

If anything more is added, it either covers up one of the prior items, concealing it,

or, if the reader if efficiently managing his desktop, he may "file" an item for later to make room for a new item.

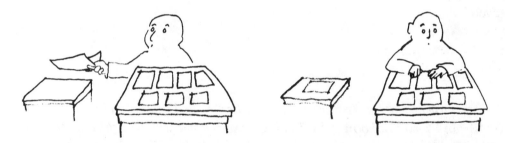

He'll then concentrate on what's in front of him—having more-or-less "forgotten" what's been filed or concealed. Unless he's prompted to do so, he won't retrieve the filed item. So it's up to you to reactivate important ideas, getting them back on the desktop so the reader will concentrate on them. That's what the revised version of "Asian corporations" did: it returned important ideas to the desktop.

An essay in which lower level material is disproportionately massive, outweighing high-level topical material, can leave the reader on his own facing a desktop covered with details. Writing out the results of your research in a first draft, you are liable to find yourself making an essay with just such disproportions—fat and sprawling at the bottom and spindly at the top.

But you can soon get that kind of essay into shape by introducing topical reinstatements that ward off ambiguity and incoherence. While these fatty disproportions may be a characteristic hazard of academic writing—which favours substantial evidence at lower levels of generality—they can be corrected by frequent and regular ascents to higher levels of generality. The following exercise will give you some practice in making deliberate, constructive ascents to topical levels.

Exercise

This exercise resembles the one you did in Chapter Two where you interpreted facts in "Brian" and "Baboons" by finding abstractions which expressed their significance. The passages below—"Transfer" and "Buffalo jump"—are like "Brian" and "Baboons" in that they are flat: they do not ascend to higher levels of generality and abstraction to claim the relevance of the data presented. From the perspective presented in this chapter, we would say they lack strong topics: although they are generally about, in one case, the mainstreaming of special-needs students and, in the other case, the practices of prehistoric hunters, the reader is still left to construct for himself the significance of this information. Readers do not perform well under these conditions. (Remember the reader who had lost sight of the topic "market-vs.-cultural-explanation-for-corporate-organization" and was lost in the valley of detail about samurai owners and the South Korean GNP.)

Your job now is to provide the reader with strong topics that will guide his effort after meaning by constructing a high-level claim that can function as a reinstated topic as the reader moves through the passage. (You may wish to refer to Figure (5) to remind yourself of a pattern for such reinstatement of topic.) Suggestions for constructing a topic follow both "Transfer" and "Buffalo jump."

(1) "Transfer"

Some children enrolled in special schools which address their particular emotional, behavioral, and educational difficulties eventually move back into mainstream schools. The passage which follows describes a sequence of activities entailed in such a move back to the mainstream.

Standard procedures govern the reintegration of special-needs students into regular classrooms. First, at a regular review meeting in the special school, the child possibly ready for transfer to a mainstream school is identified. A date is set for a second review of the the child's progress and suitability for transfer. If the child's parents are not at the meeting, they are informed of the school's intentions; teachers set up a meeting with parents to discuss the possibility of transfer. Teachers plan behavior and work targets for the pupil. The special-school head or school psychologist selects an appropriate mainstream school, and the class teacher visits the mainstream school, consulting with its special-needs or counselling teams and collecting information on curriculum and textbooks. The class teacher begins a program to prepare the pupil emotionally and psychologically for the transfer. The pupil and class teacher visit the school. The pupil and his or her parents visit the school. Staff at the special school prepare a school report. At the second review meeting, mainstream-school staff, special-school staff and parents decide terms, dates and objectives for the trial period. These objectives are discussed with the pupil. The special school sends a copy of the school report to the new school and a formal letter to the ministry of education. The trial period begins, with a follow-up meeting towards the end of the trial period. At the end of the trial period, the mainstream school prepares a report on the pupil's progress, making recommendations. The pupil transfers permanently to the mainstream school or returns to the special school. A second letter goes to the ministry of education.

To begin the process of building the passage up to higher levels of generality— endowing it, that is, with a topic—

- *find a general, possibly abstract NAME for the activities it describes; find a word or words which express what larger realm of human activities these activities belong to;*
- *find a NAME for the purpose of these activities;*

- *identify the values which would guide those who would recommend and/or perform such activities (what are the characteristics of these activities? what does each step have in common with the others?);*

- *think about whether these activities seem good or bad to you; translate your sense of goodness or badness into terms which specify the valuable or undesirable characteristics of these activities (maybe you'll sense a mix of good and bad).*

Rewrite the passage in such a way as to give it a strong topic, making paragraph divisions where necessary and keeping in mind that the divisions between paragraphs are especially suitable places to locate your ascents to abstraction and high levels of generality.

(2) "Buffalo Jump"

At ancient buffalo-jumps, like the one at Head-Smashed-In, Alberta, pre-historic hunters drove buffalo over cliffs to their death. From the beginnings of this practice, about 5,700 years ago, until about 2,000 years ago, the hunters consumed only the choice cuts of the slaughtered animals and left the rest to rot. Then practices changed. The hunters began dragging much of their kill at Head-Smashed-In to flat land close by. After drying or roasting the bison flesh on hearths, they crushed the animals' long bones into splinters, boiling the fragments to render bone grease. To boil bones, prehistoric families first had to heat stones in a fire and then drop them into a hide-lined pit filled with water. Good boiling stones were rare at Head-Smashed-In, for the local sandstone crumbled during heating. So band members brought their own stones with them — tons of quartzite and other rocks from more than a mile away. The bone-boiling process was necessary to the production of pemmican. During prehistoric times, the Peigan and other members of the Blackfoot Nation rendered bone grease to stir into mixtures of smashed dried meat and saskatoon berries, making massive 40-kilogram bags of the long-lasting food. The grease not only added to the usable protein in the meat but made the mixture extremely stable. According to one account from the Canadian fur trade, a bag of pemmican was slit open and safely consumed 20 years after it had been prepared. After techniques for producing pemmican developed, later bands began to pitch semipermanent camps in the nearby Oldman River Valley. Having extensive stores of pemmican for the winter, they no longer had to range so far afield for food.

Adapted from Heather Pringle (1988), Boneyard enigma, *Equinox*. May-June, 87-104.

To begin to build up this flat, disproportionately low-level passage,

- *find general NAMES for what it's about; find words which express what larger realm of occurrences these changes and practices belong to;*
- *identify the main characteristics of the practices and situations described;*
- *express the significance of these data: what do we learn by finding out about these ancient occurrences?*

Rewrite the passage in such a way as to make its topic clear, dividing for paragraphs where necessary.

3.8.3 List-like outlines

Because academic writing favours substantial evidence at lower levels of generality, first drafts are almost naturally prone to the disproportions that lead to incoherence. You've invested in acquiring all this evidence; now you want to get it down on paper. The drafting of research results can end up in ambiguity and in the reader feelings uncertain about how all this material fits together.

This uncertainty asks "why is *this* next to *this*? What is all this adding up to?" and it can arise as well from the conditions of another stage of the writing process, which is also deeply influenced by the imposing bulk of lower-level evidence that academic writers have to deal with. Just as in the drafting stage, you may often find yourself hostage to your voluminous data, so too in the *planning* stage you can find yourself a servant of your own thoroughness. Having collected so much information, you now have to organize its delivery to your reader.

So you begin to *sort*, grouping like items together—mentions of South Korea here, mentions of Japan over there. (Some items don't become members of a group easily; they resist and struggle until you force them to join.) Like all writers, you are feeling a bit anxious at this stage of the composing process.

So, when you remember what you were taught in school about a proper *outline*, you feel as if you might be getting somewhere. You write down

I. Introduction

and you feel a bit better. In need of good feelings at this unsettling stage of composing, you go ahead with what Mr. Jones taught you in Grade 7, or Miss Ashworth showed you in Grade 10:

I. Introduction
II.
    A.
    B.
        1.
        2.
    C.
III.
    A.
        1.
        2.
    B.
IV. Conclusion

What a relief! You've remembered that the first levels have Roman numerals, and the next levels use capital letters, and so on. You feel particularly satisfied when you remember that you can't have just *one* lower level—just *I.A.* followed by *II.* If you go lower at all, you have to go at least *two steps. I.A.* necessitates *I.B.*—minimum.

This kind of outline can be useful as a memory device: it reminds you to mention certain parts of your research. Otherwise you might forget. But this kind of outline also has serious *flaws*, and if you rely on the outline too confidently, these features can handicap you when you come to actually writing the essay. For one thing, the outline makes no estimate of the essay's *proportions*: it can fail entirely to account for the volume of each element. *I.B.2.* may be hugely disproportionate, smothering the stages of discussion which precede and follow it, littering the reader's desktop. If you rely solely on your schoolroom outline, and don't screen the product for disproportion, you can end up with an incoherent essay—despite the outline's exact and orderly appearance.

Disproportion is not the only risk you run by relying on this kind of planning. There are other potential problems as well, also to do with incoherence. Strange as it may seem, even the most intricately ordered and labelled outline can fail to generate the *strong topic* you need to keep your reader on track and to ward off ambiguity. (It was the *strong topic* that was called on repeatedly in the revision of "Asian corporations.") The schoolroom outline can mislead you into thinking that you have a topic, when really all you have is a general name for what you're talking about: "sport," "Japanese firms," "Toronto policemen," "irony in *Pride and Prejudice*." Establishing and frequently reinstating these general names is good. In fact, it's the least you can do for your reader, and he certainly expects it of you. But it's not nearly enough to control his effort after meaning (as we saw in the first version of "Asian corporations," where the most that could be said for the second paragraph was that it was mostly about Japanese firms in the twentieth-century).

To see how a schoolroom outline can fail to generate a strong topic, and can mislead you as to the coherence of your planned essay, we'll examine such an outline.

Literacy in Renaissance Italy
    I. Introduction
    II. Literacy in business
        A. Different handwriting for different purposes
        B. Notaries
        C. Numeracy
            1. Ledgers
            2. Abacus schools
    III. Domestic literacy
        A. The ricordanze (memoranda)
            1. records of family history and accounts
            2. notation of good advice, mention of local history
        B. The letters of Alessandra Macingli Strozzi to her husband
    IV. Literacy and the Church
        A. Church attitudes towards literacy
            1. illiteracy and superstition
            2. literacy and heresy
        B. Censorship

C. Keeping records of who went to confession
V. Literacy and the State
    A. Bureaucratic communication and control
        1. census
        2. passes and licences
        3. reports
    B. Literacy as a threat to secrecy
    C. Graffiti and political posters
VI. Conclusion

Material for this outline adapted from Peter Burke, "The uses of literacy in early modern Italy." In *The Social History of Language*, ed P. Burke and R. Porter (1987) Cambridge: Cambridge UP. 21-42.

Someone with an outline like this might seem ready to write.

And he may indeed be ready to go—if, that is, he's prepared to recognize and make up for the deficiencies in this plan as he goes along.

The first deficiency appears with *I. Introduction*. What's he going to *say* in his introduction? Maybe he'll write, "There was literacy in many forms in Renaissance Italy. There was literacy in business, at home, in the Church, and in the State." The writer realizes that this will not impress the reader, so he works with it, trying for something more compelling: "Literacy has been an important issue in societies throughout modern history, and Renaissance Italy was no exception. There was literacy in many forms in early modern Italy. People in business used reading and writing...." But what's the "important issue" in *that*? The writer may struggle with his introduction for a long time—maybe for an hour, maybe all day.

The outline offers no help to the struggling writer—it has, after all, constructed no topic other than the general category "Literacy in Renaissance Italy." And its weakness here is only the first sign of its deficiencies. Say the writer does

get going, composing an introduction by default, and heads into section *II. Literacy in business.* He tells about "different handwriting for different purposes" (why is handwriting significant?), and then the outline directs him to tell about "notaries"—because their handwriting was a certain way? Why are "notaries" next to "handwriting"? We could say that this outline, for all its headings, indentations, and exactness, is only a list of mentions, roughly grouped under general names. Making the outline according to Miss Ashworth's rules may have been satisfying, but actually writing the essay is not so satisfying. Having to introduce "notaries" right after "different handwriting," the writer is bound to feel uneasy about his reader's reaction: what will the reader make of this gap? How will she cross it?

Other gaps lurk throughout, ambushes waiting to overcome the reader and his intentions. Here are some of them:

- Arriving at *III. Domestic Literacy B. The letters of Allessandra Macingli Strozzi,* the writer finds he has massive data on this woman's letters about her children—their first steps, their remarks about their absent father. So he writes out all this painstakingly accumulated information. But how is the reader going to interpret this huge material, so disproportionately comprehensive that it begins to make a world of its own? The reader may begin to construct her own topic: "Renaissance attitudes towards child development." And, then, how will the reader behave when she has to make the transition from letters about children to Church ideas about superstition? What's the connection? Why are these two subjects next to each other?

Only the most strenuous and ingenious effort after meaning could construct a topical bridge between these two sections.

A READER AT THE GAP

- *IV. Literacy and the Church C. Keeping records of who went to confession* comes up against *V. Literacy and the State*. What is the connection? Is the Church *like* the state? Or unlike it? In what way? Is the reader supposed to go on to *V. Literacy and the state* expecting confirmation of what was said about the Church? Or are the state uses of literacy and their consequences revealingly different? Or is "the state" just next on the list, with no meaning intended?

- *V. Literacy and the State B. Literacy as a threat to secrecy* tells about the problems rulers had with leaving evidence behind when they or their officials wrote things down. But then comes *C. Graffiti and political posters*: posters and graffiti aren't *secret*: what's the point here?

- *VI. Conclusion*—what *is* the conclusion? What is the point of all this?

An experienced writer would be disturbed by all the gaps, disconnections, and discontinuities in this account of literacy in Renaissance Italy. He would know that his reader was going to react awkwardly—either constructing off-track meanings or, more likely, finding the effort too much and abandoning it, taking the essay as only a list of things the writer has found out.

A good writer might be able to repair these gaps in the drafting process, making connections and developing a strong topic. These repairs would be hard work, involving false starts, new starts, and serious thinking. But eventually the writer might come up with a *topic* something like this:

business & family uses of literacy show how calculation and accounting for details in *personal* affairs were valued. This could suggest that individuals saw themselves increasing their *control* of their personal lives. *But*, going beyond the individual and family domain to Church and state, while we still find literacy serving individual control (reading the Bible privately, writing graffiti), we also find literacy as an instrument of large-scale control of the population.

Do you see how this topic answers the "what-is-this-*about*?" question much more powerfully than the pseudo-topic 'literacy in Renaissance Italy'? Moreover, the topic's complex answer to the aboutness question is a sign of a how *functional* it will be for both writer and reader in establishing meaning.

- It gives the writer important things to say in his introduction, preparing the reader for the logic of the argument that follows.

- It can be *reinstated* at frequent intervals in the essay, showing the reader what to concentrate on and how to fit the parts together. It can show, for example, how graffiti relates to census-taking (they're competing effects of literacy: on the one hand expressions of individual dissent and, on the other hand, expressions of state control).

- It can guide the writer in the use of his research results, directing him, for example, to reduce material on children's first steps and emphasize instead how family letters enabled people to keep in touch and informed despite physical separation.

With this strong topic in hand, the writer is in a good position to deliver to the reader a coherent essay free of ambiguity. And the reader, instead of facing a loosely assembled list of things the writer knows, will make efficient efforts after meaning: concentrating, remembering, and reasoning productively. Once the strong topic appears on the writing scene, this story about making an essay heads for a happy ending.

This version of composing shows the writer discovering gaps and incoherence in the list-like outline and, heroically, repairing those gaps with a new-born topic. But this is only one way of telling the story of the birth of a topic. Topics don't always show up at just this point when the writer faces facts and realizes his outline is faulty. Different writers and different writing situations can await the fertile moment at different stages in the composing process. Sometimes the successful writer might conceive of his topic when he reviews his outline and spots disconnection: acutely aware of the gap, he comes up with the meaningful connection, the proposition that justifies these two things being said next to each other.

Or sometimes the topic might emerge when the writer is composing his first draft: trying to get from section III to section IV, he finds himself stuck for a "transition."

This writer who discovers connections while he's drafting might also be the kind of writer who can do a good job with an only barely coherent first draft. He reads over what he's written, predicts that his reader is going to feel stranded or confused at some points, and rewrites to establish connections and topic.

Other times, the topic arrives as the essay *plan* is developing, as the writer works on organizing his material and designing an argument. Then the outline or plan itself constructs the connections that have to be made, and itself generates the strong, complex topic that makes the essay coherent and meaningful. The drafting which follows this planning, then, is a matter of executing the design sketched in the plan.

In my own writing, I mostly favour this third way of going about things—although I support it with reading and revising the first (or second) draft to refine the topic and to make sure I really have taken account of the reader's needs. I would not claim that this strategy is the best one; it's simply the one that works for me in most (but not all) writing situations. You will have to develop your own favoured strategy. There are no rules for constructing a topic, only an unavoidable principle: an essay without a strong, complex topic risks ambiguity and incoherence.

You've already had some practice in revising for *topic*—your rewrites of "Brian" and "Baboons" in Chapter Two and of "Transfer" and "Buffalo Jump" in this chapter. Now, the three exercises which follow offer you opportunities to practise the activities involved in constructing a *topic* at other stages of the writing process:

- at the stage when you're looking at your outline, screening it for gaps and disconnections;
- at the stage when you're writing from your outline and find yourself with a passage that exposes your argument as no argument at all but only a list of mentions;
- at the planning or design stage, when you face your data and figure out what they mean.

Exercise

Some of the gaps in the "Literacy in Renaissance Italy" outline have been exposed, but others remain. Look at that outline again, and identify these gaps. Keeping in mind the topic that the writer eventually developed, plan how you would get the reader across these gaps.

Exercise

Here is an outline for an essay on revenue sources for television broadcasting.

Sources of revenue for television broadcasting
 I. State
    A. Subsidy
    B. Total support
 II. Advertising
 III. Subscription
    A. Individual
    B. Corporate

We now know that, even though this outline looks orderly and logical, it's liable to be concealing pitfalls. For one thing, it's unable to control disproportion. The writer may have abundant detail—statistics and regulations—on TV licensing revenue in Great Britain. This material would make III.A balloon and swell, disfiguring the essay, yet the outline offers no means of dealing with this disproportion. And other pitfalls are hidden in the outline's list-like logic. Say the writer gets to Section II. Advertising, and she writes out the information she has on advertising revenues.

Another source of revenue is advertising. In Italian and in some other televsion services dependent on advertising revenue there are separate times set aside for commercials. American sport is increasingly spectator-oriented and supported by income derived principally from broadcast sources which use athletic events as a vehicle for commercials.

The first sentence announces the high-level concept "advertising revenue," which shelters the lower levels of generality in the two sentences which follow. But we know that readers need more that just a name to guide their effort after meaning: they need a strong, complex topic which justifies claims being made next to each other. What is the connection between Italian and American practices? What should the reader make of these facts?

Rewrite this passage to guide the reader towards constructing the meaning of Italian TV being one way and American TV being another way. To do this, you will have to think about TV programming, audiences, commerical messages, and other related issues.

The "TV revenue" exercise tries to replicate the conditions you might experience when you construct topic in the midst of drafting or revising. Sometimes, for some writers, these occasions are especially fertile: actually writing things out, getting information down on paper, they find their brains ready to tackle anything. They feel productive, creative, ingenious.

But for other writers—or for the same writers in different situations—the gaps and discontinuities they discover in the midst of composing can be a source of *writer's block*. They see the gap, they hate it, and they want nothing more to do with it. They stop writing. If you wait till you're in the midst of writing or revising to construct your topic, you may run some of these risks.

And there are other hazards in delaying construction of the topic. What if the significance constructed for "advertising revenue" doesn't go with the claims you developed to explain the significance of the two forms of state revenue in Section I. State/A. Subsidy/B. Total support? In that case, the sub-sections of your essay may be coherent and meaningful in themselves, but the essay as a whole will be ambiguous and incoherent. (As a by-product of this condition, introduction and conclusion become very hard to write.)

Of course, you can always keep rewriting and rewriting until you get everything to fit together. But this tactic can be too time-consuming and imposing when you're facing a heavy workload. An alternative strategy is to try to construct your topic *before* you start writing—before you commit yourself to a single permanent sentence.

The next exercise gives you a chance to practise making a topic in the *planning* stage of the composing process. This strategy sees the process of *organizing* your material as fused with the process of *interpreting* your material. As you decide what to put first, what should come next, where to conclude, you also construct the *connections* between these clusters of information. These *connections* add up to your topic: the high-level, complex, interesting claim that can be reinstated to guide your reader's interpretation of the information you present.

Exercise

Below you will find two sets of data. One set—"Pacific Yew"—is small, and it has to do with forests, laboratories, and illness. The other set is bigger, and it has to do with stress and some of its social implications. In each case, the data are basically unorganized—simply listed. As far as possible, I have tried to present them in a "pre-writing" or "pre-prose" form: they are meant to resemble the brief notes you might recover from your reading and research. (Arrows /—>/ signify "cause(s)" or "lead(s) to.") Details are mixed up with higher level generalities, concrete references with abstractions.

To practise making connections and constructing a topic in the planning stage:

- *group the data in clusters of related items, establishing the main categories of information you're dealing with;*

- *construct the connections between these groups (for example, in "Pacific Yew," what does slash-and-burn logging have to do with the 80-hour work week of Florida scientists?);*

- *from the connections you have constructed, design a high-level topic which interprets the data and explains their significance;*

- *in light of this topic, decide what would be the best order of presentation—the best arrangement—of the clusters of data.*

I suggest that you try to avoid prose in this planning exercise. Instead of writing out paragraphs, experiment with graphic *techniques that let you see the whole picture at once. In this exercise, anything that isn't prose counts as "graphic." For example, you might make clumps connected by spokes:*

By keeping your plan circular, you will be able to avoid linear expression that can soon turn your plan into only a list. Or you might make a tree which shows how each cluster participates in or contacts higher-level concepts:

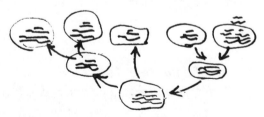

Higher nodes on the tree are the connections between lower levels. Whatever images you choose to help you design your topic (amoebas, rivers and streams, pyramids, highways and footpaths), aim to keep your planning all on one page. As soon as you go from one page to another, you risk trapping yourself in linear—and, thus, list-like—expression.

(1) "Pacific Yew"

taxol: anti-cancer drug, promising weapon against leukemia, cancer of lung, colon, breast, ovaries.

bark of Pacific Yew: only source of usable amounts of taxol

team of scientists at Florida State University: 80-hour weeks working to synthesize taxol. On the verge of creating taxusin.
   taxusin: simpler member of taxol family.
   from taxusin, knowledge of how taxol works
   from knowledge of how taxol works, ability to manufacture drug more effective than taxol itself.

for experimentation: large quantities of taxol needed

12,000 Pacific Yew trees: 1 kg of taxol

Pacific Yew forest: too slow growing to replace itself after harvest sufficient to meet medical community's demands.

from BC to northern California: 80-mile wide swath of rain forest.
   in this forest: Pacific Yew (Taxus brevifolia)

for years, Pacific Yew forests slash cut and burned.

   Adapted from Rick Boling (1988), Rain-forest dilemma, *Equinox*. Jan/Feb, 107-08.

(2) "Stress"

in the late 60s: evidence that in guinea pigs the hippocampus (region of brain important to learning & memory) damaged by massive amounts of glucocorticoids (hormone secreted during stress)

stress: emergency summoning of energy to deal with & survive crisis
     e.g. to fight or flee a predator

studies in 70s & 80s: normal concentration of glucocorticoids over rat's lifespan —> deterioration of hippocampus, ageing of the brain —> loss of ability to modulate stress response —> higher glucocortoid levels
     —> further ageing of the brain

individual's lifetime experience of stress influences conditions of ageing and its diseases
     e.g. history of prolonged stress —>
     more severe damage from strokes
     seizures

without period of rest after stress, brain cells less able to recover from glucocorticoid onslaught

60s experiments with intermittent punishments and rewards for monkeys learning a task: monkeys learning and decision-making didn't get ulcers; companion monkeys who only experienced rewards and punishments & had no control over decisions got ulcers

biochemistry of stress: secretion of hormones adrenaline and glucocorticoids.
- glucocorticoids prevent energy storage, force breakdown of energy stockpiles
     —> glucose released into blood.
- adrenaline constricts arteries —> rise in blood pressure —> quicker flow of glucose-enriched blood to muscles

during stress, suspension of less urgent physiological activities. On hold:
    build-up of fat supplies
    digestion release of reproductive hormones
    growth
    immune & inflammatory response to
    infection

prolonged stress:
    fatigue muscle wastage
    fragile bones
    infertility & impotence
    ulcers
    susceptibility to disease

80s studies of olive baboons on Serengeti savanna: social complexity, abundance of food, absence of predators

olive baboons: male hierarchy, stable status quo over long periods of time.
males at the top get shady resting places, food gathered by others, sexual partners, grooming from females
males at the bottom get harassed, get no sexual partners or grooming, have to sneak food.

in high ranked males: hydrocortisone (primate version of glucocorticoids) level is high in crisis situations, then drops off—sharp curve.
in low-ranked males: flatter curve—hydrocortisone persists in non-crisis
in low-ranked males: lower levels of "good" cholesterol that clears plaque from arteries; lower testosterone (for muscle metabolism and aggression) levels; weaker immune systems

baboon community in 1981: top male crippled —> fights for dominance —> long period of social instability —> new top males: same privileges as before but persistently elevated levels of testosterone, sluggish response to stress

Adapted from Robert M. Sapolsky (1988), Lessons of the Serengeti, *The Sciences*. May/June, 38-42.

CHAPTER FOUR

topic and meaning

4.1 Topic

In Chapters One and Two, we investigated the levels of generality in academic writing, looking at how abstractions, generalizations, and details positioned themselves in relation to one another. In your reading, summarizing, and analysis of passages, you developed your awareness of the multi-level structures of prose.

In Chapter Three, we looked into relationships between these *structures* and the *processes* associated with them—that is, between the organization of prose on the one hand and reading and writing on the other hand. Readers use the text's abstractions and high-level generalities to help them manage their comprehension efficiently. Writers—in planning, drafting, or revising—construct high-level, often abstract propositions to explain and manage lower level information.

In this chapter, the idea of *topic* will show itself once again, in a slightly refined version which confirms its prestige, its high status in readers' and writers' priorities. After acclaiming topic as the source of meaningfulness, we will go on to consider practical issues related to topic—namely, where to put topical statements. Then, proceeding further into practical realms, we will reflect on the role of some features of *sentence style* in managing the reader's comprehension, directing her to your topic. Finally, this chapter will return to wider structural issues by suggesting patterns for one type of argument: comparison.

4.1 Topic as meaning

Topic is what makes your expression of facts *meaningful*. Your topic interprets lower-level statements. Your topic claims that what you are saying is relevant to larger issues, and it says how material is relevant to larger issues. So, in a way, topic is meaning. When your topic is slight, just a noun phrase like "stress" or "advertising revenue," the meaning of your essay will be correspondingly slight. But when your topic is strong and complex, the meaning of your essay will be correspondingly rich and compelling.

4.1.2 Meaning *vs.* reference

So far, one of our tests for topic has been the aboutness question: facing an assembly of items or sentences, we ask, "What is this *about* ?" Thereby, we screen the collection or passage for connections. The items on the party tray were disconnected: they weren't about anything. The bus-stop man's sentences were disconnected: we can't say what he's talking about without repeating each item.

But we also found that, even when we *can* say what a passage is about, we can't necessarily say what it *means*. Items in a passage could show enough connection to allow us to say the passage was about "sport," or "schooling," or "Toronto policemen," or "shoe binding," but we still could not make any confident claims as to what the writer *meant*. So, now, to test for topic, we move beyond the question "What is this about?" to "What does this mean?" With this question, we expose the difference between reference and meaning.

To begin to understand this difference, we'll go back to the utterance produced by the bus-stop speaker. Taken individually, that speaker's sentences present no problem. We know what he refers to when he mentions tooth extraction, home insulation, and lawn mowing: his *reference* was clear. But his *meaning*, his reason for saying these things, was not.

Similarly, in the passage about Toronto policemen, we understand what kinds of things the writer is referring to when he mentions that many Toronto policemen had been in the armed forces, and we understand what he is referring to when he mentions the department administrators' military experience. We don't dispute the truth of these assertions (even though they may be news to us). We know—although probably only by hearsay—the phenomena the writer mentions. But we don't know *why* he refers to them: we don't know what he *means to say*.

We can observe how reference and meaning differ by looking at how the meaning of the same referring statements can change. Here is a reference to, say, a situation in a story:

(1)   The table was bare,the floor swept clean. The window was open, and a keen breeze crossed the room. The walls glimmered in the pale light.

We have no problems figuring out what sorts of entities or conditions these sentences *refer* to. We all know what "bare tables," "clean-swept floors," and "open windows" are, although each of us has different mental images of these entities. As for what the passage is *about*, it seems to be about "a room." Details have been sorted according to this implicit heading.

However, the fact that the passage does not disclose *meaning*—despite plain reference and some "aboutness"—becomes clear when we add alternative sentences at the beginning of the passage. We could say

(2)   The scene was one of desolation and abandonment, of utter emptiness. The table was bare, the floor swept clean. The window was open, and a keen breeze crossed the room. The walls glimmered in the pale light.

Now "bare table" and "open window" mean *desolation, loss, absence.*
Alternatively, the reader could approach the same sentences with a different statement of topic, a different *guide to meaning.*

(3)   All clarity and candour, the scene suggested renewal, and fresh beginnings. The table was bare, the floor swept clean. The window was open, and a keen breeze crossed the room. The walls glimmered in the pale light.

Now "bare table" and "open window" don't mean *desolation* any more. Now they mean *renewal, promise, hope.* Although the second, third, and fourth sentences continue to *refer* to the same entities or circumstances in each case, their *meaning* differs according to the sentence that introduces them. Those introductory sentences are *topic statements.* The topic statements:

- construct a higher level of generality by giving general and, in this case, abstract names to the details of the passages;
- establish the meaning of the objects and conditions referred to;
- guide the reader's interpretation of the facts mentioned.

The exercise below will give you a chance to see *meaning* developing out of mentions.

Exercise

The following passages are like the first bare-room passage in that they make clear enough reference but they do not establish meaning. Provide each passage with two, alternative topic statements to guide the reader's interpretation of the passage's mentions. These alternative topics will guide the reader to different interpretations of the phenomena being referred to. Compare your topic statements with those of your classmates.

(1) The PTL Club, an hour-long programme broadcast by the Global Television Network at 7:00 a.m., originates in North Carolina. Viewers of the PTL Club become "partners" by mailing in a monthly contribution of fifteen dollars or more, and have the option of donating a larger "one-time gift" in exchange for a record, book, art print, or other item whose monetary value is less than the contribution. The PTL Club features a resident singing group and maintains its own orchestra.

(2) When the Lethbridge Herald was purchased by Thomson Newspaper Ltd., in 1980, the publishers noted the paper's substantial legislative reporting and political commentary. They suggested less political and government coverage and more "women's news," more stories about community events, more coverage of leading citizens, service clubs, chambers of commerce, merchants.
     Adapted from Klaus Phle (1988), "The buck stops here...," *content*, Jul-Aug.

(3) In the large convent schools which educated the daughters of the middle and artisan classes of seventeenth-century France, girls who were not at work on their books worked on sewing. Where possible, specialists taught handwork, often in large, well-lit classrooms. Schools which educated girls from the upper classes taught handwork only to a certain level of expertise, highly skilled work being seen as inappropriate for "modest young women of good family." In the many pauper schools of France, reading was at best a minor concern, often overlooked altogether. Students worked in silence, sewing, knitting socks, and lacemaking while they listened to spiritual instruction.
     Adapted from Elizabeth Rapley (1987), "Fénelon Revisited: A Review of Girls' Education in Seventeenth Century France," *Histoire Sociale — Social History*, 20, 40, 299-318.

4.1.3 Reader meets topic

The alternative revisions of the bare-room passage each place the topic statement at the beginning: the reader meets the topic before she encounters the facts which develop it. We seem to be taking it for granted that this is where topic statements go—on the top, like a hat.

Perhaps we should not feel so assured. Maybe topics aren't like hats. Maybe they can be scarves or boots or belts. Before we plan our outfits, we should get a better idea of what occasions we're dressing up for.

Take for example the practice of *evaluation*, introduced in Chapter Three. In that section, I said that, in writing critical summary, you had options as to where to position your evaluation. You could show some of it at the beginning and then arrange for it to reappear from time to time throughout the summary, giving it full attention in the conclusion. Or you could save the evaluation entirely for the conclusion. Each of these choices will have different effects on the reader.

Say you tell at the start the gist of your evaluation, expressing yourself at a high level of generality and abstraction: "Although Masters relies heavily on quantitative methods of content analysis, his survey of print media does help to explain the role of newspapers in generating moral panic in national communities." As you go on to summarize the original, you keep "quantitative methods" and "moral panic" in topical focus, and in your conclusion you show what's wrong with quantitative methods, and you explain the significance of the moral panic phenomenon. In this case, your reader has your evaluation *in mind* throughout, and interprets what you report about the original in light of these claims.

If, on the other hand, you save your evaluation to the end, the reader will experience your summary differently. She will interpret material from the original without being guided by the evaluation, maybe getting ideas quite different from the ones you are heading for. The concluding evaluation may come as a surprise.

Sometimes these surprises are effective: they startle the reader into re-thinking material from the centre of the discussion. And it's possible that instructors who are used to reading critical summaries are prepared to be surprised. They are used to a reading experience that suddenly shifts perspective, and they like it.

However, critical summary may be a special case—a sub-genre in academic writing where surprises are conventional. You will remember that the revised version of "Asian corporations" in Chapter Three goes to great lengths to *avoid* surprises. The topic is repeatedly reinstated to guide the reader's interpretation of facts. The diagram which illustrates the new structure of the argument shows regular ascents to high-level topic claims.

But the diagram may be slightly misleading if we take it to be only a prescription for *formal* regularity—"Rule #1: Reinstate your topic every 250 words." In fact, in making decisions about positioning your topic statements, you should rely not on such prescriptions but on your judgements of the *reader's experience* of your writing. To make such judgements about your reader's experience, you need a reliable concept of this being who reads what you write, and in Chapter Three we started to develop such a concept, sketching a portrait of the reader. We pictured him at a desk, the top of which represented his *attention span*, his capacity for concentrating and remembering. We saw how this desktop could accommodate a certain number of items—and no more. If more items arrived, they pushed off or covered up what was already there. In effect, the reader no longer had the concealed or removed items *in mind*.

Now we will add to that portrait of the reader. We sketch in features that help us make judgements about position and frequency of high-level topic statements.

4.1.4 Keeping the desktop tidy

The reader's desktop is a finite area. It can't get bigger. In other words, the reader's attention span—or short-term memory—is inelastic. No matter how hard the reader tries (or how urgently you wish he would try), he can only concentrate on a relatively small number of things at a time. This is the way the human brain works. Writers have to learn to live with this inescapable condition of reading comprehension.

This small, inelastic space for paying attention may make the reader seem like a rather limited being, hardly worth addressing with an interesting essay. Moreover, this limitation doesn't match other qualities of our own reading experience: we read articles, chapters, books, and we have a sense of remembering a lot more than the handful of items that happened to be the last ones to pass across our mental desktops. We need to add features to the portrait of the reader—features that will account for this circumstance.

To the picture of the reader and desktop, we will add a management device. To manage the flow of information and make the most of it, the reader operates a mechanism which detects:

(a) those items which can be combined to form a single item, thus leaving room for new items to be concentrated on;

(b) those items which can be put aside on a nearby table as not centrally relevant at this point but liable to be necessary at any moment;

(c)   those items which can be neglected, left to fall off the desktop when other material arrives —

— or sent to long-term memory, which houses all we know but aren't thinking about right now.

Now that we've got the reader equipped with an information management device, we'll observe the operation of this device under certain reading conditions.

Case 1. The reader faces an essay *without* repeated reinstatements of a strong, complex topic.

(a)   He encounters a series of mentions whose relationship to each other is not explicitly expressed.

When no clear topic explains the relationship—that is, *interprets* the details—the reader can't operate the management device to combine items into a higher, more compact concept. The original items still spread out over the desktop. They take up space that's needed for new items or they simply fall off or get covered up by the next information the reader meets. In other words, the reader finds he can't concentrate on what comes next, or he simply forgets what he's just read.

Or the reader might make the effort after meaning despite the absence of topic:

These speculations—unconfirmed by the essay itself—themselves take up space on the desktop, making it harder for the reader to concentrate on new items as they arrive.

(b) When the reader's management device notices that an issue which has been important so far, and worth keeping on the desktop, suddenly recedes from the text while other issues arrive, the device has to make a decision about what to do with the now overshadowed issue.

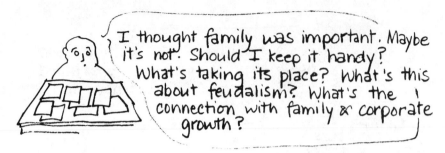

These speculations themselves take up space on the desktop, absorbing valuable processing capacity, deflecting the reader's concentration from new material to management problems. Either the device will make a default decision, letting the old material drift away randomly, or it will take the risk of investing in the overshadowed issue, keeping it nearby and referring to it from time to time, bringing it back to the desktop to check for its relevance.

Of course, the investment may be unprofitable. The issue may never come up again, yet the reader uses valuable space to entertain it.

(c) Finally, when the managment device is not properly instructed by a strong topic, it may make some very inefficient decisions about long-term storage. Encountering a big claim early in an essay, and finding it neither developed nor repeated in subsequent passages, the device may judge that it's not important enough to keep handy. So the claim gets sent to the long-term memory files – that huge, elastic capacity that houses the individual's experience and knowledge of the world.

Now the material is not exactly forgotten, but it's no longer in mind. And, stored in long-term files, it is relatively *inaccessible*, compared to items on the desktop and on temporary holding surfaces. If the device has made a mistake, and it turns out that this material *is* needed, the reader has to go and retrieve the item from the long-term files.

The retrieval takes up attention capacity. During the time the reader spends retrieving something from long-term storage (assuming he *can* retrieve it, and hasn't simply forgotten it), the desktop gets dishevelled. When he returns, he finds that things have fallen off, and have to be recalled by re-reading.

List-like essays, incoherent essays, essays without regular ascents to higher levels of generality and interpretive abstractions, essays without strong, reinstated topics—all these kinds of essays fail to trigger the efficient operation of the information- management device. The reader finds it hard to concentrate, remember, reach conclusions. The reader is not likely to appreciate the essay as meaningful.

Maybe this management device seems like a rickety contraption—prone to error, oversensitive to distractions, too liable to break down. Under the conditions of Case #1—incoherence, missing topics, list-like flatness—the device *is* a fragile, high-strung mechanism. But under other conditions, it's very efficient.

Case 2. The reader encounters an essay which repeatedly reinstates a strong, complex topic.

(a) By providing unmistakable guides to interpretation, the topic explicitly instructs the device on how to combine lower-level details into higher-level, space-saving generalities and abstractions. This combining reduces bulk on the desktop without sacrificing information, and leaves the reader room to concentrate on new material.

(b) The topic explicitly instructs the device as to which issues can be temporarily removed from the desktop but should be kept handy for later use. When they're needed, the topic explicitly recalls them, and shows how they relate to the current contents of the desktop.

(c) The topic explicitly instructs the device as to which issues are only peripheral and can be sent to long-term storage or, if worst comes to worst, even forgotten. These materials won't be needed later, and don't have to take up the reader's limited and valuable resources for paying attention.

Coherent essays with a strong topic structure activate the reader's information-management device with clear instructions. The reader concentrates, remembers, and reasons efficiently. The reader appreciates the essay as meaningful.

4.1.5 Positioning the topic

With the portrait of the reader fleshed out a bit more, we can return to the question that came up earlier: where should you situate topic statements in your essay? When this question came up before, we had only formal answers: "at the beginning," "every 250 words." Now we have access to better answers—answers based on cognitive rather than formal conditions.

Make your decisions about topic statements according to your judgements about the condition of the reader's desktop.

• If the desktop is littered with a string of mentions that the reader is liable to dwell on too much or that are simply liable to fall off, reinstate your topic to enable the management device to combine and reduce these details to a compact, meaningful concept.

- If it's time to switch the contents of the desktop from one area of your discussion to another, make sure your reader realizes that the main points of the content that's now yielding to other material have to be kept in mind, kept handy. And tell your reader how the new material relates to the points that are temporarily withdrawing.

- If you've presented information or ideas that aren't going to be needed again, make sure you let your reader know that he doesn't have to keep them handy. (Consider eliminating them altogether, to avoid miscueing the management device.) If, on the other hand, you find that later stages of your essay depend on concepts introduced much earlier and probably by now abandoned by the reader, find ways of keeping those concepts topical during the long interval when they are not in immediate use. And when you do bring them back to the centre of the desktop, remember that they have been out-of-use, and the reader may need to be reminded of their significance.

By consulting the portrait of the reader, you will probably find yourself positioning strong topical propositions at paragraph divisions: these are the sites where the management device has to make important decisions about what to do with the contents of a crowded desktop as new information shows up: forget, file, save, keep handy.

And, if you stand back a moment, and regard this reader at work, you will probably realize that it's most efficient to instruct the management device *before* it screens and manipulates the information coming its way—before it makes mistakes, before it invests in the wrong concepts, before it gets clogged with details.

In conversation, we can repair uncertainties on the spot.

In reading and writing, these opportunities for repair don't occur. (Unless you count on your reader re-reading and re-reading your essay until he constructs your topic and meaning for himself. Don't count on that.)

So, generally speaking, you'll motivate more efficient comprehension in your reader if you position your high-level, topic claims *out front*—in your introduction and at paragraph boundaries. First provide your reader with the guide to interpretation; then present the information to be interpreted.

4.2 Logical connectives

So far, our investigation of topic has concentrated on the *content* of the essay: the system of ideas and data that support one another. Our strategies for delivering this content to the reader have focussed on the design of this system.

But strategies of *sentence style* can also help to ensure a successful approach to the reader. Some of these strategies—ones which unpack congested sentences—aim for directness and clarity that relieve the reader of unnecessary processing burdens. We'll be looking at these in a later chapter. Right now, we'll explore sentence features that relate very closely to the phenomenon of *topic* itself: logical connectives.

Your strong, complex topic is an arrangement of claims linked to one another by logical relationships. Having developed it, you want to make sure the reader appreciates it, and uses it in his interpretation of your essay. One way of ensuring the topic's prominence is to reinstate it repeatedly. And, to support these repetitions, you can also choose and position certain words—logical connectives—in such a way as to call attention to the logic of your topic.

Logical connectives are powerful words and phrases that hold the parts of a text together. They signify relationships that are very often the *reason* for speaking or writing. We are going to look at three types of logical connective:

> **additive**
> **adversative**
> **causal**

This selection does not exhaust the inventory of connectives in English, but these are probably the most crucial ones, so we'll concentrate on them.

Additive connectives express the results of reasoning which discovers likeness. With additive connectives, the writer or speaker emphasizes the intellectual action of analyzing entities according to degrees of similarity or shared features. Think of additives as *"and."*

My house is brown. *And* my car is brown.

Adversative connectives express connections that are in some sense surprising or in conflict with what has been established. Think of adversatives as expressing *"but"* situations.

I like brown. *But* my car is blue.

Causal connectives express insights into causes and results. Think of causals as expressing *"because"* and *"therefore"* situations.

Because I want all my assets to be color-coordinated, I bought a brown car to match my house.

4.2.1 Additive connectives

Additives may be the simplest form of logical connective. After all, because they signify likeness, they express the "sorting" that can be, as we have seen, a fairly elementary activity in the process of developing an argument. To achieve minimum coherence, the essay writer groups information according to shared features. We know that this grouping is not enough to establish a strong topic.

Yet "sorting"—analyzing for likeness—*can* be an impressive and illuminating action when it goes beyond the primitive and obvious process of putting, say, all mentions of TV revenue from state sources in one paragraph and all mentions of revenue from advertising in another paragraph.

Sometimes sorting for degrees of likeness can reveal surprising things. For example, after having analyzed your data in an insightful and original way, you may find that there are more structural consequences of TV advertising than just the boundaries that mark where programming ends and selling begins. Under this category of structural results of advertising, you will add the phenomenon of programmes being grouped over a period of hours according to the market segment viewers are believed to belong to: this grouping is a structural feature too. The *boundaries* between programming and selling and the *market-compatibility* of elements in a broadcast sequence are like each other because they are both structural effects of TV advertising.

This kind of sorting is important, and capable of producing a powerful topic. The sorting which says "Italian TV gets revenue from advertising. American TV also gets revenue from advertising" is not so powerful, and not likely to furnish a strong, complex topic.

When you do discover an important additive relation capable of contributing to a powerful topic, you should use every means at your disposal to draw attention to it, and keep your reader focussed on it. Additive connectives—all the *"and"* words—can draw attention to the shrewd sorting you've done. Strategically used, additive connectives can dramatize your achievement by marking the logical relationships that make up your topic. And they can help your reader keep your topic in mind—help him concentrate on it.

Sentence-initial *"and"*

The words at the beginning of a sentence get more attention than those in the middle. So, if you want to thematize or emphasize the power of additive or cumulative evidence, you should try to place your additive connections at or near the beginning of the sentences that add elements to your topic. For example, to emphasize the topic of color likeness (not a very "strong" or "complex" topic, I'll admit), you look at

(1) My house is brown, and my car is brown.

and rewrite it as

(2) My house is brown. And my car is brown.

In (2), the *"and"* at the beginning of the second sentence instructs the reader to pay attention to color resemblances. In (2) *"and"*—signifying addition and connection—holds a more prominent position than it does in (1). Its prominence thematizes the idea of connection according to likeness, enforcing the idea that the resemblance of house and car is something to notice.

To exploit the resources of sentence-initial *"and,"* you may have to overcome schoolroom prejudices against putting *"and "* at the beginning of a sentence.

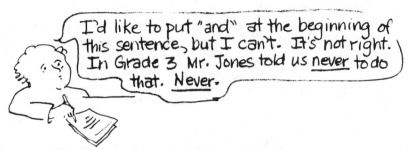

In many North American classrooms, children are prohibited from writing sentences that start with *"and."* This prohibition may have been devised to get children to write complete sentences instead of fragments.

(3) My dog eats garbage. And chases cats.

As long as *"and"* introduces a complete sentence rather than a fragment—

(4) My dog eats garbage. And he chases cats.

—you don't need to worry about harsh penalties for starting sentences with *"and."* Feel free to put *"and"* at the beginning, and enjoy the advantages it will give you in managing your reader's capacity for paying attention.

In the next passage (5), sentence-initial *"and"* emphasizes the logical connection between the two assertions, calling attention to the similarity between the reporting system and the monitoring procedures, claiming that they belong to the same category of action.

(5) Ministry officials instituted a reporting system entailing weekly up-dates. And they introduced monitoring procedures which recorded client-contact hours in regional offices.

In (5) sentence-initial *"and"* says, emphatically, "This is not the only thing they did. They did something else which added to the overall magnitude of changes." More than simply a list of changes, the sentences now make the cumulative aspect of similar actions topical.

The companions of *"and"*

"And" is by no means the only word that can perform this function of drawing attention to the cumulative energy of an argument. Other words and phrases can also show that a main topical claim is being repeatedly reinforced by new material. Here are some alternatives to *"and"*:

also	not only...but also
as well	furthermore
at the same time	moreover
in the same way	besides

(Maybe you can think of others.)

Not all of these will fit into our ministry-officials passage, but several will:

(6) Ministry officals instituted a reporting system entailing weekly up-dates.

    Moreover,
    In addition,   they introduced...
    At the same time,

Some of the other additives can accompany *"and"* for extra emphasis. Notice, for example, the emphatic quality of this version, which makes the *additive*, cumulative relation between the sentences highly topical:

(7) Ministry officials instituted a reporting system with weekly up-dates. And they not only made this change, but also introduced monitoring procedures which recorded client-contact hours in regional offices.

Exercise

In the following passages, additive connections are implicit rather than emphasized or thematized. Introduce explicit, emphatic additive connectives to these passages, making similarity topical. (As well, passages (1) and (3) dwell at a lower level of generality than (2). They would benefit from a guide to interpretation—a topic statement.)

(1) At first, a layman would not even recognize the recently-built psychiatric prison of the Karl-Bonheoffer mental hospital as a new structure. The building is integrated

into the old pavilion grounds. The walls are of yellow and red frostproof solid brickwork, following the model of the existing buildings in the hospital complex.

Adapted from "Psychiatric Prison, Berlin," *Architectual Review*, 1988

(2)   The Martha Washingtonians — temperance advocates in the years before the Civil War — were preoccupied with the meaning of gender, with an assessment of their special duties as women in the home and the community. Their sharp focus on gender permitted a penetrating analysis of the particular effects of alcoholism on female dependency. It created an acute awareness of the special vulnerability of the working and lower middle classes to the destructive power of drink.

Adapted from Ruth M. Alexander (1988), "'We Are Engaged as a Band of Sisters': Class and Domesticity in the Washingtonian Temperance Movement, 1840-1850," *The Journal of American History*, 75, 3, 763-785.

(3)   In early modern Italy, letters brought the business community news of supply, demand, and prices elsewhere. Payments could be made by particular letter forms. The Medici bank in Bruges, for example, sold what were called "letters of credit" to travellers to Italy, the letters being addressed to its Milan branch; the travellers bought the letters in one local currency and redeemed them for the other on arrival. In the fifteenth century, bills of exchange were in general use in the form of letters which allowed the advance of funds in one place and repayment in another.

Adapted from Peter Burke (1987), "The uses of literacy in early modern Italy." In *The Social History of Language*, ed. P. Burke and R. Porter. Cambridge: Cambridge University Press, pp. 21-42.

4.2.2 Adversative connectives

Adversatives link conflicting ideas. Very generally, we can say that adversatives signify a connection between facts or ideas that are in whole or in part contrary.

(8)   Our boss was invited to the party. But she didn't come.

In (8), *but* says "contrary to the expectations that have just been established." In (8), the first sentence establishes the expectation that the boss came to the party. The second sentence denies that expectation, and *"but"* signifies this denying relationship between the two sentences.

These kinds of denying or conflicting relationships between ideas or facts are often the motive for speaking or writing. There's a lot of *"but"* talk around us:

(9) Throughout the election campaign, the government promised to reduce the deficit. But they have actually increased spending during their first months in office.

These inconsistencies in experience, where promises are unfulfilled, or where surprises overturn the normal run of things, or where new developments make us revise our view of the world, are interesting and worth talking about. *"But"* situations make us want to say something.

And it seems that the relationships that are signified by *"but"* (and "however" and "nevertheless" and other members of the family of adverstive connectives) are especially prized by academic writers and readers. These revealed conflicts and discrepancies are often at the core of a strong, complex topic. Scholarly writers make the most of these adversative relationships, drawing their readers' attention to them. In the following passage, which appears in the first paragraph of an article on early labour activism in the Canadian West, the writer points to a discrepancy between common assumptions about pioneer opportunities and some actualities of frontier life.

(10) The frontier has been called the great leveller which broke down class distinction because men were equal, free and far from the traditional bonds and constraints of civilization. On the frontier every 'Jack' was as good as his master. But the settlement of the agricultural frontier was only part of the total picture of western development. An urban-industrial and a hinterland-extractive frontier was being opened at the same time which underwent spectacular productive expansion and attracted many thousands of pioneer workers. Most of these men had gone to the frontier pushed by the same ambitions and seeking the same opportunities as other immigrants. But once in western Canada most entered into closed and polarized communities and were forced to work in dangerous or unrewarding occupations. For these men there was little upward mobility, little opportunity for improvement. They were not free and were not as good as their masters.
From David Jay Bercuson (1982), "Labour Radicalism and the Western Industrial Frontier: 1897-1919." In *Readings in Canadian History: Post-Confederation*, ed. R.D. Francis and D.B. Smith, 156-175, pp. 156-57.

This writer uses sentence-initial *"but"* to thematize the logical profile of this element of his topic. Like *"and," "but"* can appear at the beginning of sentences to emphasize logical connection. And, like *"and"*, it has some semantic cousins which can also signify adversative, contrary relations.

however	despite (this)
yet	nevertheless
although	while
on the one hand...on the other hand	

Some of these adversative connectives can be used together, doubled to really enforce the writer's claim.

(11) Nevertheless, despite this promise of equality, most industrial workers found themselves dominated by powerful companies and labour-erratic markets.

Exercise

In the following passages, adversative connectives are only implicit. Rewrite, introducing explicit connectives to emphasize the contrary or conflicting logical relationship between ideas.

(1) Educators in seventeenth-century France, the France of the Sun King, agreed that schooling was necessary to train children for their station in life. The child should receive the education proper to the estate to which he or she had been called, and no more. The poor learned the deference proper to their condition. Girls learned to live inside the narrow intellectual and occupational limits society assigned to them. The reason that families, even poor families, were ready to forego their children's assistance in home or workshop, by sending them out to school, must have been that by doing this they hoped for their social promotion. It appears that schools offered something of material value: an instruction in basic skills, and a behaviour training for a society that was becoming more polished, more demanding.
   Adapted from Elizabeth Rapley (1987), "Fénelon Revisited: A Review of Girls' Education in Seventeenth Century France," *Histoire sociale—Social History*, 20, 40, 299- 318.

(2) Originally, the Martha Washington societies incorporated women alcoholics and supported them in their efforts to reform. By the mid-1840s female Washingtonians had lost much of their sympathy for female alcoholics. They saw them as defying

the parameters of acceptable womanhood. Female Washingtonians still treated male inebriates as reclaimable by womanly persuasion. They came to see female inebriates as lacking the moral will essential to "true women."

Adapted from Ruth M. Alexander (1988), "'We Are Engaged as a Band of Sisters': Class and Domesticity in the Washingtonian Temperance Movement, 1840-1850," *The Journal of American History*, 75, 3, 763-785.

(3) The concept of the family farm determined the nature of the land units made available to settlers, and this concept became enshrined if not fossilized in the 160-acre farm. Such a farm may have been suitable for family subsistence and family labour in eastern North America. It was hopelessly inadequate in parts of the more arid American West. It was tenaciously retained as the basic land unit, and suggestions that much larger units were required in the west were stubbornly rejected until the early decades of the twentieth century. By then, many homesteaders in the drier areas had given up the unequal struggle to survive on a 160-acre farm.

Adapted from A.S. Mather (1986), *Land Use* London: Longman.

4.2.3 Causal connectives

In speech, explicit causal connectives are often missing.

The speaker intends that his failure to wear a hat be understood as a cause of cold ears. (Or, at least, that could be his intention: maybe his frozen ears were tender and swollen, and, as a result, he couldn't wear a hat.) Cause is his reason for expressing these two notions—frozen ears and hatlessness—next to each other.

Whether the connection be causal or otherwise, speech situations often provide extra-lingual means of establishing logical connections: means such as voice intonation, facial expression, body gestures, elements of the immediate setting. It may be because these other means are available that implicit, unexpressed connectives are more frequent in speech than in writing. Or it may be that the causal connections expressed in formal writing (such as those between, say, the discount rate on treasury bills and the fluctuations in the equity market) are more difficult and unfamiliar than those expressed in informal speech (such as the causal connection between cold ears and hatlessness). As a consequence, written communication benefits from more *explicit expression of causal relationships.*

Besides, academic readers and writers especially appreciate explanations of cause and effect. Just as they value the discovery of adversative relationships in data, so too do they value the discovery of causal relationships. Writers foreground these relationships, drawing readers' attention to them with causal connectives.

"Because" is the most famous causal connective, and it, like *"and"* and *"but,"* is eligible for sentence-initial position.

(11) Because the 160-acre farm was typical of eastern North American family landholdings, it also became the measure of allotments in the West.

Yet many student writers are shy about putting *"because"* at the beginning of the sentence—for the same reasons that make them nervous about sentence-initial *"and"*: schoolroom prohibitions. Long ago, someone decided that children shouldn't start sentences with *"because."* This measure was probably intended to eradicate the dreaded sentence fragment.

(12) I miss my dog. He had to go away. Because he ate garbage.

Teachers want children to write:

(13) I miss my dog. He had to go away because he ate garbage.

One way of getting them to do this is to tell them never to begin a sentence with *"because."*

While this prohibition may get rid of some sentence fragments, it also deprives the writer of one form of emphatic expression of causal relationships:

(14) I miss my dog. Because he ate garbage, he had to go away.

As long as the *"because"* clause isn't standing by itself, trying to be a sentence, starting with *"because"* will not produce a fragment.

Like *"and"* and *"but,"* *"because"* has semantic cousins which can also thematize logical relationships. Here is a partial catalogue of other words and phrases which signify that the connections between ideas are relations of cause and effect:

therefore	as a result
so	for
hence	for this reason
consequently	because
because of this	owing to

Although each of these words or phrases has some restrictions on its position in the sentence, most are relatively mobile: writers can manipulate the position of these causal connectives to emphasize their topic's logical structure.

Exercise

The following passages express implicit causal relationships. Rewrite them, introducing explicit connectives that bring their logic into the foreground.

(1) In the years before and after the American Civil War, male artisans and apprentices were forced out of small home-based workshops and into an industrial wage economy. They lost immediate oversight of domestic affairs. Working-class women's responsibilities in caring for the needs of the family gained in scope and importance.

Adapted from Ruth M. Alexander (1988), "'We Are Engaged as a Band of Sisters': Class and Domesticity in the Washingtonian Temperance Movement, 1840-1850," *The Journal of American History*, 75, 3, 763-785.

(2) On the basis of salary and residential condition, police in early twentieth-century Toronto can be grouped with the lower middle class whose ranks included skilled workers. Police work was year-round and relatively permanent. Workers in the manufacturing and building trades were subject to seasonal lulls. Police enjoyed an economic advantage over these workers.

Adapted from M. Greg Marquis (1987), "Working Men in Uniform: The Early Twentieth-century Toronto Police Force," *Histoire Sociale — Social History*, 20, 40, 259-277.

(3) Proverbs are impersonal. They have an air of authority. They offer stereotyped advice on recurrent problems. They take no notice of what individuals in a situation may feel to be unique or personal about it. They make their point in an indirect, third-person manner. They leave it to the hearer to draw his own conclusions. Proverbs are anonymous and traditional. They have an existence of their own, independent of speakers and hearers alike.

Adapted from James Obelkevich (1987), "Proverbs and social history." In *The Social History of Language*, ed. P. Burke and R. Porter. Cambridge: Cambridge University Press, pp. 43-72.

4.2.4 Connectives and coherence

The study of logical connectives in language is a large domain: books and many articles have been written, and continue to be written, about the ways that units of text are logically hinged and attached to one another to produce intelligible discourse. What I have said here about additive, adversative, and causal connectives is only a very superficial introduction to the topic. I offer this information not to give you whole, technical understanding of this issue, but to give you a framework for observing the appearance and function of logical connectives in your reading and your writing.

Prominently placed and emphatic logical connectives contribute to coherence, topic, and meaning. They help to guide your reader's interpretation of facts, warding off ambiguity. They help to answer the reader's perpetual question: "Why is this being said to me now?"

- The reader encounters an emphatic additive connective.

Decisions about land use probably never conform to classical economics' purely rational model. This model assumes that decision-makers have full information, but common sense suggests that this condition of full information is unlikely to be fulfilled in ordinary circumstances. *Moreover*, decision-makers are prone to habitual behavior: having interpreted one land-use situation in a certain way, they are liable to make similar decisions in future situations, even when those situations may — rationally — call for different decisions.

With *moreover* the writer addresses the reader emphatically.

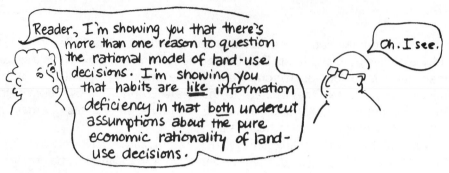

- The reader encounters an emphatic adversative connection:

Economics is an important influence on type and intensity of land use. But users may regard land as more than just a factor of production or a marketable commodity. And all decisions about land use cannot be understood in terms of economics alone. Land use is the product of human decision, and not just blind and impersonal economic forces.

With sentence-initial *but* the writer addresses the reader emphatically.

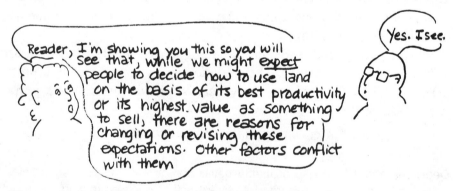

- The reader encounters an emphatic causal connective:

Owing to improvements in transportation and reductions in transport cost, huge areas of land remote from transportation centres were brought into use in the nineteenth century. As a result, relatively unpeopled areas like the American Mid-West could address the needs of distant centres by specializing in cash crops like wheat.

With sentence-initial *owing to* and *as a result*, the writer addresses the reader emphatically.

Discovering likenesses, conflicts, and causes is basic to intellectual activity. Writing that foregrounds or emphasizes them will be more likely to show a strong, complex topic to the reader.

Exercise

Like the passages in the three preceding exercises in this chapter, the passages below depend on implicit logical relationships.

(a) *Rewrite the passage to make the connections — additive, adversative, cause-and-effect — emphatic.*

(b) *Compose a topic statement that expresses the significance of the information and the relationships you have emphasized.*

Although this exercise has two steps, one following the other, you may find that, after you have worked on expressing the larger significance of this information, you will feel some incentive to go back to Step (a) and improve your emphatic expression of logical connections.

(1) One firm that owned several kinds of businesses had expanded too much and its profits started to decline. Management couldn't keep track of the firm's diverse operations. The firm decided to sell many of the businesses it owned. The managers could now focus on the remaining businesses. Now the company's earnings are much higher, and the price of its shares has risen.

(2) In seventeeth-century France, the classrooms of schools for girls were filled with scores, sometimes hundreds of children. Many of the children had no previous schooling. They were not used to orderly behaviour. Methods were developed to manage these crowds. Students were divided into smaller groups, at first according to subject: the *Filles de Notre Dame* divided their children into classes, for reading, writing, sewing, and handwork. The division which came to prevail was division according to ability and knowledge. The Ursulines of Dôle decided to divide their children into six grades. Fourier advised his canonnesses to use three levels: those who were learning their letters, those who were learning to read printed books, those who were able to read handwritten texts. Within these classes, there were divisions into benches, of ten or twenty students to a mistress. Each mistress had to keep her instruction within the limits assigned to her. The *Intendante*, or Mistress of Studies, reviewed the students' work several times a year, and the girls who had mastered the knowledge pertaining to their benches were promoted to a higher level. In time, uniform textbooks were introduced.

Adapted from Elizabeth Rapley (1987), "Fénelon Revisited: A Review of Girls' Education in Seventeenth Century France," *Histoire Sociale — Social History*, 20, 40, 299-318.

(3) Japanese patterns of late-life work and leisure differ from those in comparable countries. Japanese work longer and in fact prefer this situation in their attitudinal responses relative to other peoples. It is often thought that low pensions and social security benefits explain this situation. The ratio of the public pension to previous wage in Japan is higher than in the U.K., West Germany, the U.S.A., and Canada. It is true that some Japanese have been "underpensioned" as a result of job changes. This phenomenon is much more widespread in Australia and not unknown in any pension system with a significant occupational component. While pensions, at relatively good rates, are available, Japanese wage rates decline after retirement age is reached for both men and women. On average, rates are less than two-thirds of the peak seniority rates reached at about age 50. The phenomenon of seniority wages being revised downwards at retirement is exclusive to Japan. In other countries, constant rates and continuity of employment in the same job are the common pattern.

Adapted from John McCallum (1988), "Japanese *Teinen Taishoku*: How Cultural Values Affect Retirement," *Ageing and Society*.

Exercise

Review the plans you made in Chapter Three—your topical designs for writing about stress and about the Pacific Yew. Try to position the main logical connections in your plan: where are you claiming likeness *(additive or "and" connections);* conflict *(adversative or "but" connections);* cause-and-effect *(causal or "because" connections)? Write "and," "but," and "because" at the crucial logical junctions of your plan.*

4.3 Strategies for comparison

Logical connectives are part of topic structure: they guide the reader's interpretation of facts, signalling likeness, conflict, and causality. We know that such topic signals provide essential instructions to the reader's information-management device. To make their readers' comprehension as efficient as possible, writers repeatedly reinstate the topic and emphatically signal connections. These strategies keep the topic alive over long stretches of text, where the reader's desktop is liable to be overwhelmed by incoming detail.

And those long stretches of text extending from one landmark to the next always have the potential to put topic and meaning at risk. While "development" and "proof" expand, ambiguity and uncertainty are liable to set in. Although topic and purpose may be very clear in your mind (or, on the other hand, they may be not so very clear), the reader can easily forget a topic statement—even a startling or exact or sensational topic statement—she encountered at the beginning of a ten-page essay. Even by page two or page three, the reader may be so occupied with the local details of the discussion that the topic may be not only out of sight but also out of mind.

This final section of this chapter focusses on a type of argument which is particularly vulnerable to incoherence, and to the high-risk zones between landmarks in long stretches of text: comparison. Any form of argument or reasoning presents challenges to both the reader and the writer who try to keep the whole picture in mind. But comparison presents special challenges because it is by its very nature not one whole picture but two (or more) pictures.

Yet, despite its inherent difficulties, comparison is an illuminating and admired scholarly activity, capable of generating powerful and interesting logical structures. To get the most out of this powerful means of inquiry, academic writers develop skills in handling two (or more) entities at once, steering through likeness and difference. You should have the skills, too, so the rest of this chapter is devoted to strategies for comparison. But just before we go into these strategies and their rationale, we will look at a characteristic product of comparison, to get a sense of the kind of skilfull manoeuvres academic writers can execute when they compare two phenomena.

In Chapter Two you read and summarized an excerpt which described and interpreted nineteenth-century educational practice in North America. The beginning of this excerpt compared Canadian and American ideologies. That passage is presented again here. To draw your attention to the writers' sentence-level techniques, comparative expressions are printed in **bold**.

Late-19th-century literacy instruction in Canada **differed** in one crucial respect from its American counterpart. For **whereas Canadian schools** imported curricula from England, **teachers in America** were by this time provided with locally developed textbooks, in the tradition of the McGuffey readers. Noah Webster's American Spelling Book (1873), the most widely used textbook in United States history, not only promoted American history, geography, and morals, but was itself a model for an indigenous vocabulary and spelling. Textbooks and dictionaries of this period attempted to engender a national literacy and literature free of European "folly, corruption and tyranny," in Webster's words. **In Canada, by contrast**, classrooms featured icons of colonialism: British Flags and pictures of royalty adorned the walls, younger students were initiated to print via the Irish readers, and literature texts opened with Wordsworth's and Tennysons's panegyrics to the Crown. **In Canada**, the reduction in pauperism and crime associated with illiteracy was seen as requiring the preservation of British culture and a colonial sensibility; **in the United States**, "custodians of culture" (May, 1959, p.30) sought to assure economic independence and political participation. The match between these

differing societal and educational ideologies and the "civilizing" effects of traditional three Rs and classical education was near-perfect.

The comparative connectives keep both the U.S. and Canada in mind at once, as contrasting entities. The second-to-last sentence uses a semi-colon to signal to the reader the importance of keeping both phenomena close to each other. Then the final sentences claims that, despite conspicuous differences, both these ideologies were served by the same educational practice.

This passage is a good model. But it's also very short, and, moreover, it's the end product of a long process. How do you get to this point where you present your reader with a tightly woven frabric of comparative claims? How do you manage five or ten pages of comparison?

Writers normally tackle comparative projects by means of one of two different comparative strategies. We'll look at the first of these strategies in some detail, and the second more briefly.

4.3.1 First discuss A; then discuss B.

Maybe the most obvious way of going about a comparison is to let the two-part structure of your data dictate the organization of your essay: the essay has two parts, too. Figure (1) below shows the shape of the kind of essay that results from this approach. Discussion of A is represented by ~ ~ ~ ~. Discussion of B is represented by = = = = = =.

Figure (1)

This essay could fracture right down the middle, splitting along the fault lines which separate A and B from each other. While readers advance through B, they're on their own in interpreting B in light of A. And we know we can't leave readers on their own to interpret the facts. Moreover, by the time readers are immersed in B, they have, for all practical purposes, forgotten what the writer said about A.

However, despite the natural or inherent divisiveness of the A-then-B comparison, you can still turn it into a coherent and meaningful text. You can overcome inherent divisiveness by applying what we've learned about *topic statements* and their power to guide the reader's interpretation of facts and mentions.

We know what topic statements are: they're the claims at higher, often abstract levels of generality which represent the significance of lower level information. In Chapter Three, where disproportion had left the reader constructing her own topics from long stretches of detail about Asian firms and samurai owners and the South Korean GNP, we saw how revision corrected this disproportion by reinstating topical material at intervals throughout the passage. The same strategy, in a slightly more complex form, can also repair the fault line in the A-then-B comparison essay. While your first draft may resemble Figure (1) above, the version you deliver to your reader should present a structure more like the one diagrammed in Figure (2) below. Figure (2) shows main claims about A as ●●●●, and supported by lower level material ~ ~ ~ ~. These main claims about A, once established, are then carried forward, where they appear next to main claims about B—represented as ◊◊◊◊. These topical claims about B are supported by lower level information = = = =.

Figure (2)

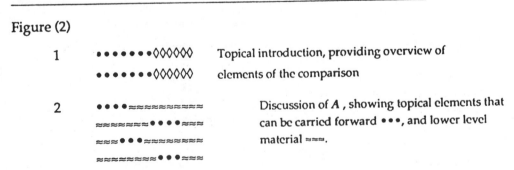

1 ● ● ● ● ● ● ●◊◊◊◊◊◊   Topical introduction, providing overview of
  ● ● ● ● ● ● ●◊◊◊◊◊◊   elements of the comparison

2 ● ● ● ●≈≈≈≈≈≈≈≈≈   Discussion of *A* , showing topical elements that
  ≈≈≈≈≈≈≈● ● ● ●≈≈≈   can be carried forward ● ● ●, and lower level
  ≈≈≈● ● ●≈≈≈≈≈≈≈   material ≈≈≈.
  ≈≈≈≈≈≈≈≈≈● ● ●≈≈≈

3	• • •◊◊◊====== ==• •◊◊◊===== =======◊◊◊• •== =============== • • •◊◊◊====◊◊◊	Discussion of *B*, showing topical elements from discussion of *A* recalled and set next to topical claims about *B* ◊◊◊ which are supported by lower level material ===.
4	• • • •◊◊◊• • • •◊◊	Conclusion, which reviews comparison, explaining the significance of its findings.

In this structure, readers are never left on their own to speculate on the reasons for certain features of the two entities being mentioned. Readers' information-management devices are consistently instructed—and reminded—as to what's important and what has to be kept in mind. The first section prepares them for the main issues that will be treated in subsequent sections; the second unit controls what use readers make of material about A and packages that material in convenient, portable bundles ● ● ● that can be carried forward to the discussion of B. In the third section, topic statements ¤¤¤ guide the reader's interpretation and management of information about B, and provide efficient points of comparison for the statements about A that have been carried forward.

Below is a brief example of how such a structure might work out in prose. (Its brevity makes comparison easier than it would be in longer texts, but the strategies used here are also applicable to those longer texts, where they are actually *more* important to coherence.) To emphasize the weaving together of topical claims in the third section, words and phrases that remind the reader of the main elements of the comparison are printed in **bold** font.

Alice Munro's *Lives of Girls and Women* and Isabel Huggan's *The Elizabeth Stories* each describe childhood and adolescence in small-town Ontario, reviewing the process of growing up against a background of the community's character. Both these collections of stories depend on the special qualities of the child's point of view—a naive perspective revealing secret life beneath social surfaces. But their narrators occupy different positions in the community: Huggan's story-teller is socially central, Munro's off-centre. Finally, these different orientations distinguish their voices from one another. While the child on the edge of social life earns some privacy from her lack of social prominence, the child at the centre becomes a spectacle, and the object of relentless pressures to conform. Accordingly, Munro's narrator addresses her hometown with some charity—alienated but still sympathetic. Huggan's narrator, on the other hand, finds nothing to sympathize with, finds only a harsh motive to repudiate the site of childhood.

Del Jordan, heroine of *Lives of Girls and Women*, narrates the stories that present the child's small-town world. She tells both what is going on within—her own changing anxieties and fantasies and perplexities—and what is going on beyond herself—the array of practices and characters which comprise Jubilee. She and her family do not quite fit into the Jubilee social scheme: they are outsiders, somewhat estranged from the town's social patterns. Del's father's fox farm on the outskirts of town, her mother's intellectual antics, Del's own detachment from goings-on she watches with both desire and aloofness—all these elements make Del's experience slightly off-centre. Being off-centre leads to embarrassments. But, in all, Del seems to live in a private world, mostly unnoticed, from which she observes the community around her.

That community is full of peculiar passions and odd distortions that Del, as narrator, watches with powerful interest. Pork Childs and his peacock, Miss Farris and her lonely, theatrical convictions, Naomi's adolescence subsiding into a gruesome marriage: these are stories Del reports with a detached ruthlessness that is at the same time somehow sympathetic. The final scene of the book, where Bobby Sherriff pirouettes, is a sign of the narrator's chill love for the grotesque.

Huggan's Elizabeth is the narrator of her own childhood, **too: like Dell**, she monitors her own **internal scene** while she keeps an eye on **the world around her. Unlike Dell, however,** who occupies an **off-centre** position in the town's social scheme, Elizabeth and her family are thoroughly **integrated** into the upper social levels of Garten. Her father is a banker; her mother performs the regular social rituals and urges Elizabeth to **conformity**. But, surprisingly, this **integration** with the community is finally a **more** painful circumstance **than Del's estrangements. Whereas Del's embarrassments are sheltered by her obscurity**, Elizabeth's are **conspicuous**, and amount to **shame and humiliation** rather than mere **embarrassment**. The uproar that follows her attack on her sickly companion, the outcry that follows her sexual encounter with the butcher's son, the nightmarish exposure of her bulky physique at the ballet recital—all these are huge, **public mortifications**. Elizabeth is as much **observed as observer. Del's position in her community, on the other hand**, makes her more **spectator than spectacle**.

Elizabeth's position in the community influences the attitude of her portrayal of that community. **While Del watches with ruthless but sympathetic eye**—detecting **grotesquerie** but somehow **cherishing** it—Elizabeth's outlook is

brutal and utterly **hostile**. Her **contempt** for the town at large is clear enough. But it is her loathing of her own family, her father in particular, that reveals the savage energy behind her portrait of life in Garten. Her father is so mean-spirited, so lacking in ordinary sensibility as to seem scarcely human. Del **exposes but sympathizes**; Elizabeth **exposes and repudiates**.

At the end of **each book**, the narrators prepare for departure. Yet they turn away from these places with very **different** gestures: Elizabeth **slams the door shut** on the place that **mortified** her and made a **spectacle** out of her, **while** Del turns away **more gently**, with a motion that suggests she will be looking over her shoulder as she goes, fascinated if not fond.

Had this been a longer piece, I would have developed elements of it, spending more time at lower levels of generality. In the section on *Lives of Girls and Women*, I would have examined more thoroughly Munro's treatment of Del's family and of Del's watchfulness, citing material from the novel. And I would have demonstrated more thoroughly the element of public shame in *The Elizabeth Stories* by analyzing instances of it. Moreover, I would have "proven" my claim about Elizabeth's father by referring to specific passages from the book.

Had this passage grown up into a full-blown academic essay, comparative strategies would have been even more crucial to *coherence*, as paragraphs multiplied and the reader faced long stretches of detail and analysis. These strategies involve not only repeated reinstatements of topic, but also features of sentence style: useful words and phrases like "whereas," "unlike," "like," "while," "on the one hand...on the other hand."

Now we will look, more briefly, at the second principal mode of comparison.

4.3.2 Discuss A and B alternately.

If the writer chooses to discuss A and B alternately instead of one after the other, she can begin her planning by identifying parallel elements in A and B. For example, material on *Lives of Girls and Women* and *The Elizabeth Stories* can be divided into five main categories.

how the story is told
the position of the narrator's family in the community
embarrassment
narrator's attitude towards those around her

departure

Having found these parallel categories, the writer can arrange her discussion this way, weaving A and B together:

Figure (3)

1	≈≈≈≈≈≈≈≈≈≈ A ≈≈≈≈≈≈≈≈≈≈ ============= B =============	How *LGW* tells the story, compared with how *ES* tells the story
2	≈≈≈≈≈≈≈≈≈≈ A ≈≈≈≈≈≈≈≈≈≈ ============= B =============	The narrator's community status in *LGW* compared with the narrator's community status in *ES*
3	≈≈≈≈≈≈≈≈≈≈ A ≈≈≈≈≈≈≈≈≈≈ ============= B =============	The narrator's embarrassments in *LGW* compared with the narrator's embarrassments in *ES*
4	≈≈≈≈≈≈≈≈≈≈ A ≈≈≈≈≈≈≈≈≈≈ ============= B =============	*LGW*'s narrator's attitudes compared with *ES*'s narrator's attitudes
5	≈≈≈≈≈≈≈≈≈≈ A ≈≈≈≈≈≈≈≈≈≈ ============= B	*LGW*'s narrator's departure compared with *ES*'s narrator's departure

---

Section 1 tells about how each story is told; Section 2 tells about each narrator's position in the community, and so on.

This structure seems tight-knit. But it does have a serious shortcoming in the way it fragments each of the compared entities. *You* may have a bright, fresh picture of the whole character of A and the whole character of B, but your *reader* may not.

The 'alternately' pattern—tight as it appears on the surface—may actually make your discussion appear piecemeal to the reader as it constantly fluctuates between one entity and the other. Strong topic statements that introduce each section and carry forward important material from previous sections can help to overcome the inherent fragmentation of this scheme.

I recommend the first method—A-then-B—for academic writing, as long as the topic structure is made strong by repeated reminders of earlier claims. But I know that technical writers—report-writers, especially—often favor the second method. Since the forms of technical writing generally evolve from the need for perfect clarity and readability, I know there must be some real virtues in the second way of going about comparison.

4.3.3 Finding a focus for comparison

Let's say you have to write a comparison of two articles on testing in early-childhood education. Your first job is to master the contents of each article: you prepare for summary, identifying in each article its crucial claims and the relationships between them. You already have experience doing this.

But when you put the two sets of material for summary together, you find that some things from A have no counterpart in B, and vice versa. The first article dwells on tests of visual acuity; the second doesn't even consider these measures. The second goes into curricular implications; the first only mentions such issues. In this situation, with all these loose strands, how do you accomplish the close-woven fabric of the coherent, meaningful comparison?

Look at the problem from the reader's point of view: he expects that the parts of the essay will combine into a meaningful whole, bound together by a strong, complex topic. If some parts have no bearing on other parts, they will produce ambiguity and disorder on the reader's mental desktop. To satisfy the reader's expectations, and the conditions of efficient comprehension, you need to find a focus that embraces both articles. You need to construct the categories that show up in both articles, and from this common ground develop your topic.

At the same time, you may want to let your reader know that you are aware that you are not accounting for every aspect of each article. You can do this openly, directly, near the beginning of your discussion where you provide an overview of the argument you will present.

Curtis examines curricular implications in much more detail than Zowolski does, while Zowolski provides a more complete inventory of testing procedures. Where these two researchers do explore common ground is in their respective discussions of institutional contexts for testing. Whereas Curtis' research suggests that testing is too often an open-ended process unchecked by reference to classroom experience, Zowolski's studies focus on mismatches between testing parameters and the expertise of those who administer the tests. Each writer evaluates the connections between test and institution, but they do so from different perspectives on educational practice.

As long as "curricular implications" and the "complete inventory" are not developed, and the topic of "institutional contexts" is repeatedly reinstated and supported by extensive development, the reader will probably be ready to concentrate on the "common ground" and interpret information accordingly.

4.3.4 Differences and similarities

A strong topical focus will let your reader see how every aspect of A you develop relates to B. The simplest level of relationship is difference and similarity: B is different from A in this respect, the same in this other respect. But, finally, difference and similarity do not by themselves constitute a strong, complex topic. Your reader will still need to know what the pattern of similarities and differences adds up to. Comparison in itself does not relieve you of the responsibilities described in the section on evaluation at the beginning of Chapter Three.

Comparison is a powerful instrument of reasoning and analysis. But its products still need to be interpreted for the reader. Having discovered these similarities and differences, you need to evaluate their significance. What do they mean?

Exercise

Following the A-then-B model, write a comparison of the two types of families described by the data below. Compose an introductory paragraph that names the essential issues to be considered, and the connections between them. Write one section on one type of family, and then another section on the other type of family. (In doing so, feel free to go ahead and develop lower-level material that demonstrates the generalizations provided in the data. Consult your own expereince and observation of family life.) In the section on the second type of family, remind the reader of the relevant points of comparison from the description of the first type of family. (Practise using the words and phrases that draw attention to comparisons: "whereas," "like," "unlike," and so on.) Compose a concluding paragraph that confirms the main points of the comparison and speculates on the significance of these matters.

"Two kinds of families"

parents reason with child, pointing out positive or negative consequences of his or her behavior for other people	parents use highly forceful discipline
parents explain reasons for rules and prohibitions	parents deprive children of rights and privileges; use frequent or severe physical punishment
parents provide guidance and control reflecting at least minimal standards of behavior	parents are critical and rejecting
parents are models of positive behavior	coercion is dominant mode of relating among family members
children are repeatedly led to help others (e.g. taking toys to hospitalized children)	*result:* child is more aggressive
result: child sees other people as benevolent and trustworthy; develops feeling of responsibility for other peoples welfare; feels self-esteem	child regards aggression as normal and even necessary for defending himself and for influencing others

Adapted from Ervin Staub (1988), "The Evolution of Caring and Non-aggressive Persons and Societies." *Journal of Social Issues*, 44, 2, 81-100.

CHAPTER FIVE

quotation and documentation

5.1 Proof

Aware now of the way academic prose moves up and down through the levels of generality, we know that as writers we must give our readers high-level, often abstract guides to interpretation of facts in order establish meaning and avoid ambiguity. But we also know that those high-level statements must be *developed, demonstrated, supported*—in other words, *proven*.

In a way, this need for *proof* is an ordinary part of day-to-day communication. Newcasters *prove* their headline that inflation is down—or up—by repeating statistics. Or they *support* a claim that spousal assault is a serious social problem by referring to a study by experts. Even advertisers, whose claims are often doubtful, must offer at least the appearance of proof to make consumers pay attention to their assertions: the excellence of a type of beer is "proven" by pictures of actors enjoying themselves.

And I have just "proven" my statement that the "need for proof is an ordinary part of day-to-day communication" by presenting these examples from news broadcasts and television advertising. Perhaps you think that your English teachers have nagged too much about the need to "use examples," but their advice was sound. Without some demonstration or development of our assertions—however true they may be—our utterances seem merely stubborn or opinionated (unless the listener is in complete agreement anyway and would have said the same thing himself).

Moreover, readers are much more likely to absorb claims that are demonstrated through descent to lower levels of generality. Although they may forget the details of an argument, readers' comprehension seems to benefit when they experience these lower levels of generality which show how the topic works in more specific domains of information.

So your English teachers gave you good advice when they told you to provide examples. However, some ways of delivering this advice may misrepresent the reasoning that goes into writing. When someone instructs you to "give examples to support your thesis," that person may seem to be assuming that first you have your main idea and then you find the information that makes this idea true. Yet, in their natural sequence, our reading-thinking-writing processes most often start with the particulars that later become "examples" and "proof" for the reader. Lower-level information arrives for your analysis, generalization, and interpretation. Those analyses and interpretations develop into your topic—the complex, interesting, high-level claims that hold your essay together.

In academic essay-writing, most of the particulars that initiate your reasoning come from your reading experience. When these particulars later become "examples" and "proof" for your reader, you introduce them into your essay as summary, paraphrase, and quotation. Proof from reading requires a rather elaborate frame before it can be introduced into your essay. We've already discussed some elements of that framing: naming sources and using certain phrases to establish clearly the extent of another writer's contribution to your ideas. Now we will look at more techniques involved in this conventional framing of proof—in particular, those techniques that allow you to introduce quotation.

5.2 Quotation

Everybody knows that material from other sources has to be identified as such: you have to put quotation marks around other people's words when you use them in your own writing. But not everybody is sure about how to fulfill this obligation. Where do the quotation marks go in relation to other punctuation marks? What counts as "other people's words"? And, beyond the technical level, many student writers don't have very reliable methods for integrating quotations into their own prose. The following discussion of quotation will address not only the technical level but the content level as well: it will show how to make your quotations coherent elements of the whole argument, rather than pasted-on afterthoughts.

5.2.1 Quoting a whole sentence

The simplest type of quotation is that which introduces into your essay a complete sentence from a book or article which is one of your sources of information. Passage (1) below is an example of that kind of citation. It shows the writer leading the reader to the material from the outside source (Colin Platt, *The English Mediaeval Town* (1979)), paraphrasing the original to emphasize the points that the reader should be keeping in mind. Notice in particular that, even though the quotation is a complete sentence, it is not left to speak for itself.

(1)

Platt explains that in the medieval town business and residential districts were not separate because town-dwellers liked to live where they did business: "Characteristically, the failure to distinguish a residential from a commercial sector made of each street a market of its own, the better for being more accessible."

FRAME identifies the source of information

PARAPHRASE summarizes the context of information and guides the reader's interpretation of the material that will be quoted; the paraphrase is a complete sentence.

COLON separates the writer's own sentence from the quoted sentence.

QUOTATION MARKS surround the exact repetition of material from the source.

5.2.2 Quoting parts of sentences

When you quote less than a full sentence, you are liable to run into problems of two kinds: first, deciding where to place quotation marks—deciding, that is, which words are the author's property and which are part of the "public domain"; second, making the quoted material grammatically compatible with your own sentence.

When to enclose words and phrases in quotation marks

Sometimes some of the words you use in a summarizing paraphrase will be the same as the words and phrases that appear in the text you are paraphrasing.

Sometimes these words that are the same need quotation marks, and sometimes they do not. To illustrate the criteria by which the essay writer decides when to use quotation marks, I will show you first a passage from a source and then a passage of my own writing that makes use of the source.

Here is a passage from Platt's book of medieval English towns. In this passage, Platt discusses the relationship between business confidence and capital expenditures by local governments. (It's a relationship that is still an issue in the minds of today's taxpayers and politicians.) In this case, the instance of capital expenditure is the construction of walls around newly established market towns.

> Well illustrating the attractions of a work that had more than military objectives to recommend it, the great fortified circuit of Coventry was constructed only after the borough had secured its independence. Over the 200 years it took to complete, the Coventry defensive system absorbed much of the surplus revenue of the borough, but it stood, even while building, as a notable expression of corporate independence and pride. Promising security and good government, it attracted trade to the town. In contemporary Hull, it was precisely this quality in the enhancement of trade which was advanced by the burgesses in 1321 as their first reason for walling the town. Prosperous, like Coventry, while other towns were suffering a decline, Hull built itself, through the second half of the fourteenth century, a massive circuit wall studded with interval towers, one of which has recently been excavated. Constructed of locally manufactured bricks, it was probably the first major public work in mediaeval England to have been carried out in this new material.

Passage (2) puts the original to use in a mixture of paraphrase and quotation. Some words that repeat the original appear in quotation marks. But others do not. For the purposes of the discussion that follows Passage (2), these repeated words without quotation marks are printed in *italics*.

(2) Although costly, the construction of walls around medieval towns had some effects on the business life of these towns. To illustrate these effects, Platt refers to the construction of Coventry's *defensive system*. Despite the 200 years it took to build, and despite the burden it imposed on *borough revenues*, Coventry's *defensive system* was an important asset that expressed "corporate independence and pride." Because the project promised "security and good government," it inspired commercial confidence and *attracted* business to Coventry.

The words and phrases in *italics* are the same as words and phrases in Platt's writing, yet I have not enclosed them in quotation marks. I decided that they belonged to the "public domain": anybody discussing the construction of medieval town walls is almost obliged to use terms like *defensive system, borough,* and *revenue.* Moreover, *attracted* expresses an event-phenomenon inherent in the topic of business confidence, and can hardly be said to be the exclusive property of Colin Platt. (Notice, though, that the second sentence of my version of this information clearly establishes my overall indebtedness to Platt: I certainly would have very little to say about proud, confident buisness people in walled towns if it weren't for Platt and his book.)

The words and phrases in quotation marks also coincide with material from the original. In my judgement, they are the property of the writer because they are interpretive and they could not have been predicted as terms likely to be used in a discussion of this topic. With the quotation marks, I acknowledge my summary's specific debt to the language with which the original writer expresses his valuable insights.

You can see that judgement plays a part in this kind of decision: I think that "revenues" is predictable, while "corporate independence and pride" is interpretive and unpredictable. Other people might make different judgements. The following exercise gives you a chance to exercise your judgement on these matters, and compare the results with the judgements your classmates and instructor make in the same situation.

Exercise

This exercise presents first an excerpt from a source, and then a summary of that excerpt. The summary takes some words directly from the original.

Read both original and summary. Introduce into the summary quotation marks where you judge them to be necessary. Compare your version to those of your classmates.

Original

Reading the world always precedes reading the word, and reading the word implies continually reading the world. This movement from the word to the world is always present; even the spoken word flows from our reading of the world. In a way, however, we can go further and say that reading the word is not preceded merely by reading the world, but by a certain form of writing it or rewriting it, that is, of transforming it by means of conscious, practical work. For me, this dynamic movement is central to the literacy process.

For this reason I have always insisted that words used in organizing a literacy program come from what I call the "word universe" of people who are learning, expressing their actual language, their anxieties, fears, demands, and dreams. Words should be laden with the meaning of the people's existential experience, and not of the teacher's experience. Surveying the word universe thus gives us the people's words, pregnant with the world, words from the people's reading of the world. We then give the words back to the people inserted in what I call "codifications," pictures representing real situations. The word "brick", for example, might be inserted in a pictorial representation of a group of bricklayers constructing a house.

Paulo Freire (1987) "The Importance of the Act of Reading," in Paulo Freire and Donaldo Macedo, *Literacy: Reading the Word and the World*. Massachusetts: Begin and Garvey, 29-36, pp. 35-36.

Summary

Paulo Friere's literacy program focusses on words from the learner's—not the teacher's—experience. In describing the principles which direct his literacy projects, Friere says that reading the world always precedes reading the word: that is, people's talk about their world is itself a reading, and our conscious, practical work—our action—is itself a writing or rewriting of the world. With this in mind, teachers using his method respresent to their students the students' own world, and in these representations they embed the words to be read. As an example of this practice, Friere suggests a pictorial representation of a group of bricklayers constructing a house—a codification of the learners' world—with the word "brick" inserted into the picture.

How to make the quoted material grammatically compatible with its surroundings

The occurrence of the enclosed phrases in (2)—"corporate independence and pride" and "security and good government"—also illustrates another aspect of the process of quoting parts of sentences: grammatical integrity. The words you quote must fit into the grammar of your own sentence. Sometimes you have to do some fiddling to achieve this fit.

In the original text, "corporate independence and pride" is part of a longer sequence: "as a notable expression of corporate independence and pride." This original sequence wouldn't fit into the sentence I had written as its vehicle. Sentence (3) doesn't sound right at all:

(3) Coventry's defensive system was an important asset that "as a notable expression of corporate independence and pride."

But this mis-fit was no reason to abandon either the sentence or the quotation. I simply had to make some grammatical adjustments. To get the original material to fit into my sentence, I kept the meaning of "expression" but changed it from a noun into a verb: "expression" (noun) —> "expressed" (verb). Having made this grammatical change, I had to exclude the grammatically altered word from the surrounding quotation marks.

(4) Despite the 200 years it took to build, and despite the burden it imposed on borough revenues, Coventry's defensive system was an important asset that expressed "corporate independence and pride."

The second quoted element—"security and good government"—also underwent grammatical adjustments: "promising" would not fit into the grammar of my sentence:

(5) Because the project "promising security and good government," it inspired commercial confidence and attracted business to Coventry.

"Promising" became "promised", and like the altered "expression," it was excluded from quotation marks:

(6) Because the project promised "security and good government," it inspired commercial confidence and attracted business to Coventry.

Sometimes the incompatible relations between a quotation and its environment don't show up in grammatical clashes within the sentence or clause or phrase. These other types of incompatibility often show up in ambiguities associated with pronoun reference.

Pronouns are function words like "it," "she," "they," which stand in for nouns. In *Some instructors gave Albert high marks, but they rarely praised him*; "they" stands in for the noun phrase "some instructors," while "him" stands in for the noun phrase "Albert." "Him" refers to "Albert"; "they" refers to "some instructors."

As you can see, the operation of *pronoun reference* depends on the relationship between the pronoun and preceding discourse: what has already been said. When you introduce quotations, you compose the preceding discourse, and then you switch to someone else's writing to continue. This switch can lead to problems with pronoun reference. Now we'll look at these problems and techniques for solving them.

Here is a sentence from Platt about medieval suburbs:

Characteristically, they stretch out in an untidy ribbon along the lines of the principal approach roads, clustering in particular about the enlarged open spaces that were usually to be met with about the gates.

Here is the same sentence as a quotation, preceded by an introductory paraphrase:

(7) Medieval suburban development was disorderly and ragged: "Characteristically, they stretched out in an untidy ribbon along the lines of the principal approach roads, clustering in particular about the enlarged open spaces that were usually to be met with about the gates."

What does "they" refer to? In the preceding discourse, there is no plural noun for which pronoun "they" can be standing in. As a result, the quotation is *grammatically incompatible* with its surroundings.

There are three ways of repairing this incompatibility.

(a) Start the quotation later.

Medieval suburban development was disorderly and ragged: the suburbs "stretched out in an untidy ribbon along the lines of the principal approach roads, clustering in particular about the enlarged open spaces that were usually to be met with about the gates."

However, if the writer wanted to keep "characteristically," she would have to choose one of the two other solutions to the problem.

(b) Alter the quotation to make it fit. Introduce the noun that "they" stands in for, thus correcting the pronoun reference fault:

Medieval suburban development was disorderly and ragged: "Charac-teristically, they [the suburbs] stretched out in an untidy ribbon along the lines of the principal approach roads, clustering in particular about the enlarged open spaces that were usually to be met with about the gates."

The square brackets [ ] signify that the words inside them do not appear in the original text, and that they are a change introduced by the present writer.

(c) Change the introductory sentence to provide the noun "they" refers to.

Medieval suburbs were disorderly and ragged: "Characteristically, they stretched out in an untidy ribbon along the lines of the principal approach roads, clustering in particular about the enlarged open spaces that were usually to be met with about the gates."

Now "they" clearly refers to "medieval suburbs," and the quotation is grammatically compatible with its environment.

When this kind of grammatical incompatibilty confronts you, you always have the choice of altering either the quotation or the surrounding text. On the whole, it's probably better to leave to quoted material intact, and avoid square-bracket intrusions. But sometimes the words you have chosen to introduce the quotation may be very important to your topic, and you won't want to change them. For example, the writer of (7) may really want to say "suburban development " and not "suburbs": "development" is topical and important to keeping the reader concentrating in the right direction. Then she can use the square-bracket device to preserve her own word choice.

Quotation marks are not syntactic markers: that is, unlike commas, periods, semi-colons, and so on, quotation marks are not dictated by sentence structure. In fact, they have nothing to do with sentence structure. This circumstance may suggest to some writers that sentences with quotation marks don't have to obey the same constraints as ordinary sentences.

So, what do I have so far? Town-dwellers valued the borough defences quote stood as a permanent reminder of important legal & social distinctions unquote — that doesn't sound right. But I have quotation marks. It's probably OK.

Quite the contrary is true: quotation marks do not confer on the writer licence to compose peculiar sentences. The same conditions for grammaticality apply whether the sentence has quotation marks or not. If you're in doubt about the compatibility of quoted material and its surroundings, try taking the quotation marks away: does the sentence sound acceptable? If not, make adjustments along the lines suggested in this section.

5.2.3 Quoting sentences with parts missing

Very often, quotation is part of the summarizing process and, therefore, part of the process of *condensing, reducing, economizing.* However, as writers, we often feel the urge to quote very freely and generously, to represent more completely our reading experience. The economy of summary and the urge to quote freely often conflict.

To reconcile these competing goals, writers sometimes use ellipsis. Ellipsis, in this case, is the *omission of words, phrases or sentences from a quoted passage.* Such omissions are marked by a series of three dots— ... —called ellipsis points.

Say I find a sentence in Platt that says something I really want to get across. Aware of the goal of economy, but wanting to preserve the structure of the sentence, I select the part of the sentence least crucial to my message. In this case, it's a part that only elaborates or enforces another part of the sentence.

> The borough defences would have stood as a permanent reminder of an important legal and social distinction, *built up over many years and at great cost*, between the town and the countryside beyond.

I can delete the material in *italics* without destroying the meaning or grammaticality of the passage. Everything in italics—including the commas which surround the deleted phrase in the original—will be replaced by three ellipsis points.

(8) Town dwellers, on the whole, preferred to live within the town walls: "Borough defences would have stood as a permanent reminder of an important legal and social distinction...between the town and the countryside beyond."

The same procedure applies to deleted words and phrases which in the original passage occur at the end of a sentence. Still on the topic of walls and their meaning, I have found another sentence in Platt. Here it is, with potentially deletable material in italics.

> Although commonly within the franchise of the town, the suburb stood physically in relation to its begetter rather as did the surrounding countryside, *firmly excluded by its walls.*

The words in italic font can be deleted without destroying the meaning or grammaticality of the passage. In (9) I introduce and present the passage, replacing everything in italics by three ellipsis points.

(9) Even though the suburban cottages nestled close to the gates of the town and enjoyed close economic ties with the town, they were clearly distinguished from it: "Although commonly within the franchise of the town, the suburb stood physically in relation to its begetter rather as did the surrounding countryside...."

You may think that I've broken the three-point rule by ending the quotation with four points. But I have only followed previous practice: I have replaced omitted words with three ellipsis points. The period at the end of the original sentence is not part of the omitted material (any more than it was in the previous example), and it must be retained to preserve the grammaticality of the quotation.

Ellipsis can also occur in quotations shorter than sentences. Here is a passage from which I, as writer of an essay about the economy and arrangement of medieval towns, want to cite a small piece. Platt is referring to a fifteenth-century terrier (a register of property owned by individuals or corporations); the particular document he has in mind listed property assessments in medieval Southampton.

> Conceivably, the poorest dwellings at Southampton were not listed in the terrier, as not liable to defence charges. Yet the document itself is exceptionally complete, sufficient evidence for a convincing map to be compiled of the tenement pattern in the late-medieval town, and the small total of cottages recorded there can suggest only that the labouring poor lived, for the most part, outside the defended enceinte of the borough, and that the very poorest, unidentifiable in any surviving record, are likely to have done the same.

Wanting to repeat these ideas as important to understanding the character of the medieval suburb, and wanting to establish the fact that the suburb didn't leave records of its existence the way the wealthier town did, I summarize and quote this way:

(10) From evidence available in a fifteenth-century list of taxable properties in Southampton, Platt infers that the poorest laborers "lived...outside the defended enceinte of the borough," for borough records show no trace of them.

The three ellipsis points mark the omission of "for the most part" from the original "lived, for the most part, outside the defended enceinte of the borough." But no ellipsis points appear at the beginning and ending of the quoted material, although, obviously, masses of material have been left out. The ellipsis points don't appear at the beginning and ending because it is so obvious that material has been omitted. Any reader would know that "lived...outside the defended enceinte of the borough" must have appeared as part of a sentence in the original text, and that the surrounding words have been left out. However, it would not be at all obvious that a word was missing from "lived outside the defended enceinte of the borough," and that's why ellipsis points are there.

Use ellipsis points to signal omissions that would otherwise not be recognized by the reader.

A writer uses ellipsis

Below is an example of a writer using ellipsis extensively to condense quoted material. The passage comes from an article by William Lanouette called "A High-Risk Numbers Game" (*The Atlantic*, Dec. 1984). In this article, Lanouette describes the practice of making money on the stock market by buying and selling futures contracts on stock indexes (the Dow Jones Industrial Average is one such index). In the part of the article from which the passage comes, Lanouette explains the degree of risk involved in this complicated practice. To do so he cites material from the Commodity Futures Trading Commission, the U.S. agency that monitors futures trading and requires brokers to explain the risk involved to their clients.

One CFTC risk-disclosure statement cautions: "The high degree of leverage that is often obtainable in futures trading because of the small margin requirements can work against you as well as for you. The use of leverage can lead to large losses as well as gains." The agency warns that "you may sustain a total loss of the initial margin funds and any additional funds that you deposit with your broker.... If the market moves against your position, you may be called upon by your broker to deposit a substantial amount of additional margin funds, on short notice, in order to maintain your position.... Under certain market conditions, you may find it difficult or impossible to liquidate a position.... Placing contingent orders...will not necessarily limit your losses to the intended amounts, since market conditions may make it impossible to execute such orders."

Notice that the writer has carefully designed the ellipses to preserve the grammaticality of the quotation and its surroundings.

A caution about ellipsis points

In your university writing, you should not use ellipsis points for purposes other than those we have examined here in connection with quotation. Do not use ellipsis points to let provocative or mysterious statements trail off coyly.

(11) Modern urban dwellers, proud of their impeccable lawns and imitation-tudor mansions, might be surprised to hear about the early history of suburban development...

What should the reader take this to mean? Why would people with nice lawns be surprised? Ellipsis points say that something is missing, and that's acceptable in quotation. But your own argument is supposed to be complete and thorough, not impressionistic or mysterious. Outside quotation marks, ellipsis points are too informal for academic writing, although their secretive suggestiveness may be useful to you on literary or personal writing occasions.

5.2.4 Quoting more than one or two sentences

When you feel like quoting a substantial part of a paragraph, or even more than a whole paragraph, think twice before you do so. Substantial quotation is a heavy burden for an essay to carry, and your essay will have to be very robust if it's to make any headway once it's burdened with huge quotations.

Can you paraphrase instead, using quoted phrases and sentences to establish the source's contribution and to authenticate your summary? Take another look at that paragraph you want to quote in its entirety. Can you make do with the one or maybe two sentences that best convey the gist of the passage?

If the answer to both these questions is "no"—you must cite this big passage—go ahead and introduce it (keeping in mind that your instructor may very well have already read it in its original context, and may not welcome its full reappearance). But introduce it very carefully, taking care on two levels: the mechanical level, which is no big problem, and the level of coherence, which is more of a problem.

The mechanical level

In academic writing, passages that will take up more than four typed lines should normally be set apart in your essay. They should be separated from the surrounding text, which may be entirely your own writing, or a mixture of paraphrase, quotation, and original explanation. Here is how you make the separation.

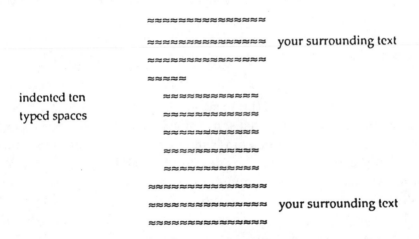

No quotation marks appear around passages set apart in the text. The separation, enforced by the indentation, says, in effect, "This is a quotation. These words are accurately copied from another writer." The separation—the placement of the passage on the pages—replaces the quotation marks. It's not an insignificant error to use both indented separation and quotation marks. It's misleading to the reader, for it signifies, conventionally, that the passage was in quotation marks in the original text. So, if there are not quotation marks in the original, none should appear in your set-apart quotation.

However, if you are repeating material from a passage enclosed in quotation marks in the original, then those quotation marks will show up in your set-apart quotation. Here, as an example, I will cite a passage from Alice Munro's *Lives of Girls and Women*. The passage comes from a chapter which tells about the high school's production of its annual operetta. This year and every year, Miss Farris is in charge of the production.

(12) In Jubilee, aesthetic vision can make one conspicuous, although sometimes such eccentricity can serve the town's ritualized ways of expressing romantic ideas. One of those rituals is the high school's annual operetta, and it is Miss Farris' vision that forces the romantic idea into being. Miss Farris is carried away by the planning and arranging that create the spectacle. Her excitement is a kind of managerial passion, and it is slightly hysterical. Addressing the girls who will be members of the cast, she lurches and leaps from one notion to the next:

> "Girls, stay, help me sort out. What have we got here that will do for a village in the Middle Ages, in Germany? I don't know, I don't know, I don't know. These dresses are too grand.... Would the breeches fit the mayor? That reminds me, *that reminds me* — I have to make a mayor's chain! I have to make Frank Wales' costume, too, the last Pied Piper we had was twice as big around. Who was it? I even forget who it was. It was a fat boy. We picked him solely for the voice."

Wholly absorbed by what she has in mind, Miss Farris seems frantic and flighty, herself a spectacle. But her vision prevails, despite its garbled expression, and she can make others participate in what she foresees. Her obsession is authoritative, and her managerial excitement brings about the annual spectacle and its temporary romance. *The Pied Piper* takes place, acknowledged by everyone.

Because Miss Farris' words are enclosed in quotation marks in the original text, they are also enclosed in quotation marks in my citation of them. Had I quoted a smaller portion of her speech, one that did not have to be set apart from the text, I would have used double quotation marks to show its status in the original:

(13) Miss Farris lurches and leaps excitedly from one idea to the next: "'That reminds me, that reminds me—I have to make a mayor's chain! I have to make Frank Wales' costume, too....'"

The coherence level

Quoting long passages poses special challenges to the coherence of an essay. When the selection you cite from another writer is long, both you and the reader are liable to slip into the priorities and direction of the original—priorities and direction that serve another argument. Returning to your own argument, both you and the reader are liable to have trouble picking up where you left off—reinstating or recovering the essay's or the paragraph's topic.

For these reasons, you must thoroughly introduce the long quotation before it appears: you must state very clearly how the upcoming quotation fits into your topic structure, telling readers what to look for as they make their way through the cited passage. And after the quotation, you must reinstate and recover your topic by summarizing the relevance of the quoted material.

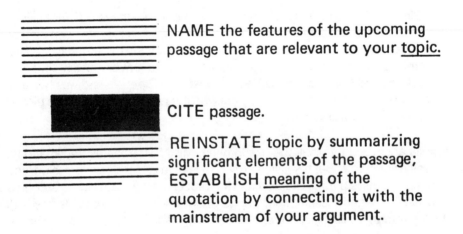

NAME the features of the upcoming passage that are relevant to your <u>topic.</u>

CITE passage.

REINSTATE topic by summarizing significant elements of the passage; ESTABLISH <u>meaning</u> of the quotation by connecting it with the mainstream of your argument.

Without this substantial environment for quotations, your essay can become little more than a list of passages you've copied from your reading. The quotations will dominate your essay, throwing it off balance and overshadowing your own argument.

Sample (12) shows a quotation firmly lodged in its environment. First, the sentences that introduce the quotation name the features of the passage which I want the reader to watch for: being "carried away" by planning; the passion for management; the incoherence ("lurching") of Miss Farris' speech. But, more important than this, they connect the passage with larger elements in the essay's topic structure: aesthetic versions of experience, and the town's capacity to accommodate an "artistic" outlook. (Other parts of the essay would develop other aspects of the uneasy relationship between social conformity and the individualism of aesthetic impulses.) The introductory sentences also explain the context in which the passage occurs: Miss Farris is talking while students listen.

Right after the quotation, the reader is reminded of the significance of the passage: Miss Farris makes a spectacle out of herself by talking in this flighty way. I then go on to confirm the connection between the quotation and the main stream of the discussion: although Miss Farris is so eccentric as to be nearly incoherent, she can nevertheless get the people around her—indeed, the whole town—to cooperate in her romantic ideas. With this, I have returned to the mainstream, and I can go on to develop my topic: the way the town can accommodate certain kinds of eccentricity associated with "artiness" while it cannot acknowledge other kinds.

The introductory statements with which you approach a cited passage and the summarizing statements with which you follow the quotation are not mere formalities: they are crucial to the coherence of your essay. Just as high-level topic statements are essential to establishing the meaning of lower-level details and facts, so too are the topical statements that introduce and summarize quotations essential to guiding your reader's interpretation of the quoted passage.

Think of the quotation as a "fact"—a fact like the bareness of the table or the swept-up condition of the floor in the paragraph we looked at in Chapter 4. Like those facts, the quotation is potentially ambiguous. Making the effort after meaning, readers could have interpreted Miss Farris' excited ramblings as signs of feeble-mindedness or mental deterioration. But the introductory and summarizing remarks prevent them from doing so. These statements are a guide to interpretation, ensuring that readers take the quotation as evidence of the way Miss Farris executes her eccentric vision. The material surrounding the long quotation establishes the topic of the paragraph; when the quotation appears, it serves that topic, supporting and developing it.

And once you are in the habit of supplying a rich environment for the quotations that support your case, you will never be stuck with unattractive wordings like these to get your quotations onto the page:

(14) In this quote Miss Farris is arranging the production of *The Pied Piper*.
   or
   This quote shows Miss Farris talking to the girls.

Readers will not react favourably to "this-quote" constructions. And their negative responses are not only a sign of their aversion to "quote" being used instead of "quotation." As well, readers sense that "this-quote" sayings are evidence that the quoted material is not thoroughly incorporated into the writer's argument, that it is little more than an element in a list.

In fact, the practice of surrounding your quotations with a strong topical environment is probably of more consequence than the correct use of quotation marks, ellipsis points, and indentation. The latter is an important formality: it shows that you can mark the relations between reading and writing with the conventionally accepted devices. But the former—the conceptual connection between your writing and someone else's—is even more important. It shows you putting your reading to use, making something new.

This chapter has so far argued for the necessity of making quotations coherent with the essay that is their host. Quotations of sentences or parts of sentences must be grammatically coherent with the sentences in which they are embedded, or the sentences that surround them. And they must be conceptually coherent with their surroundings: paraphrase should lead the reader right up to the words that are imported from another writer's work. When the quotation is longer, you need to make even greater efforts after coherence, fully controlling your reader's processing of the quoted passage. Clearly, your ability to do so will depend partly on your sense of your own topic—the main claims and logical connections that dominate your argument.

In the exercises which follow, you won't have a bona fide topic to guide your quotation strategies: you will have to pretend to have a topic. Nevertheless, despite this artificial condition, these exercises will still give you practice in introducing other writers' words into your own prose—achieving grammatical and conceptual coherence.

Exercise

A. *Paraphrase the substance of these passages, quoting the <u>underlined</u> parts of sentences.*

SAMPLE

Original, from Suzanne de Castell and Allan Luke (1986), "Models of literacy in North American schools: social and historical conditions and consequences." In *Literacy, Society, and Schooling*, ed. S. de Castell, A. Luke, and K. Egan. Cambridge: Cambridge University Press. 87-109, p. 101.

While our inheritance from the Army testing of the First World War was the concept of "IQ" as a measure of ability (Gould, 1981), the educational legacy of World War II may have been <u>functional literacy as a measure of vocational and social competence</u>. Throughout the 30-year development of the technocratic model, functional literacy remained a goal of North American schools, leading ultimately to the Competency Based Education movement of the 1970s.

Quoted

De Castell and Luke suggest that the first traces of the technologizing of literacy instruction in North America show up in the testing performed by the U.S. Army during World War II — testing which isolated "functional literacy as a measure of vocational and social competence."

1.

   Original, from Anne Martin (1988), "Screening, Early Intervention, and Remediation: Obscuring Children's Potential," *Harvard Educational Review* 58, 4, 488-501, p. 489.

A flexible kindergarten program can accommodate wide diversity in children's backgrounds, maturity, temperaments, interests, talents, abilities, and skills. In this important introduction to school, every child should have the chance to grow, to be appreciated, and to learn to be a contributing member of a group. It seems, however, that schools are increasingly unwilling to accept all children and to adjust to their particular needs. I remember one meeting of kindergarten teachers in which the suggestion was made that we should visit all the preschools in our district to identify and head off problem children before they registered for kindergarten. But even without such extreme measures, our entering children tend to be <u>labeled and pigeonholed through screening and testing procedures.</u>

2.

Original, from Martin, p. 490.

The language used to describe children in professional reports, whether written by school personnel or by outside clinicians, may seem to be just current professional jargon, but its implicit meanings are actually highly significant. For instance, the phrase "children at risk" has become a familiar one, picked up frequently by the media in reference to a variety of probems like poverty, hunger, lead poisoning, AIDS, or teenage pregnancy. The words have a dramatic ring that catches people's attention. The expression "children at risk" is explicitly a prediction of danger and implicitly a call for immediate strong action to avert disaster. Obviously, some of the issues where children are seen to be at risk are actually life-and-death matters. In schools, however, the phrase can be casually applied to almost any concern, from trivial matters such as a handwriting deficiency to the possibility of total school failure.

3.

Original, from Martin, pp. 489-90.

I had repeatedly rejected not only the particular instrument of our screening tests (which happens to be one that I find especially objectionable) but the whole idea of sorting out children into categories and giving them numerical scores for isolated skills. I have maintained that there is no way that a twenty-minute contact and a set of test scores can adequately describe a child's potential to learn. All children come to school as complex persons with their own unique backgrounds and sets of experiences. For me the fascination of each new school year is the gradual revelation of this complexity as I observe the children and develop a relationship with each child and the whole group. It is only through living in the classroom together that we start to understand one another and begin to get a sense of each other's strengths and vulnerabilities.

B. *Write a sentence to lead the reader to a quotation of all or part of the* <u>underlined</u> *material.*

1.

     Original, from Rapley, p. 312.

The accent on horror of sin, "particulièrement de ceux qui sont opposés à la pureté," was more marked in feminine than in masculine pedagogy. Fourier, and others after him, saw the innocence of early childhood as a gift which could be preserved by careful upbringing. The child, if shielded from bad influence, could grow up in ignorance of all signs of impurity. This principle, added to the nuns' natural reserve, made direct reference to the sins of impurity almost unthinkable. <u>Sexual reticence was pushed to such lengths that some nuns were reluctant to discuss the details of the Incarnation, or to mention the word "marriage." It is not surprising, then, that they taught purity mostly through indirect reference.</u>

2.

Original, adapted from de Castell and Luke, pp. 88-89.

In the European Protestant educational tradition on which the public schools of the New World were first based, commonality of religious belief was central to literacy instruction. The "criss-cross row" — the first line of the earliest 17th-century English reader, the Horn Book—was a graphic representation of the Cross, invoked to speed and guide the beginner's progress through the text. The expansion of literacy in Europe was initially inseparable from the rise of Protestantism, and the erosion of the Church's monopoly over the printed word. The intent of the 16th- and 17th-century educational reformers was that "whosoever will" should have access to the word of God. It was believed that individual access to the Word, even though it might involve uncomprehending repetition, would improve the soul of the reader without the necessity of authoritative mediation by a cleric. This explains, in part, the importance ascribed in European schools to repetition and recitation of texts which children could not have been expected to "comprehend"—a religious and pedagogical tradition inherited by North American education in its earliest days.

3.

Original, from de Castell and Luke, p. 94

Following the European model, reading [in 19th-century North American schools] took the form of oral performance to an audience. Individual reading time was limited, and all students progressed at a fixed rate through the text. Both in grade and secondary schools, each student, in turn, would read passages aloud; those not reading were expected to listen attentively to the reader, since the intent of oral reading instruction was not merely to ascertain the reader's ability to decode the text, but to develop powers of effective public oration. Pronunciation, modulation, and clarity of diction were stressed. In the 19th-century classroom, reading was neither a private nor a reflective act, but a rule-bound public performance.

4.

Original, from de Castell and Luke, p. 98.

Beginning in the 1910s and 1920s, American prescribed and authorized readers, also used in Canada, reflected the dominant values and popular culture of commercial and industrial life. Stories of "adventure" and "friendship" featured vignettes of family life, work, and play, and encouraged community service and individual achievement. Dick and Jane usurped Arthurian heroes; by the 1930s discussions of the latest "moving pictures" and radio programs coexisted in secondary classrooms with the study of Shakespeare. <u>Literacy texts portrayed a vision of a harmonious American social community, blessed with the gifts of technological advancement and material prosperity.</u>

C. *Introduce the reader to the cited material (<u>underlined</u> in the original passage) by paraphrasing and contextualizing the original author's message and by directing the reader to the significance you intend.*

SAMPLE

Original, from Rapley, pp. 308-09.

The rules and manuals of the teaching congregations described, in detail, even the most basic procedures. The rules, once formulated, soon tended to harden, so that further adaptation was difficult. Thus, after a flurry of creative activity at the beginning, literal observance of the original teaching methods very swiftly became an obligation, and the rule was inscribed:

Les Maîtresses maintiendront exactement l'ordre des exercices...et n'y pourront rien changer, qu'avec la permission de la Supérieure at Maîtresse genérale.[1] (The Mistresses will maintain the exact order of these exercises, changing nothing except with the permission of the Mother Superior or Mistress of Studies.)

<u>Innovation was considered to be disobedience to the rule; any nun guilty of it could be reprimanded or removed. The communities were ardent guardians of custom. Rigidity, not laxity, was their invariable tendency; their pedagogical methods were virtually unchanged at the time of the the Revolution.</u>

1   Reglemens des ursulines (1705), p. 33. In this case, the practice under discussion was the folding of the boarders' linen.

Cited

Rapley's account of developments in pedagogical methods shows that school organization—while at first innovative and goal-oriented—can quickly sink to the most trivial levels of regimentation. She cites an admonition from the Ursuline manual which insists that even the folding of linen be controlled by standard, unyielding ways of doing things. Individuality, adaptation, and change were smothered by institutional authority and routine:

Innovation was considered to be disobedience to the rule; any nun guilty of it could be reprimanded or removed. The communities were ardent guardians of custom. Rigidity, not laxity, was their invariable tendency: their pedagogical methods were virtually unchanged at the time of the Revolution.

Although the schools had arisen in response to social change, once established they assumed an unchanging, authoritative character.

1.

Original, from Rapley, p. 316.

There was a bundle of overlapping prejudices against women who could write. For the upper classes, writing, insofar as it was a trade, still carried a taint of servility. "Ecrire, c'est perdre la moitié de sa noblesse," wrote Mlle de Scudéry. ("To write is to lose half of one's nobility.") Among the writing professionals, the maîtres écrivains, there was no anxiety to see women invading their profession. "Cet art étroit attaché au sexe masculin." Some moralists saw it as a dangerous skill, which would allow women to carry on underhanded liaisons. But the chief argument against writing seems to have been that it undermined the existing order. The later seventeenth and the eighteenth century saw a strong resurgence of the opinion that education should be tailored to the station in life of the students. "On excluerait de l'écriture ceux que la Providence à fait naistre d'une condition — labourer la terre." ("Those whom Providence has assigned to till the soil one would exclude from writing.") What applied to the lower classes applied also to women: they should not exceed the limits of their condition.

A century later, Restif de la Bretonne stated the case succinctly:

Il faudrait que l'écriture et méme la lecture fussent interdites — toutes les femmes. Ce serait le moyen de resserrer leurs idées et de les conscrire dans les soins utiles du ménage, de leur inspirer du respect pour le premier sexe qui serait instruit de ces mêmes choses avec d'autant plus de soin que le deuxiéme sexe serait négligé.

(Writing and even reading should be forbidden to all women. This would be the means of fixing their ideas and containing them within useful household concerns, inspiring them with respect for the first sex who would teach them those things with as much care as the second sex would lack.)

2.

Original, from de Castell and Luke, pp. 92-93.

Late-19th-century literacy in Canada differed in one crucial respect from its American counterpart. For whereas Canadian schools imported curricula from England, teachers in America were by this time provided with locally developed textbooks, in the tradition of the McGuffey readers. Noah Webster's *American Spelling Book* (1873), the most widely used textbook in United States history, not only promoted American history, geograpghy, and morals, but was itself a model for an indigenous vocabulary and spelling. Textbooks and dictionaries of this period attempted to engender a national literacy and literature free of European "folly, corruption and tyranny," in Webster's words. In Canada, by contrast, classrooms featured the icons of colonialism: British flags and pictures of royalty adorned the walls, younger students were initiated to print via the Irish readers, and literature texts opened with Wordsworth's and Tennyson's panegyrics to the Crown. In Canada, the reduction in pauperism and crime associated with illiteracy was seen as requiring the preservation of British culture and a colonial sensibility; in the United States, "custodians of culture" (May, 1959; p.30) sought to assure economic independence and political participation. The match between these differing societal and educational ideologies and the "civilizing" effects of traditional three Rs and classical education was near perfect.

3.

Original, from de Castell and Luke, p. 104.)

[The] claim to "neutrality" and cross-contextual validity places literacy instruction in line with the dominant belief that North American schools should assume no particular moral or political bias; there is an explicit avoidance of any story content or language that might appear to discriminate against or exclude any subcultural viewpoint. The result is an inherent blandness, superficiality, and conservatism in the texts children read. What standardized readers communicate to children is "endlessly repeated words" (Bettelheim and Zelan, 1981). In order to capture the multinational market, publishers and editors must create a product that will pass as culturally significant knowledge in diverse social contexts, without offending the sensibilities of local parents, teachers, special interest groups, politicians, and, of course, administrators who decide purchases. The result is a watering down of the content for marketing purposes. As mass-marketed commodities, the children's readers follow a pattern identified by Raymond Williams (1976): The larger the audience of a given communications medium, the more homogeneous becomes the message and the experience for its consumers. Technocratic literacy systems posit an imaginary "everystudent", much as telelvison networks seek to identify and communicate with "the average viewer."

5.3 Documentation

Your answers to the exercises you have just completed will show some of the polish and finesse your readers expect in academic prose that cites outside sources. But they are not yet completely polished. There's still something missing: namely, documentation. This passage quoting another writer—

(14) De Castell and Luke suggest that the first traces of the technologizing of literacy instruction in North America show up in the testing performed by the U.S. Army during World War II — testing which isolated "functional literacy as a measure of vocational and social competence."

—needs to be inscribed with indications of the exact source of the quotation:

(15) De Castell and Luke (1986) suggest that the first traces of the technologizing of literacy instruction in North America show up in the testing performed by the U.S. Army during World War II — testing which isolated "functional literacy as a measure of vocational and social competence" (101).

In turn, these inscriptions require back-up entries somewhere outside the boundaries of the essay itself:

(16) de Castell, S., & Luke, A. (1986) Models of literacy in North American schools. In S. de Castell, A. Luke, & K. Egan (Eds.) *Literacy, society, and schooling.* Cambridge: Cambridge University Press.

Such inscriptions and entries are instances of documentation. Documentation is the whole system of page numbers, dates, titles, footnotes, bibliography, and so on, that officially specifies and locates the writer's indebtedness to other writers and researchers.

As you are probably aware, documentation practices are highly formal and conventional: that is, you can't just make up your own way of telling on what page a quoted passage appears, and you can't design your bibliography page in just any way that strikes you as interesting.

You have to follow rules. Because these rules are intricate and sometimes hard to remember, you may have negative feelings about them. They may seem like nothing more than a complicated body of restrictions and obligations devised to harass students and to give teachers something to mark wrong. However, documentation practices are actually more than formalities cherished by teachers and more pitfalls feared by students. They express essential features of scholarly activity, and they reflect essential features of the reading process.

We have already observed that scholarly writing is a special compound of indebtedness and originality: your readers expect you to have outside sources of information, and, at the same time, they appreciate your own interpretations of those sources. They have the same attitude towards the work of their colleagues in their disciplines. While they expect that what they read will contribute something new and original to research on a subject, they do not expect that it will be a bolt out of the blue, a shot in the dark. They expect that it will be a recognizable step forward in a territory already heavily mapped with prior contributions to the research. (Sometimes these steps forward are very tiny, scarcely discernible, and then they arouse little interest. Other times they are big steps, almost leaps, and then they excite controversy.) When the scholarly writer offers her step forward, she shows, as exactly as possible, its location on the map of previous research; thus she displays her indebtedness, and provides her readers with means of measuring the significance of the step she has taken.

But the scholarly process doesn't end there, with the new step. The new step becomes an established location, from which other scholars can now embark. To make sure they're heading in a legitimate direction, they need to master the points of departure of the writer who has proposed the step-just-taken. In other words, they need to read the contributions that have taken research this far. *Documentation* tells them *exactly* where to find those sources: what books and journals they appeared in. Documentation makes possible the on-going process of scholarship. Documentation practices, then, must provide all the information the academic reader needs to get hold of the contributing sources himself.

At the same time, however, the reader has to pay attention to the current argument—the logic of this proposal—and not be distracted by all this information about the location of sources. So documentation techniques are designed to *interrupt the reading process as little as possible.* Properly presented, documentation should pose no threat to the orderliness of the reader's mental desktop. You can see in Sample (14) how unobtrusive the documenting inscriptions are: in a sense, they don't have to be "read" at all.

5.3.1 The status of rules

Rules govern documentation in such a way as to satisfy the conditions described above: the requirements of on-going scholarship, and the limits of the reader's capacity for paying attention. What are these rules?

No doubt, you have already received instruction in documentation, probably in some previous English class, maybe as long ago as your days in elementary school, and often thereafter. But you have probably also experienced some difficulties in applying the rules. Some of these difficulties may be only a nuisance factor: you have trouble remembering the rules.

But other difficulties may be more than just the nuisance of looking up the rules once again. Having documented an essay according to the procedures recommended by your English teacher, you get the essay back from your Economics or Philosophy or Education instructor, and you find your practices condemned or corrected. You do what your History instructor wants, and your Psychology instructor complains. It seems that the operation of rules makes things obscure rather than exact.

In this situation, you are in the midst of discovering that different disciplines subscribe to different rules, and that, even within the same discipline, different people have different visions of the rules. Preparing this chapter, we tried to determine which practices were most common in scholarly journals: from this information, we hoped to provide you with a set of general rules which would hold for most cases. So we reviewed many journals across the disciplines, gathering data and calculating instances of certain practices.

Unfortunately, what we discovered was not a legible pattern, pointing firmly to inescapable conclusions. Instead, we discovered variation in almost *every feature* of documentation. Sometimes we found these variations in a *single edition of one journal*: evidently, the editor let the contributors follow whatever rules they chose. At first, we were dismayed by our findings: how could we provide you with all-purpose rules that would hold for most cases? But then we began to look at our findings for their positive value: they explained the disorientation student writers feel when they document their papers. What should be one of the simplest, most mechanical aspects of essay-writing, only a matter of following rules and observing technicalities, was in fact a systematic confusion. When students have learned in their English classes that *this* and *only this* is the way to document sources, they are naturally disoriented by their encounters with contradictory evidence.

So, rather than present you with yet another set of rules that you will have to revise, set aside, or ignore, or that you will simply forget, we will provide you with samples of documentation from the journals we surveyed. From these data, you will not only infer the principles that govern academic writers' documentation techniques, but also experience the range of variation in these techniques. At the same time, we hope to show you that you don't need to have the rules of documentation imprinted indelibly on your memory, never to be erased. To document acceptably, all you need is one or two samples of published work from reputable journals in the discipline you're working in: from these samples taken out of journals available in the periodical section of your university library, you can deduce the principles that should govern your own practices.

5.3.2 The two-part system

Now that I have described the chaotic results of our survey, you may have small hopes of discovery any tangible patterns in the samples that will appear below. But we will be simplifying the issue in two ways. First, we have narrowed the selection of samples, excluding the most eccentric instances and concentrating on ones that seem to represent mainstream practices. And, second, we will be offering you samples that all operate within the *two-part system* of documentation. The two-part system prevails in *most* (but not all) disciplines in the humanities, having superseded, in most (but not all) disciplines, the old system of footnoting which depended on those "ibid.," "op. cit.," "loc. cit." inscriptions that you may have learned in school.

This prevailing system depends on two complementary parts which work together to ensure that (a) the reading process is interrupted as little as possible, and (b) readers can fully inform themselves about the writer's sources. One part appears in the body of the essay; the other part appears separately after the end of the essay under the title "References" or "Works Cited."

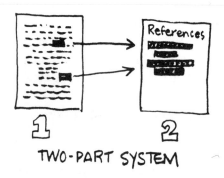

The pair of Samples (15) and (16) at the beginning of 5.3 shows the cooperation of the two parts.

(15) De Castell and Luke (1986) suggest that the first traces of the technologizing of literacy instruction in North America show up in the testing performed by the U.S. Army during World War II — testing which isolated "functional literacy as a measure of vocational and social competence" (101).

(16) de Castell, S., & Luke, A. (1986) Models of literacy in North American schools. In S. de Castell, A. Luke, & K. Egan (Eds.) *Literacy, Society, and Schooling.* *Cambridge: Cambridge University Press.*

Encountering (15) in the body of the text, the reader can, if she wishes, turn to the alphabetized "References" at the end, and find an entry (16) for "de Castell, S., & Luke, A." whose date (1986) corresponds to the one cited in the text. (On the other hand, if she wishes to concentrate on the argument and not get burdened with distracting information, she can ignore the documenting signal.) From this entry, she can retrieve full information on the source: its title, the title of the book in which it appears, its circumstances of publication. Both parts of the system enable the reader to proceed efficiently: Part 1 (15) contains just enough information to direct the reader to the relevant entry in the "References" list; with the information in Part 2 (16), the reader could actually put her hands on that book in the university library. Notice that this information includes both the title of the book in which the article appears and its editors. It is under these names that the source will be catalogued; without them, the reader would not be able to find the source.

The exercise that follows will provide you with examples of the two-part system in operation. You will see it at work in passages from the body of the text, parenthetically directing the reader to entries in "References." And you will see it at work in the entries themselves, providing full information which exactly locates the source. As you inspect these samples, you should watch for techniques for presenting and positioning authors' and editors' names, titles of sources, and dates of publication. You should also be on the lookout for variations which relate to different kinds of sources: books, articles in journals, articles in books. You will find that different kinds of sources activate different documentation techniques: articles in journals, for example, are located not only by year of publication, but also by volume and (sometimes) issue number. You will also need to take account of patterns of punctuation and capitalization.

This exercise will give you firsthand contact with the practices of documentation, showing you that they are things people do, not just lists of rules hoarded by English teachers. It will show you, too, that there's enough variation in these practices to permit you to be sceptical about claims that proper documentation is performed one way and one way only. And I hope this exercise will also show you that the rules are accessible to you from any sample: they are not occult or sacred but open to your discovery.

In addition, this assignment asks you to report your findings. So it will give you practice in organizing abundant detail and presenting it in compact, readable form—practice in getting useful points across without simply listing every single thing you found out. In a sense, this assignment puts you out in the field, gathering data firsthand rather than from someone else's research.

Exercise

Inspect the samples of documentation practices presented below. Write 500-700 words reporting the pattern of resemblances and differences you discover in these practices. Organize your report under these headings:

Introduction	Define documentation (its characteristics, function, and occurrence). Explain the purpose of your inquiry.
Method	Describe your method of inquiry: how you collected and analyzed your data; what aims or principles governed your procedures.
Results	Present the results of your research—the patterns and variations you discovered.
Discussion	Draw your reader's attention to your main findings, explaining their significance and their relationship to one another.
Conclusion	Identify the clearest conclusions you have been able to reach and the areas of uncertainty your research has revealed. Suggest what forms of future research would resolve these uncertainties.

Case 1: American Sociological Review, *1989, 54, 3. Howard Shuman and Jacqueline Scott, Generations and Collective Memories.*
Passage from body of article, showing documenting clump.

Even for memories that have more apparent relevance to the future, for example, memories of the divisiveness of the Vietnam era, there may be quite contradictory lessons drawn, some people focusing blame on the government or the military, some on the press or on liberal critics of the war. These two different lines of political interpretation correspond roughly to Mannheim's (1952) distinction between the perspectives of different "generational units," and they indicate again the danger of moving too quickly from one's own views of the lessons of the war to predictions of the views, let along future behavior, of others. In addition, the general public was less concerned about the larger moral issues of the war than about the likelihood of winning or losing it (Schuman 1972), so the most obvious implications for decisions about future American intervention are contingent on that aspect of a new situation, with enthusiastic backing of what seems like a painless intervention (e.g., Grenada), but reluctance to support what is thought to be riskier involvment (e.g., Central America).

Passage from list of references; *** indicates that this excerpt omits preceding or following entries.

REFERENCES

***

Knoke, David. 1984. "Conceptual and Measurement Aspects in the Study of Political Generations." *Journal of Political and Military Sociology* 12:101-201.

Mannheim, Karl. [1928] 1952. "The Problem of Generations." Pp. 276-322 in *Essays on the Sociology of Knowledge*, by Karl Mannheim. London: Routledge and Kegan Paul.

Markus, Hazel and Robert B. Zajonc. 1985. "The Cognitive Perspective in Social Psychology." Pp. 137-230 in *Handbook of Social Psychology*, vol. I, edited by Gardner Linzey and Elliot Aronson. New York: Random House.

Marwell, Gerald, Michael T. Aiken, and N.J. Demerath III. 1987. "The Persistence of Political Attitudes Among 1960s Civil Rights Activitists." *Public Opinion Quarterly* 51:359-75.

Mueller, John F. 1973. *War, Presidents and Public Opinion*. New York: Wiley.

Neisser, Ulric. 1982. "Snapshots or Benchmarks." Pp. 43-48 in *Memory Observed: Remembering in Natural Contexts*, edited by Ulric Neisser. San Francisco: Freeman.

Riley, Matilda White, Ann Foner, and Joan Waring. 1988. "Sociology of Age." Pp. 243-90 in Neil J. Smerlser, *Handbook of Sociology*, Newbury Park, CA: Sage.

Rintala, Marvin. 1968. "Political Generations." In *International Encyclopedia of the Social Sciences*. Vol 6:92-96. New York: Macmillan and the Free Press.

Rosow, Irving. 1978. "What Is a Cohort and Why?" *Human Development* 21:65-75.

Rubin, David S., ed. 1986. *Autobiographical Memory*. New York: Cambridge University Press.

Rubin, David C., Scott E. Wetzler, and Robert D. Nebes. 1986. "Autobiographical Memory Across the Lifespan." Pp. 202-21 in *Autobiographical Memory*, edited by David C. Rubin. Cambridge, England: Cambridge University Press.

Ryder, Norman B. 1965. "The Cohort as a Concept in the Study of Social Change." *American Sociological Review* 30:843-61.

Schuman, Howard. 1972. "Two Sources of Antiwar Sentiment in America." *American Journal of Sociology* 78:513-36.

Schuman, Howard and Jacqueline Scott. 1987. "Problems in the Use of Survey Questions to Measure Public Opinion." *Science* 236: 957- 59.

Schwartz, Barry. 1982. "The Social Context of Commemoration: A Study in Collective Memory." *Social Forces* 61:374-402.

***

Case 2: The Rand Journal of Economics, *1988, 19, 2.*
Passage from body of article, showing documenting clumps.

Mathewson and Winter (1984) assume that territorial protection takes the form of closed territorial distribution: "...the assignment to each retailer of exclusive rights to all consumers within a territory" (p. 27). It is important to recognize that this is a two-part restriction. First, in the words of European Economic Community law, it imposes upon distributors "...the obligation to refrain, outside the contract territory and in relation to the contract goods, from seeking customers..." (European Economic Community, 1983). But, in addition, it imposes a duty on distributors to ascertain whether prospective consumers reside within the specified territory and to refuse service to those do not. It is perfectly possible that the first part of this restriction is enforceable, but that the second part is not.[2]

2   Broadly speaking, incidentally, this is the position under European Economic Community law.

List of references

References

ARCHIBALD, G.C., EATON, B.C., AND LIPSEY, R.G. "Address Models of Value Theory," chap. 1 in J.E. Stiglitz and G.F. Mathewson, eds., *New Developments in the Analysis of Market Structure*, London: Macmillan, 1986.

BLAIR, R.D., AND KASERMAN, D.L. *Law and Economics of Vertical Integration and Control.* New York: Academic Press, 1983.

BOARD OF TRADE. "The Motor Trades in 1962." *Board of Trade Journal*, Vol. 186 (1964), pp. 842-846.

_____. "The Motor Trades in 1967." *Board of Trade Journal*, Vol. 198 (1970), pp. 1238-1241.

DEPARTMENT OF THE ENVIRONMENT. *Transport Statistics Great Britain 1964-1974.* London: Her Majesty's Stationery Office, 1976.

DIXIT, A. "Vertical Integration in a Monopolistically Competitive Industry." *International Journal of Industrial Organization*, Vol. 1 (1983), pp. 63-78.

EATON, B.C. AND LIPSEY, R.G. "Freedom of Entry and the Existence of Pure Profit." *Economic Journal*, Vol. 88 (1978), pp. 455-469.

MARSHALL, A. *Principles of Economics*, 8th ed. London: Macmillan, 1920.

MATHEWSON, G.G. AND WINTER, R.A. "An Economic Theory of Vertical Restraints." *RAND Journal of Economics*, Vol. 15 (1984), pp. 27-38.

REY, P. AND TIROLE, J. "The Logic of Vertical Restraints." *American Economic Review*, Vol. 76 (1986), pp. 921-939.

RHYS, D.G. *The Motor Industry: An Economic Survey.* London: Butterworths, 1972.

SCHMALENSEE, R. "Entry Deterrence in the Ready-to-Eat Breakfast Cereal Industry." *Bell Journal of Economics*, Vol. 9 (1978), pp. 305-327.

WARD, T.S. *The Distribution of Consumer Goods.* Cambridge: Cambridge University Press, 1973.

Case 3: British Journal of Criminology, *1989, 29. 2. Ngaire Naffine and Fay Gale, Testing the nexus: Crime, gender, and unemployment.*
Passage from body of article, showing documenting clumps.

The few attempts to correlate female employment and crime indicate that they may well be related in some way. In the United States, Jane Roberts Chapman (1980) has produced some indirect evidence. She compared the female labour force participation rates from 1930 to 1970 with the arrest rates for the same period and found that the smallest increases in female arrests coincided with the periods of greatest increase in economic acitivity. This suggested that the absence rather than the availability of employment stimulated female involvement in crime. In the United Kingdom Steven Box and Chris Hale (1983, 1984) examined the effects of both employment and unemployment on adult female crime from 1951 to 1980. Unemployment, rather than participation in the work force, emerged as a positive correlate of female offending.

Further evidence that suggests that unemployment may encourage offending in women comes from the researches of strain theorists. They have examined the effect on young females of blocked educational and occupational opportunities and have found them to be anxious about their work prospects (Datesman et al. 1975; Smith 1979; Cernkovich and Giordano 1979; Simon et al. 1980).

Passage from list of references; *** indicates that this excerpt omits preceding or following entries.

REFERENCES

***

BOX, S. (1981), *Deviance, Reality and Society*, 2nd edn. London: Holt, Rinehart, and Winston.
BOX, S. and HALE, C. (1983), 'Liberation and Female Criminality in England and Wales', *British Journal of Criminology*, 23/1:35.
_____ (1984), 'Liberation/Emancipation, Economic Marginalization, or Less Chivalry', *Criminology*, 22/4:473.
_____ (1985), 'Unemployment, Imprisonment and Prison Overcrowding', *Contemporary Crises*, 9:209.
BRAITHWAITE, J. (1979), *Inequality, Crime and Public Policy*. London: Routledge and Kegan Paul.
CERKNOVICH, S.A., and GIORDANO, P.C. (1979), 'Delinquency, Opportunity and Gender', *Journal of Criminal Law and Criminology*, 70/2:145.
CHAPMAN, J.A. (1980), *Economic Realities and the Female Offender*. Lexington: D. C. Heath.
COHEN, A.K. (1955), *Delinquent Boys*. New York: Macmillan.
DATESMAN, S.K. et al. (1975), 'Female Delinquency: An Application of Self and Opportunity Theories', *Journal of Research into Crime and Delinquency*, 10 July: 7.
FARRINGTON, D.P. et al. (1986), 'Unemployment, School Leaving and Crime', *British Journal of Criminology*, 26/4:355.
GALE, F. (1985), 'Seeing Women in the Landscape: Alternative Views of the World around Us', in J. Goodnow and C. Paterson, eds., *Women, Social Science and Public Policy*. Sydney: George Allen and Unwin.

***

Case 4: Canadian Journal of Education, *1988, 13, 2. G. Malicky, W. T. Fagan, C.A. Norman, Reading processes.*
Passage from body of article, showing documenting clumps.

Most research into French immersion reading has studied success achieved by readers in French immersion classes on English-language reading tests at various grade levels (Edwards, 1976; Genesee, 1978; Lambert & Tucker, 1972;

Swain & Lapkin, 1981). These studies generally showed that, after an intial lag in reading English in the primary grades, immersion students achieve at least as well as their peers in Egnlish programs after approximately one year of instruction in English language arts.

*Passage from list of references, ***** indicating that this excerpt omits preceding or following entries.*

REFERENCES

***

Edwards, H.P. (1976) Evaluation of the French immersion program offered by the Ottawa Roman Catholic Separate School Board. *Canadian Modern Language Review*, 33, 137-142.

Fagan, W.T. (1984). *Categories for protocol analysis*. Unpublished manuscript, University of Alberta, Edmonton.

Genesee, F. (1978). A longitudinal evaluation of an early immersion school program. *Canadian Journal of Education*, 12, 71-77.

Goodman, K.S. (1970). Behind the eye: What happens in reading. In K.S. Goodman & O.S. Niles (Eds.), *Reading process and program* (pp. 3-38). Urbana, IL: National Council of Teachers of English.

***

Case 5: Qualitative Sociology, *1988, 11, 4, _____, Aural assault: Obscene telephone calls.*
Passage from body of article, showing documenting clumps.

My findings parallel those in Davis's (1978) account of the feelings of women who encountered exposers and Janoff-Bulman's analysis (1979) of self-blaming reactions among rape victims. Janoff-Bulman distinguishes between behavioral and characterological self-blame: the first concerns a woman's judgement of her behavior in a specific situation, the second involves her negative evaluation of herself as a person. The different types predicted a victim's sense of having the control to prevent a rape in the future.

*Passage from list of references; ***** indicates that this excerpt omits preceding or following entries.*

References

***

Cooley, C.H.
1981 "Self as Social Object." In Gregory P. Stone and Harvey A. Farberman (Eds.). Social Psychology Through Symbolic Interaction. Pp. 169-173. New York: Wiley and Sons.

Davis, S.K.
1978 "The Influence of an Untoward Public Act on Conceptions of Self." Symbolic Interaction 1:106-123.

Goffman, E.
1977 "The Arrangement Between the Sexes." Theory and Society 4:301-331.

Henley, N.
1975 "Power, Sex, and Nonverbal Communication." In Barrie Thorne and Nancy Henley (Eds.). Language and Sex: Difference and Dominance. Pp. 184-203. Rowley, MA: Newbury House Publishers.

Janoff-Bulman, R.
1979 "Characterological Versus Behavioral Self-blame: Inquiries into Depression and Rape." Journal of Personality and Social Psychology 37:1798-1809.

Hopper, C.
1987 "Obscene Calls: Impersonal Sex in Private Places." Unpublished paper. Presented at the annual meeting of The Popular Culture Association, Montreal, March 26.

Kollock, P., Blumstein, P. &Schwartz, P.
1985 "Sex and Power in Interaction: Conversational Privileges and Duties." American Sociological Review 50:34-46.

***

Case 6: Canadian Journal of Archeology, *1986, 10. Roger Marios and Edward Jelks, Comparative study of French, English, Spanish, and Portuguese terms related to pre-historic pottery decoration techniques.*
Passage from body of article, showing documented clump.

The permutation of the alterations constituting the arrangement might undergo considerable variation, depending on the creativity of the potter, on knowledge transmitted from one generation to the next and on the influence of other communities. The decorative elements, on the contrary, were produced by the combination of an instrument and a motion (or action), both offering somewhat limited choices. The production of alterations and their arrangement, therefore, are different phenomena that may be usefully distinguished for the purposes of analysis and that have accordingly been designated respectively as "production elements" and "constituent elements of the decoration (Marois 1984:169). The principles of the permutations that create the arrangements of the elements have been elucidated in another work (Marois 1984:42-6) based on Canadian pottery. The present study will deal specifically with the production elements of the decorations.

Passage from list of references; *** indicates that this excerpt omits preceding or following entries.

REFERENCES

Balfet, H., M-F Fauvet-Berthelot and S. Monzon
1983 *Pour la normalisation de la description des poteries.* Editions du Centre national de la recherche scientifique. Paris.

Camps-Farber, H.
Matière et art mobilier dans la préhistoire nord-africaine et shararienne. Centre de recherches anthropologiques, préhistoriques et ethnographiques, Mémoire 5. Alger, Algeria.

Chymz I., ed.
1976 Terminología, arqueológica brasileira para a ceramica. *Cadernos de arqueológica* 1(1):119-147. Paranagua, Brazil.

Emerson, J.N.
1968 *Understanding Iroquois Pottery in Ontario: A Rethinking.* Ontario Archaeological Society. Toronto.

Finlayson, W.D.
1977 *The Saugeen Culture: A Middle Woodland Manifestation in Southwestern Ontario.* 2 vols. National Museum of Man Mercury Series, Archaeological Survey of Canada Paper 61. Ottawa.

Keenlyside, D.L.
1978 *Late Prehistory of Point Pelee, Ontario, and Environs.* National Museum of Man Mercury Series, Archaeological Survey of Canada Paper 80. Ottawa.

Marois, R.J-M.
1975 *Quelques techniques de décoration de la céramique impressionée: correspondence des termes français et anglais.* National Museum of Man Mercury Series, Archaeological Survey of Canada Paper 40. Ottawa.
1984 *Canadian Prehistoric Pottery: A Tentative Systematization of Decoration Analysis.* National Museum of Man Mercury Series, Archaeological Survey of Canada paper 127. Ottawa.

***

Case 7: British Journal of Psychology, *1989, 80, 2. D.V.M. Bishop, Does hand proficiency determine hand preference?*
Passage from body of article, showing documenting clump.

An alternative way of measuring handedness is to assess relative proficiency of two hands in carrying out skilled activities. This approach allows very fine distinctions between degrees of handedness on a quantitative scale. Furthermore, we can use tasks where subjects have not received specific training. Reliability of handedness measures based on relative skill of the two hands will depend on the particular task used, but several tasks have been found to give acceptable test-retest correlations (Annett, Hudson & Turner, 1974; Todor & Doane, 1977).

Passage from list of references; *** *indicates that this excerpt omits preceding or following entries.*

References

Annett, M. (1970). A classification of hand preference by association analysis. *British Journal of Psychology*, 61, 303-321.

Annett, M. (1985). *Left, Right, Hand and Brain: The RightShift Theory*. London: Erlbaum.

Annett, M., Hudson, P.T. & Turner, A. (1974). The reliability of differences between the hands in motor skill. *Neuropsychologia*, 12, 527-531.

Annett, M. & Kilshaw, D. (1983). Right- and left-hand skill: II. Estimating the parameters of the distribution of L-R differences in males and females. *British Journal of Pschology*, 74, 269-283.

Benton, A.L., Meyers, R. & Polder, G.J. (1962). Some aspects of handedness. *Psychiatric Neurology (Basel)*, 144, 321-337.

McManus, I.C. (1985). Right- and left-hand skill: Failure of the right shift model. *British Journal of Psychology*, 76, 1-16.

***

CHAPTER SIX

descriptive definitions

6.1. Remembering the role of abstraction

In Chapter Two, we saw how one of the efficiencies of reasoning is translated into prose and offered to the reader: we saw how an abstract term at a high level of generality could interpret facts, gathering and condensing scattered data.

The writer offers these abstract interpretations of specific data to the reader, constructing meaning:

(1) The hierarchical social structure of some primate groups confers on certain group members excessive privilege, while it deprives others of even the most basic social and physical amenities. Among the olive baboons of the Serengeti savanna, some male indiviuals get the shady spots....

Without these high-level interpretative abstractions about "hierarchical social structure" and "privilege," the report of olive baboon behaviors is liable to be merely a list, fulfilling only the minimum conditions of topic (generally about baboons, but what about baboons?). The reader will make diligent efforts after meaning, trying to construct what the writer has not, and hoping to have his attempts confirmed. Or he will abandon the effort, processing and storing information randomly, forgetting most of what he reads as items slip off his mental desktop willy-nilly.

When you come up with interpretive abstractions, you are making sense of what you have observed. When you offer them to your reader, foregrounding them at the beginning of paragraphs, repeating them at transitional points, you construct meaning for your reader and instruct his filing device as to the best use of the information you present.

But you can do more. You can get hold of those high-level names for things and make them work harder for you—directing your reader into complex and convincing arguments that break new ground.

6.2. Making abstractions work harder

In the passages which follow, you will see abstraction working hard, going beyond naming. Each passage dwells on the high-level name that represents the essential features of the lower-level cases. Each passage not only introduces the name for the phenomenon on which it focusses, but also defines the phenomenon. Read the passages to see how these definitions develop.

(2) "Salutation"

Salutations are verbal and physical gestures by which individuals acknowledge one another at the beginnings and conclusions of encounters. They are conventional systems of greeting and leave-taking that express social bonds and accord, however temporary or tentative those bonds and accord might be. The handshake, for example, marks the boundaries of social encounters in communities where the absence of physical or verbal recognition can be interpreted as a sign of hostility. Mutual performance of this hand ritual assures individuals of their acceptance or membership in a group. Or the performance may only appear to make such assurances, masking actual hostility, indifference, or competing interests. The handshake seems to signify a suspension of hierarchical relationships: it expresses symbolically a social equality. This symbolic expression may take place despite one participant actually having the "upper hand" in the relationship.

Other forms of salutation in face-to-face encounters depend on verbal expression, accompanied by conventional facial expression: smiling, one participant in a social encounter may initiate the exchange by offering a ritual inquiry into the welfare of another participant. Like the handshake, the inquiry and its response comply with formulaic, culture-specific patterns: in North America, an individual who responds to a ritual inquiry with detail about kin and household will be seen as failing to observe the conventions of salutation.

Handshaking, ritual inquiries and responses, and other forms of salutation are signs of the cooperation and mutuality that promote human association and enable productive transactions. Depending on conventional procedures, salutation shows that, whatever else may divide individuals and their interests, they are at least united in their shared knowledge of this ritual and can cooperate in its performance. Salutation supports and reflects larger cultural systems of social coherence which incorporate individuals into groups, recruiting the single actor into community purposes.

(3) "Cybernetics"

Cybernetics is the science of maintaining order in a system, whether that system is natural or artificial. Since all things in the world have a tendency to become entropic, disorderly, their random deviations from order must be corrected continually. This is accomplished by using information about the behaviour of the system to produce different, more regular behaviour. By such means the system is kept on course. The term cybernetics comes from a Greek word meaning steersman, and it carries the sense of stability, of constant, correct functioning. Illness is entropic, irregular, an error in the living system, while healing is cybernetic, restoring the body to its original state, correcting the error. Natural selection is also cybernetic, disallowing genetic mutations which deviate from the norm in undesirable ways. Wiener regarded a human society as a self-regulating system kept orderly by the cybernatic mechanism of its laws. Cybernetics enforces consistency. It permits change, but the change must be orderly and abide by the rules. It is a universal principle of control, and can be applied to all kinds of organization, just as Shannon's theorems applied to communication of all kinds. It does not matter whether the system is electrical, chemical, mechanical, biological, or economic.

Jeremy Campbell (1982). *Grammatical Man*. New York: Simon and Schuster. 22-23.

(4) "Ethnostatus distinctions"

Ethnostatus distinctions are those distinctions which an individual or population makes concerning themselves, and the significant others in their lives, in which the factors of legal status and cultural affinity play a varying role. Ethnostatus distinctions can also develop as a product of ascription to a particular cultural group or legal category by individuals or agencies external to the community. In the western Canadian subarctic, government legislation and policy implementation at both the federal and provincial levels have probably played the most prominent role in the development and maintenance of such distinctions. The product of these distinctions is the development of separate ethnostatus identities which may shift and surface from time to time in different socio-political contexts or situations. In this sense, the concept of ethnostatus precludes the identification of "ethnic" groups as defined in the anthropological literature.

Barth, in his classic essay on "ethnic groups and boundaries," argued that membership in a particular ethnic group effectively governed all behaviour in virtually every social situation, and further "that it cannot be disregarded and temporarily set aside by other definitions of the situation" (1969:17). As I shall demonstrate, ethnostatus distinctions rarely produce "ethnic groups" in this sense, since, according to my conception, the identities formulated tend to govern behaviour only in certain contexts and can be readily set aside or altered as the situation dictates. Further, it is evident that a concentration on boundaries between ethnic groups, as Barth suggests, would not prove fruitful in understanding ethnostatus distinctions precisely because such boundaries are too amorphic. While ethnostatus distinctions have the potential of forming ethnic groups, the existence of such groups must be demonstrated and cannot be presupposed.

In a similar vein, ethnostatus groups are not the equivalent of "factions," as defined in the literature. Nicholas (1965:27-29) has presented five characteristics which define "factions": they are political groups; they are conflict oriented; they are not corporate groups; members are recruited by a leader; and recruitment occurs according to a variety of criteria, such as religion and kinship. As Nicholas (1966:52) notes, factions are primarily involved in political activity, "the organized conflict over public power." As I shall demonstrate, ethnostatus distinctions by-and-large do not reflect groups organized by a leader to achieve a political goal, and certainly there is no active recruitment.

James B. Waldram (1987), Ethnostatus distinctions in the western Canadian subarctic: Implications for inter-ethnic and inter-personal relations. *Culture*, 7, 1, 29-37, p. 31.

The three passages develop their definitions in a variety of ways, using strategies we will look into later in this chapter. But each has in common one feature in particular: a core statement which defines the phenomenon as an equivalence, saying, in effect,

x = y
Salutations **are** verbal and physical gestures....
Cybernetics **is** the science of maintaining order in a system....
Ethnostatus distinctions **are** those distinctions which an individual or population makes concerning themselves, and the significant others in their lives....

Writers tend to position these core statements of equivalence at the beginning of their definition: these statements become the footing on which the rest of the definition is constructed.

Once these footings are established, writers develop the defintion. They may "double" the core defintion, as in the "Salutation" and "Ethnostatus Distinctions" passages, adding more of the features which distinguish the phenomenon. Or, as in the "Cybernetics" sample, they may mention the conditions which explain the fact of the phenomenon's existence. If the writer thinks the information will be useful to developing his claims, he may linger at the word itself: "The term cybernetics comes from a Greek word meaning steersman, and it carries the sense of stability, of constant, correct functioning." The writer can also compare the phenomenon with similar ones, pointing out the differences: ethnostatus distinctions create groups that in some ways can resemble "ethnic groups" and "factions," but, in other important ways, also differ from them. The writer may also put the phenomenon into context, showing its operation in the larger system of which it is part: salutations are part of systems of social coherence; cybernetics plays its role in the universe itself (the biggest system of all).

And each passage uses examples to develop the definition: handshakes, healing, social differentiation in the western Canadian subarctic. But it is the definition of ehtnostatus distinctions that most clearly shows us the role of descriptive definition and its supporting examples in academic writing. The writer tells us he has specific evidence to confirm the claims he is making as he defines ethnostatus distinctions: "As I shall demonstrate...." Although he presents the definition before the examples that support it, we might very well assume that, in real life, the evidence came first, and the name which interpreted the evidence, along with the definition which refined it, came after. In his article, the definition is a management device, on the one hand interpreting scattered data from his research, and on the other hand offering the reader a clear focus for a complex argument.

Finally, the cluster of data, the interpretive name, and the descriptive definition are reciprocating elements of the writer's product:

DATA

ABSTRACTION interprets data by naming the phenomenon

DEFINITION explains the phenomenon and the data, which become examples that develop the definition

You may find it hard enough to come up with the abstraction which interprets the data—"privilege" or "hierarchy," for example, in the case of the olive baboons. But the result is worth the trouble. In fact, your reader and your essay can hardly do without it. Now the descriptive definition, which dwells on the interpretive name, asks that you make even greater effort. This effort is also worthwhile, for, under certain conditions, it can provide your writing with the focus and complexity that make strong arguments. Also, there are techniques that sweeten the effort; we will survey these in the next section. First, though, the following exercise gives you a chance to practise dwelling on a phenomenon you have identified by defining it.

Exercise

The second exercise in Section 2.2. in Chapter Two asked you to find abstract words to name the conditions described in "Baboons" and "Brian." Focus on those

abstractions now, defining them. Integrate specifics about baboons and Brian as examples which develop the definition.

6.3. Techniques for developing descriptive definitions

Material for the descriptive definition will come from your research, from your experience of life, and from your own powers of reasoning. There are no rules which dictate exactly what a descriptive definition should look like, but Figure (6) below shows how a fully developed definition can have three focal nodes.

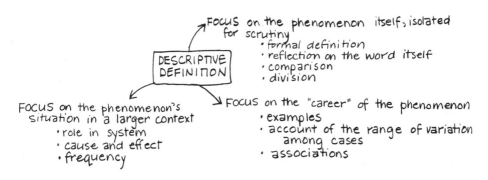

In the sections which follow, we will look at how writers can fulfill each of these nodes and their constituents, keeping in mind the fact that essay writers who use descriptive definition are under no obligation to track through every station on the map. These locations represent not rules but strategies. The writer uses only that material which convincingly and efficiently supports an argument. Sometimes the structure of the descriptive definition is the structure of the whole essay. Other times, the definition is only a part of the essay's structure, an attentive moment where assumptions and distinctions are established.

6.3.1. Focus on the phenomenon itself

When the defintion focusses on the phenomenon itself, it isolates the entity for scrutiny, separating it from the accidents, mix-ups, and blurry boundaries that surround entities in the real world. So we could say that this focus is ideal. If I claim that

(7)   Day-care is the institutional provision of care-taking services to young children, these services including feeding, supervision, shelter, and instruction.

I am ignoring cases where it's hard to distinguish between baby- sitting and day-care, where children are not exactly fed but feed themselves (or refuse to eat), where care is provided on so informal a basis it might not be called "institutional" at all. I am providing an ideal, formal definition of day-care, offering a statement of equivalence. On one side of the equation is the phenomenon—

Day-care

—and on the other side is the definition:

the institutional provision of care-taking services to young children, including feeding, supervision, shelter, and instruction.

The defining side of the equation first enlarges our view by identifying the larger class to which day-care belongs—

Day-care is the institutional provision of care-taking services

—and then narrows our view again by identifying the features which differentiate day-care from other members of this class (from, for example, health care, corrections, education):

Day-care is the institutional provision of care- taking services to young children, these services including feeding, supervision, shelter, and instruction.

The following definition shows the same pattern of *enlargement to classify* and *reduction to differentiate*. This is the classical pattern of formal sentence definition. Sample (8) also shows one of the development options open to the writer: following the formal definition, the writer can "double" the definition by saying what the phenomenon *does*.

(8)   Broadcasting is a system of social control which, through the transmission of electronic signals, normalizes the diverse experiences of individuals. Broadcasting

interprets events and life conditions in ways which confirm society's ideological centre.

In (8), the definition first *expands* our focus by identifying the *class* to which broadcasting belongs (systems of social control), and then *differentiates* it from other members of the class (laws or customs, for example). Moreover, Sample (8) shows as well that the formal definition can be in itself a step in an argument. Someone else could have defined broadcasting differently—as a result of having interpreted data differently, or of having different data to interpret.

(9) Broadcasting is a system of communication which, through the transmission of electronic signals, illuminates public and private life alike. By linking widespread communities through a shared network of information, broadcating ensures that citizens in democratic societies recognize common and crucial features of their experience, and enables them to respond to those features as issues.

Clearly, definitions (8) and (9) would serve different arguments, This disparity won't surprise you if you remember that definition is the development of the *interpretive name* the writer assigns to a cluster of data. We know we have to offer our readers these interpretive names in order to guide their use of the facts we present: the data don't speak for themselves. So the definition is bound to be an expression of the reasoning and insight which led us to assign the name in the first place.

For example, if I interpret the conditions of Brian's experience as "therapeutic supervision," and I go on to define that phenomenon, my definition will reflect my reasoning which produced the name—reasoning which detected in Brian's case the features of constraint, surveillance, and correction of deviance.

(10) Therapeutic supervision is a form of social restraint which targets an individual as deviant and then, through management and monitoring of the individual's daily experience, seeks to adjust his behavior to conform to a recognized norm.

The formal definition, with its practice of classification and differentiation, sounds "scientific" (if we think of science as pinning things down absolutely, once and for all, so everyone would agree). Yet, in a sense, these definitions are only hypotheses—plausible and rational ones, but hypotheses nonetheless. From another point of view, or later on, after more evidence is in, Brian and broadcasting could be seen as meaning something else. In other words, the writer stipulates the definition of the phenomenon, for the purposes of the current argument, in the service of a particular interpretation of a particular set of data. Of course, the stipulation can't be outlandish:

(11) Therapeutic supervision is the celebration of the individual spirit in communion with the natural world.

It has to respect the reader's common sense. But neither should the definition simply reiterate an all-purpose, dictionary definition:

(12) Webster's defines broadcasting as "...."

Dictionary definitions will not have the reciprocating relationship with the data and their interpretation that the stipulated defintion has. In an essay, dictionary definitions are liable to sit like wallflowers, never invited into the core of the argument.

The following exercise asks you to practise writing formal definition. The exercise is artificial in that it does not take into account the real process of descriptive definition, in which the stipulation reflects the analytical, interpretive activities that yield the name for the phenomenon: here you'll just be assigned the term. Nevertheless, the exercise will give you the chance to try classifying and differentiating.

Exercise

Write formal definitions of the following terms:
- dissent
- retirement
- computer-aided instruction

Or choose a term which names a phenomenon you are studying in another course (narrative, *for example, or* clan).

After you have composed your formal definition, you may feel like adding more, saying what retirement *or* dissent *does. Go ahead. Say more.*

Further focus on the phenomenon itself

To establish more firmly the sense of the phenomenon you wish to convey, you can direct your reader to pay attention to the word itself:

(13) Earlier uses of the term "broadcasting" referred to sowing by scattering seed widely, over a broad area. Modern, electronic broadcasting suggests the same wide scattering: broadcasting focusses not on unique, individual receptors, but on large expanses of population.

(14) As the term suggests, therapeutic supervision combines surveillance with calculated practices designed to correct behavior that has been diagnosed as pathological.

In addition to directing your reader's attention to the word itself, you can *analyze* the phenomenon to which the word refers, *dividing* it into *parts*:

(15) The two main elements of broadcasting are (1) the technical apparatus which create, transmit, and receive the electronic signal, and (2) the editorial processes which gather and transform information for conversion to electronic signals. As we will see, the characteristics of the editorial process were, for a long time, dependent on the features and capacities of the technical apparttus. Recently, however, innovations in editorial process have begun to influence the design and development of technical apparatus.

(16) In a program of therapeutic supervision, the chief actors are the clinician and the subject who has been targeted for correction. But the relationship between these actors is determined by other elements of the program: the institutional settings which host therapeutic supervision, and the body of knowledge which directs the clinician to interpret the subject's behavior and respond to it in systematic ways.

Besides focussing on the word itself, and analyzing the phenomenon into parts, you can also direct your reader's understanding of the phenomenon by comparing it to its near neighbours:

(17) Like broadcasting, the print media, particularly daily newspapers, disseminate information to a wide audience. And the reader, like the viewer or listener, always has the option of calling a halt to the process: the reader can put down the newspaper; the viewer can turn off the TV and the listener can turn off the radio. But broadcasting differs from the transmission of information by means of print in the degree of control it exercises over the individual's reception of information. While the reader can select the articles or advertisements he will read, the order in which he will read them, and the pace at which he will absorb information, the viewer has less control: once he begins to watch, he receives information in the order and at the pace the broadcaster has determined.

(18) Like the healing techniques of modern medicine, the techniques of therapeutic supervision address individuals' problems and afflictions with recognized expertise. But, unlike the practice of medicine, therapeutic supervision regards the subject's whole character, not just his affliction. The deviation—from health, from normalcy—is seen as logically entwined with the individual's conduct of his daily life, and every aspect of his daily life becomes an object of expert analysis, interpretation, and adjustment.

Each of these three strategies—focus on the word, analysis into parts, comparison—can develop the definition's focus on the phenomenon itself. But they are not self-justifying strategies. That is, if "focus on the word" contributes little or nothing to the main claims of your argument, then this entry will be only a distraction for your reader. Similarly, your comparisons and analyses into parts are meant not simply to fulfill the requirements of definition but to advance your interpretation of data—the interpretation that led you to identify this phenomenon in the first place. Like any essay, the essay based on descriptive definition has to be coherent. The reader shouldn't be left with irrelevant comparisons or analyses on his mental desktop, taking up scarce resources and confusing the filing system.

Exercise

Test these three strategies—focus on the word, analysis into parts, comparison—for their capacity to develop your definition of

- dissent

- retirement
- computer-aided instruction

or the term you have selected from your studies in another course. When you find the strategies that can contribute to your argument, write out an expanded version of your original definition.

6.3.2. Focus on the "career" of the phenomenon

This phase of definition releases the phenomenon from its isolation in an ideal domain and, relocating it in the real world, investigates its career there: its forms of occurrence, the local conditions of its occurrence. In many academic writing situations, this phase generates the main bulk of the text, for it is the phase that introduces examples: specific instances of the phenomenon. As we saw earlier, the specific data which lead to the interpretive abstraction are, in the process of descriptive definition, converted into examples. You know from your experience in summarizing academic prose that the lower-level information that reports specific cases takes up a lot of space. You can expect that your essay structured according to descriptive definition will also spread out when you present actual instances of the phenomenon. (You will have experienced this spreading in the assignment you did in Chapter Five. While your definition of "documentation" was probably enclosed in a compact passage in your introduction, your presentation of your data—actual instances of documentation—will have bulged out into long, detailed passages in the centre of your report.)

> The essay which bases itself on a descriptive definition of "broadcasting" would turn from definition of the phenomenon to presentation of the data which led the writer to identify the phenomenon and to identify its essential features: statistical evidence, for example, which counted the frequency of reports of certain "events and life conditions"; description and analysis of specific transmissions to show "normalization" towards an "ideological centre."

> The essay which bases itself on a descriptive definition of "therapeutic supervision" would go from definition of the phenomenon itself to Brian and other cases like his. The accounts of Brian and other cases would consistently confirm the essential features of the phenomonen as the definition presented

them: surveillance, constraint, interpretation of daily conduct, prescription of adjustment measures.

Looking at the individual cases, you will also be in a position to observe and report the range of variation among specific instances: all cases will not conform in the same way to the ideal. And, once you have relocated the phenomenon in the real world, you may find that you have a chance to observe its associations with nearby phenomena. The cases of "therapeutic supervision," for example, may tend to occur in conjunction with poverty, or formal schooling, or systems of professional accreditation which license the clinician.

The exercise which follows asks you to exemplify the phenomenon you have defined. In most writing situations, you would be working in the other direction—constructing a definition from a cluster of instances, rather than constructing examples to support a definition. But I assume you got your definition from some form of specific experience—your knowledge of anti-abortionists' practice of dissent, for example, or your knowledge of your co-worker's retirement. Now you can retrieve that original source to compose examples of the phenomenon you are defining.

Exercise

Provide examples which support your definition of

- dissent
- retirement
- computer-aided instruction

or the term you have selected from your studies in another course. Present the examples in such a way as to confirm the essential features identified by the definition.

6.3.3. Focus on the phenomenon's situation in a larger context

A third phase in descriptive definition accounts for the phenomenon's role in the system of which it is part. Sometimes the surrounding system which the writer identifies is conspicuous, one most people would notice as the design which assigns the phenomenon its role and its operation. Medical diagnosis, for example, is part of the larger system of medical treatment.

But other times the writer's way of putting the phenomenon in context is noticeably interpretive: plausible but not inevitable. Just as the definition itself is a hypothesis—one way of organizing and interpreting the data—so too is the contextualizing of the phenomenon a hypothesis. In Samples (19) and (20) below, centralization and professional expertise are plausible contexts in which to situate broadcasting and therapeutic supervision, and they are compatible with earlier entries in the definition. But they are not the only conceivable contexts for these phenomena.

(19) Modern broadcasting contributes to the functioning of centralized societies. As commercial and government authorities locate themselves beyond neighbourhoods and communities, local resources are no longer adequate to explain the individual's role in the marketplace or his obligations and privileges as a citizen. Broadcasting is one of the mechanisms that replace the traditional, face-to-face interactions which formerly oriented people in public life.

(20) The practice of therapeutic supervision is part of a larger occurrence—that of professional expertise in post-industrial societies with strong institutional sectors. These forms of expertise depend on well-defined inventories of knowledge (such as, for example, counselling psychology) which the expert acquires and then confirms by applying them in specific cases. Both the knowledge and its application depend on institutional settings—to house and disseminate the knowledge by creating experts and to provide occasions for the application of the knowledge in programs like therapeutic supervision which permit experts to observe and adjust the behavior of non-expert individuals.

Putting the phenomeon in context, the writer reveals its significance in a bigger picture: the conditions which cause its appearance, the effects which it contributes. The bigger picture can also reveal the phenomenon's history, its emergence or disappearance according to the forces and tendencies which shape contexts.

Like other phases of descriptive definition, context depends on the writer's original interpretation of the data. If the writer had analyzed Brian's case or certain television transmissions differently, she would have located therapeutic supervision and broadcasting in different contexts: healing practices, for example, or marketing.

Definition arranges data into meaningful patterns, but it does not fix them forever in those patterns. The data are still there, living lives of their own, open to new interpretations, ready to be regrouped into new sets, awaiting new perspectives from observers who approach them from a different avenue of inquiry. These revisions and innovations and re-definitions are features of scholarly activity.

Exercise

Put

- dissent
- retirement
- computer-aided instruction

or the term you have chosen from your studies into context, explaining the role of these phenomena in the larger system of which they are part. Contextualize the phenomena in such a way as to confirm your earlier entries in the descriptive definitions.

6.4. Invention

Definition is itself a phenomenon. We could compose a descriptive definition of definition, writing a core statement of equivalence, comparing it to other forms of analysis, providing examples of its occurrence, accounting for its range of variation, and situating it in a larger cultural context.

If our definition of definition took into account the presentation in Sections 6.3. through 6.3.3., we could say that definition is also an invention strategy: that is, a device to help writers come up with ideas. As long as you were writing summaries, you didn't need invention strategies so much (although the techniques for evaluation proposed in Chapter Three could qualify as an invention strategy). Having identified the original writer's main claims and the connections between them, your principal concern was to develop a structure for the summary which would take account of the reader's capacity for paying attention.

Summary is an important part of most academic writing assignments, but you have no doubt discovered that many assignments present you with tasks that require more than summary:

- Discuss the controversies surrounding the 1984 Olympics.
- Describe the role of reciprocity in trading practices among the Nishga.

In fulfilling these assignments, you will need your summarizing skills to handle your sources of information. But you will need more besides: you will have to have some way of generating main claims of your own, and constructing the connections between them.

Recognizing the need for generative techniques, many composition teachers and most composition textbooks suggest invention strategies: orderly procedures for coming up with ideas. Often, these procedures occur in the form of a series of questions the writer can ask herself about a topic. The answers to these questions provide material for her essay. Another name for these orderly procedures is *heuristic*.

Some of these invention strategies are very efficient. They help the writer come up with ideas she otherwise might never have thought of.

Interestingly, invention strategies seem to be becoming more and more common as computers are increasingly called upon to help in composition instruction.

Programs "prompt" students to enter ideas on the screen in response to orderly questioning from the computer.

But invention strategies also have shortcomings. For one thing, invention strategies don't normally provide the writer with means to cope with outside sources of information. This is probably why invention strategies work best in schoolroom situations where the ability to come up with ideas out of the blue is highly valued. The academic writing situation differs from the schoolroom: at university or college, readers want to see ideas which develop from careful study of reliable sources of information. Surrounded by copious results of diligent research, the writer may have trouble getting the invention mechanism started up and operating smoothly.

And, second, there is not a lot of clear evidence that invention strategies are transferable. In other words, if you learn to use a particular heuristic successfully in your writing course, we can't guarantee that that heuristic will work efficiently in other academic writing situations. Maybe you'll forget to use it. Or forget how to use it. Or maybe it just won't fit in. When you are asked to "Write a descriptive definition of dissent," it's easy enough to get the invention mechanism going, but, beyond the writing classroom, you'll probably never be asked to do such a thing. Certainly, publishing scholars don't see themselves as setting out to use a particular invention strategy. They see themselves as setting out to gather and interpret evidence, consult authority, and publish a contribution to the research.

Third, most invention strategies provide no check for coherence. Having complied with the heurisitc procedure, the writer comes up with a list of ideas that are often no more than a list of loosely connected items. If the writer goes straight from the invention strategy to drafting an essay, she may find herself with no core argument and no clear relation between the points it makes.

Like any heuristic, the invention-through-definition strategies offered in this chapter are open to all these charges and complaints. They defend themselves in several ways.

Defence against the charge of schoolroom ideas

This chapter asks you to look at definition as emerging not out of the blue but from the interpretation of data—presumably, data gathered from reading and research. As I have pointed out, the exercises which keep step with each phase in the process of definition are misleading in their suggestion that the word comes first and the examples follow. In actual practice, definition is a strategy for expanding, developing, and refining the reasoning that names the common and significant features of a cluster of data: Brian's day-to-day experience, for example, or the behaviors of olive baboons. Without the interpretive claim and its abstract name, the data are only a list of mentions—ambiguous and not memorable. With the interpretive claim, they begin to take on the shape of argument. With the expansion of the interpretive name through definition, they become even more meaningful and significant.

Defence against the charge of non-transferability

Knowing how to write a descriptive definition will not do you much good in situations outside the composition classroom if you don't know how to apply this knowledge. You need to be able to spot the occasions for definition, keeping alert to the emergence of a key term that efficiently names crucial features of the data you are working with. When such a term emerges, and you test it to see if it will sustain development through definition, then you can entertain the possibility of using definition as a controlling device in your essay.

The exercise at the end of this chapter gives you a chance to begin to train yourself to detect the occasions for definition. Like the planning exercises in previous chapters, this exercise presents unorganized clusters of data. These are intended to resemble the notes you might end up with when you've completed your research of a topic. The exercise asks you to write an account of these data based on descriptive definition. But it doesn't tell you what to define. You have to figure that out for yourself from your interpretation of the data.

Defence against the charge of incoherence

As I explained the phases of the definition process, I argued that each entry in the definition should contribute to an overall argument, one originating in the interpretation of data. But I realize that these arguments could fall on deaf ears—or on ears deafened by the noise of the invention mechanism in operation, chugging away, spewing out ideas. So here I will suggest ways that you can add coherence monitors to the invention mechanism. These coherence monitors are meant to ensure that the heuristic doesn't produce an essay that is just a list of unrelated points.

Coherence monitors

(1) Before you begin to draft your essay, arrange your material according to the planning style you have developed. By passing your material through the planning screen, you will test for connections and focus. If some entries in the definition don't connect easily with other entries, rewrite them or eliminate them. (The one entry you can't eliminate is the formal sentence definition which classifies and differentiates the phenomenon. But you can rewrite it.) If some entries seem almost inaccessible from the main focus of your discussion – your most important claim – get rid of them. Remember, too, that the order of information in your essay should obey not the heuristic's steps but the reader's needs. For example, if you think the reader should know about the "larger system" right from the start, include this entry in your introduction.

(2) When you have written your draft, check again for coherence by glossing the draft. You gloss your draft by answering these questions about each paragraph in the body of the essay:
- what is the main thing my reader should keep in mind from this paragraph?
- what does this main, memorable thing have to with the preceding paragraph?
- what does it have to do with the main claims of the whole essay?

The answers to these questions will supply material with which you can revise the topic statements of each paragraph or section: these revisions will lasso wandering parts of the essay and pull them back to the central focus of the argument. And if, confronting certain parts of your discussion, you can't come up with answers to these questions, you should consider eliminating those parts from the essay.

This coherence monitor that glosses the draft is applicable to any draft—not only the draft of any essay based on definition.

Exercise

Apply the coherence monitor (1) to the entries you have developed in your definition of

- dissent
- retirement
- computer-aided instruction

or the term you have selected from your studies.

Exercise

Abstracted from The British Journal of Special Education *(Denis O'Connor (1987) Glue sniffers with special needs. 14, 3, 94-97), the data below are about glue-sniffing. Read through these notes, looking for connections and ways of interpreting the phenomena reported. From this analysis, find a key term that names the aspect of the data you want to focus on. Use descriptive definition to develop that interpretive name. Write 600-800 words which present and explain this information about glue-sniffing, using descriptive definition to develop you argument. (Note that "glue-sniffing" is an obvious target for definition—but it's certainly not the only one expressed or implicit in these data. Don't settle for "glue-sniffing" before you have considered other possibilities.)*

practice of inhaling volatile substance — common name 'glue-sniffing'
technical name 'volatile substance abuse' (VSA)
not only glue — also gasoline, thinners, clothing dyes, typing eraser liquid, nail polish & remover, aerosols

evidence of VSA: empty containers (tubes, tins, bottles, cans); freezer bags, milk bottles

effect on behavior:
first, excited, loud, aggressive, hyperactive, moody, easily annoyed, expressions of feelings of hate then, depression, sleepy, can't concentrate, yawning, dizziness, slurred speech
overall effect:
decline in school performance, stealing, secretiveness, isolation, family quarrels, morbid attitude towards health

some patients at clinic report VSA helped them endure boredom & stress of schooling

addiction to VSA is possible

especially at risk—children without emotionally supportive family life; children with emotional &/or physical impairments

occurrence of VSA: especially in large comprehensive (non-academic stream) urban schools also in residential facilities—hospital schools, observation or assessment centres

with peer group pressures: epidemic-like spread of VSA through school population

effects of VSA: emotional comfort, release of stress, reduction in anxiety, disinhibition of personality. In half the cases: illusions; wish-fulfilling, dream-like states. Minority of cases: hallucinations

associated with VSA: social disadvantages; disorganized home life. Often also disabilities — > feelings of inferiority

sniffer's appearance: facial blemishes, cracked lips, paleness, tired look

tolerance to VSA develops — > increase in VSA — > use of other drugs

most likely ages for VSA: 13-17; as young as 8; as late as 18 or 19 (then associated with unemployment)
more boys than girls

therapeutic counselling teaches young person to live without solvents

teachers don't know much about VSA

adults see VSA as problem. Sniffers see VSA as solution to problems—e.g., violence in the family, family break-ups, loss of beloved family member, feelings that can't be expressed. Punitive reaction from adults makes matters worse

counselling: advice on basic routines of living; encouragement to modify behavior

one case: Brian, 14, slight brain damage at birth, moderate learning difficulties; needed sustained learning assistance.
at school, his behavior disturbs staff & other students; older boys teach him glue sniffing — > his behavior becomes more aggressive at home & at school; complaints of indecency; other students start to bully him
counselling: constant supervision—escorted to and from school, jobs at class breaks, 2 evenings a week at youth club, weekends with church group, one morning a week at intermediate treatment centre; one morning at clinic for group counselling and activities like painting & modelling. Brian's VSA contained, but several relapses

experience of threat from environment: VSA's appeal
VSA: release from anxiety, from boring routines of living, from struggle

deliberate inhalation of volatile substance can kill even on first attempt one case: Sally wanted to stop sniffing; parents refused counselling services.

Counselling sessions videotaped, then reviewed with Sally: how would she like to improve herself?

Sally notes that sniffing leaves little time for self-improvement — > weekly programme drawn up: Sally chooses Friday for self-improvement; comes to clinic Saturday, looks much better, sees before-&-after videos, very pleased with herself, staff take her shopping for new blouse and cosmetics; new contract for more improvement. Sally progresses. Parents refuse to cooperate. Sally graduates to helping new clients.

products containing volatiles: plentiful, cheap, legal controls ineffective

CHAPTER SEVEN

reader-friendly styles

7.1 Style

The coherence monitors introduced at the end of Chapter Six respect what we know about readers' behavior and capacity. We know that readers will make sincere efforts after meaning even in discouraging situations, but we also know that their ability to construct meaning from written texts is limited by the inelastic dimensions of short-term memory. The reader's mental desktop is a confined area, liable to congestion and disorder when the traffic of information across it is unorganized and random. The coherence monitors go to work to organize this traffic and keep the reader's desktop orderly.

We could say that coherence is a text-level condition: it pertains to the overall management of concepts and information; it has to do with the content of the essay. But text-level contact is not the reader's only experience of the essay. In fact, the reader's first contact with the essay is much more local: the reader first experiences the argument at word- and sentence-level. If conditions at word- and sentence-level are obstructive and troublesome, the reader will never get to the text-level of ideas and information. In other words, if the writer's style is obscure, her way of wording things awkward and confusing, the reader will stall in these local conditions and never get to the point of absorbing and appreciating the argument.

This chapter focusses on style. It looks at the role of word choice in furthering or impeding the reader's efforts. It looks at those features of sentence structure that can speed the reader on his way to comprehending content, and at those features that can block him. It looks at ways of managing sentence boundaries and their punctuation. Then, approaching text-level once again, it looks at the role of repetition and commentary on the argument itself in keeping the reader working efficiently.

7.2 Additions to the portrait of the reader

"Style" may suggest to you matters of taste and flourish, personal expression and literary values. Style *can* make such suggestions in many situations, but in the academic writing situation, we're better off thinking of style as one of the conditions of the reader's work. We already know that the writer's way of arranging information determines what the reader is going to be able to do with that information. An essay which fails to instruct the reader as to the priority of certain items will leave the reader making long, distracting searches through long-term memory to retrieve items he had taken to be marginal, and dispensable. Or he may be led to hold on to other items only to find that they are minor players in the argument, and a bad investment for processing energies. These are poor working conditions for the reader.

But before the reader ever gets to that level of processing, where the overall structure of the argument is at stake, he has to go through more local levels of processing. He has to, first, decode words, and, second, sort out sentence structure. Both these processes make claims on the same mental resources that the reader applies to concepts and information. And they make *prior* claims. In other words, if the reader has to think twice about what words mean, he will have to use valuable processing energy to decode those words. That means he'll have

"If in an epistemological figure characteristics of objectivity and systematicity are present then it may be defined as a science, on the other hand where these criteria are absent, as is the case in Foucault's view in respect of the human sciences, we may only speak of a positive configuration of knowledge being present."

fewer resources left over for understanding the argument. If the reader encounters a long, syntactically complex sentence whose core subject and verb are buried in a pattern of dependencies and qualifications, he will have to use valuable processing energy to discover the structure of the sentence. Both these expenditures of energy come *before* the reader's processing of the argument itself. After all, if the reader hasn't understood the words and untangled the sentences, he is in no position to master the argument.

So far, our portrait of the reader has shown him at his mental desk, concentrating on some ideas by keeping them on the desktop, putting some ideas aside but keeping them handy for later use, and sending other ideas to longer-term storage. Now we show him with other material crossing his desktop: words and their references, sentences and their structures. This material takes up space on the mental desktop—space we have already measured and found to be limited and liable to congestion. If the new material—vocabulary and syntax—is demanding, there will be scarcely any room left for ideas and information. "Reading" becomes a process of grinding through the local features of the text, never catching a glimpse of its global structure, its meaning.

These are poor working conditions for the reader. And he will perform poorly—missing the point, getting discouraged. You don't want your reader working under these conditions. The following sections will suggest ways you can improve your reader's working conditions.

7.3 Words

The vocabulary of academic writing is under a lot of pressure to complicate itself. Some of this pressure is cultural—a matter of tradition and custom. In Chapter Eight, we will look into the current status of the traditions and customs that select hard words and reject easy ones. But other circumstances also lead to complicated wordings.

Academic writing takes issues that are, in ordinary life, referred to loosely, in general terms, and analyzes those issues, differentiating them into smaller parts scarcely visible to the untrained observer. For example, we all know that there is such a thing as "thinking." But, probably, only specialists know that there is such a thing as "nonspecific goal strategy in problem solving." Nonspecific goal strategy in problem solving is an object of study for some researchers in cognitive science. When they report their studies, they say "nonspecific goal strategy in problem solving." They don't say "thinking." "Thinking" would not be precise enough.

Although some reasonable people would complain that "nonspecific goal strategy in problem solving" is an unnecessarily complicated way of speaking, I think we have to accept the fact that these specialist terms are inevitable. As long as current academic practices prevail, scholars will come up with these cumbersome terms. You are going to have to use them, too, in your essays. And even the specialist finds these terms a heavier burden than words like "car" or "fish" or "breakfast."

Given that academic writing will be laden with these inescapable terms, we can predict that the reader's desktop will have to devote an unusual amount of space to decoding words—figuring out or remembering what they refer to. And then we have to add to this circumstance the fact that the *content* of academic writing—the array of information and its explanation—is typically more complex than the content of most messages. The reader has to really concentrate on content. So anything the writer can do to clear desktop space will improve the reader's working conditions. One of the things the writer can do is to attend to her style, getting rid of hard words—wherever she can—and replacing them with easy words. If "nonspecific goal strategy in problem solving" has to stay, the writer can give the reader more room to work on it by replacing other difficult words with simple ones.

What distinguishes easy words from hard ones? A practical answer to this question is that easy words are the most common ones, the words we learn earliest in life. Semanticists or philosophers would probably not entirely approve of this criterion: they could very well claim that "thinking" is, in some ways, more problematic than "nonspecific goal strategy in problem solving." There is something to be said for their point of view. But for academic writers, the earliest-learned criterion is useful and sensible. If a writer wants to describe the set-up of a complicated experiment designed to explore people's complicated reactions to something, he may find himself saying

(1) Subjects were cognizant of the fact that....

He has no reason to burden his reader with "were cognizant of" when he could just as easily say

(2) Subjects knew that....

"Know" is an early-acquired word, effortlessly processed by everybody. Even four-year-olds process "know" without difficulty. "Be cognizant of," on the other hand, comes late on the acquisition calendar, as a rarely used and attention-seeking entry. Four-year-olds neither produce nor receive "be cognizant of."

There is *nothing wrong* with "be cognizant of." It's perfectly respectable English, and speakers or writers who want to swell their utterance with it may legitimately prefer it over "know." But academic writers can't really afford to indulge such preferences, for they are liable to take up space on the reader's desktop—space that's in high demand. Academic writers are better off translating what words they can to match the four-year-old's vocabulary. (This doesn't mean that the four-year-old could understand the argument—only that he would be able to decode these translated words.)

Observe this rule-of-thumb in word choice: *the more complicated the argument, the simpler the words should be.*

Exercise

Translate the following words into words a four-year-old could understand.

magnitude	eliminate	place of residence
ascend	delineate	purchase (verb)
descend	incarcerate	attempt (verb)
apparel	commence	ascertain
comprehend	initial (adjective)	perceive
concept	bestow	epistle
assistance	dispatch (verb)	domicile
alteration	anxiety	facilitate
obtain	traverse	intractable
monetary resources	fabricate	
possess	employ	
proximity	terminate	

Sometimes the fancy word will be the one you want: it says what no simple word can say. But other times your meaning can be much more directly expressed by the ordinary words we use in conversation.

7.3.1 The structure of the noun phrase

The English noun phrase is just about the most elaborate element of the English sentence—even more quirky and intricate perhaps than the verb phrase with all its features of tense and aspect and its partitions into auxiliaries and participles and so on. You will be relieved to hear that we will make no effort to account for this elaborateness. We will only look at one crucial feature of the noun phrase which has a direct influence on the reader's working conditions. That feature we can witness simply by observing the structural difference between the noun phrase "thinking" and the noun phrase "nonspecific goal strategy in problem solving."

(3)   **thinking**
                          NOUN HEAD

(4) <u>nonspecific goal</u> strategy <u>in problem solving</u>
Premodifier   NOUN HEAD   Postmodifier
adjective + noun   preposition + Noun Phrase
                                         Premodifier + NOUN HEAD
                                         noun

Most people wouldn't like to see these analyses of noun phrases. They might find the analysis of (4) particularly disturbing.

Displays of technical analysis of speech seem to make people doubt their mastery of their own language and to think that they don't know the grammar of English. Actually, they *do* know the grammar of English. If they didn't, they wouldn't understand what was said to them. And they wouldn't be able to say understandable things to others. They wouldn't even be able to say "I don't know grammar." People shouldn't let grammatical analyses undermine their confidence in their own competence as speakers. Especially, *writers* shouldn't think that the ability to analyze grammatical structures has anything to do with writing competence.

You can be an efficient, effective writer without ever acquiring the technical know-how that enables analyses like the one in Sample (4). However, you can take advantage of the analysis presented in (4) to confirm what is visible to the naked eye, without research instruments: the noun phrase in (3) is *much simpler* than the noun phrase in (4). Sample (4) has modifying wings on each side of the noun head, each of which covers its *own* noun or noun forms ("goal" and "problem" and "solving"). Two of these nouns ("goal" and "problem") are themselves modifiers, not heads. Although it's probably true that all mature and normally experienced users of English have the grammatical competence to read (4) properly, this heavily winged noun phrase makes much greater demands on that competence than does noun phrase (3) "thinking."

The difference between (3) and (4) demonstrates the noun phrase's most interesting feature—and the one most relevant to writers who want to manage the reader's working conditions productively: the noun phrase is capable of *expanding* by picking up other sentence elements and installing them in the modifying wings around the Head. In the series that follows, you will see the noun phrase grow by absorbing material from other parts of the sentence.

The noun phrase absorbs an adjective
(5)

    This **behavior** is <u>criminal</u>.
                                   adjective
    This <u>criminal</u> **behavior**....

The noun phrase absorbs another noun
(6)

    The **reports** record <u>offences</u>.
                                      noun (object)
    The <u>offence</u> **reports**....

The noun phrase absorbs a predicate—verb and adverb
(7)

    Some **strategies** <u>work forward</u>.
                              verb + adverb
    <u>Forward-working</u> **strategies**....

The noun phrase absorbs a predicate—verbs and its noun object
(8)

    Strategies <u>solve problems</u>.
                             verb + noun (object)
    <u>Problem-solving</u> **strategies**....

There are some limits to what the noun phrase can absorb, but Samples (5)-(8) don't even approach these limits: (5)-(8) exemplify some of the simplest forms of noun-phrase expansion.

And you can see that the noun phrase's capacity to expand is one of the normal *economies* of English. By installing, in (7), "work forward" in the noun phrase, the writer leaves the rest of the sentence free to carry other information:

(9) Forward-working strategies enable the problem solver to explore the problem space to see what moves are possible.

Speakers of English use the capacity of the noun phrase all the time to achieve economies of expression. Instead of saying

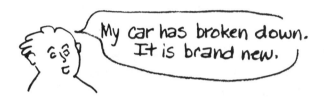

the speaker can economize, presenting the same information fewer words:

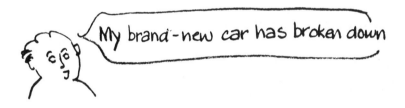

But, especially, *writers* are liable to load up noun phrases. Writers have more time to gather scattered elements and compact them in heavy noun phrases. While (10) below is probably more characteristic of speech, (11) shows the kind of wording a writer could come up with.

(10) A study recently compared costs of developing and maintaining multiple-family housing. It was based on 1986 construction experience, and it showed that three-storey buildings ultimately provided cheaper housing than high-rises.

(11) A recent comparative study of multiple-family development and maintenance costs based on 1986 construction experience showed that three-storey buildings ultimately provided cheaper housing than high-rises.

Like all writers and speakers of English, you already know how to exploit the grammatical capacity of noun phrases: you know how to construct a noun phrase like the one at the beginning of (10), and you know how to make a noun phrase like the one at the beginning of (11). The following exercise is meant to show you your own grammatical competence in handling noun phrases. And the experience you get from this exercise will help you understand some of the implications of noun-phrase structure for style—the reader's working conditions. We will look into these implications in Section 7.3.2 below.

Exercise

In the following passages, underlined sections are candidates for inclusion in earlier-occurring noun phrases (printed in **bold***). Rewrite these passages to incorporate underlined material in the noun phrase.*

SAMPLE

Models have been described in the research. <u>They are separate. One is oriented to working forward. The other is oriented to working backward.</u>

Separate forward- and backward-oriented models have been described in the research.

(1) In the case of both the Lutheran Reformation and the French republic, central authorities supported **evaluations of literate practice** to monitor the penetration of ideological orthodoxy. <u>These evaluations were extensive and difficult.</u> In both cases, **new relationships** were intended to replace **earlier relationships**. <u>The new relationships were literate and compelled by law. The earlier relationships were oral and local and sanctioned by community loyalty.</u>

Adapted from Carolyn Marvin (1988), Attributes of authority: Literacy tests and the logic of strategic conduct. *Communication*, 11, 63-82, p. 70.

(2) To compare societies' use of prisons, criminologists have studied **rates from different nations**. <u>These rates show how often nations incarcerate criminals. These rates are based on surveys of victimization.</u>

Adapted from James P. Lynch (1988), Comparison of prison use in England, Canada, West Germany, and the United States: A limited test of the punitive hypothesis. *Journal of Criminal Law and Criminology*, 79, 1, 180-217, p. 187.

(3) The system of subcontracting connects **large firms** with **small firms**. The large firms are in charge of raw materials. The small firms transform these materials into manufactured goods.

Adapted from Gary G. Hamilton and Nicole W. Biggart (1988), Market, culture, and authority: A comparative analysis of management and organization in the Far East. *American Journal of Sociology*, 94, S59-S94, p. S59.

7.3.2 Processing the noun phrase

In the exercise above, you packed noun phrases with materials from other parts of the sentence and from other sentences. The results of the exercise probably left you with mixed feelings. Sometimes, loading a noun phrase clearly saves words: that saving should relieve your reader of some processing burdens. He has fewer words to get through. But other times the heavy noun phrase grows strange and awkward—and seems likely to impose more rather than fewer burdens on the reader. Moreover, you may have found that, in arranging for noun phrases to absorb more material, some information got lost. For example, if you wrote

victimization-based incarceration **rates** from different nations

you lost "criminals" and "surveys." In fact, most heavy noun phrases print only traces of the arguments with which their meaning was originally associated.

The transformation shown in (12) reverses the procedure you followed in the last exercise. It unpacks the heavy noun phrase, showings its elements in a more complete environment.

(12) nonspecific goal **strategy** in problem solving

Strategy helps thinkers solve problems. Some strategies are directed towards specific goals: the answer to, for example, "How fast is the car travelling?" Other strategies are directed towards nonspecific goals: response to, for example, "Calculate the value of as many variables as you can."

If, up to this point, you didn't know what "nonspecific goal strategy in problem solving" was, or you had some ideas about what it was but couldn't say for sure, you are probably glad to see the elements of the term spread out in their sentence environments. Although the unpacked version uses 44 words—more than seven times as many as the heavy noun phrase—it will have communicated to you more efficiently. The long version will actually have imposed *fewer* processing demands than the short version. If you had encountered "nonspecific goal strategy in problem solving" in an article you were reading, it would have caused problems on your mental desktop—blocking the arrival and processing of new information while you entertained several hypotheses about what it might mean. Or it might have just fallen off the desktop, unprocessed and unavailable for interpreting later parts of the argument.

The noun phrase can absorb material from other parts of the sentence or from other sentences. This capacity can produce economies on the page: more information in fewer words. Sometimes these economies are desirable. Once the meaning of "nonspecific goal strategy in problem solving" has been established, it can efficiently compact that meaning in later references. But other times those economies are false ones. Using more words actually provides the reader with easier access to information. Exercises at the end of this section will give you a chance to use your judgement about these matters, and to practise unpacking noun phrases to improve the reader's working conditions.

Before you get to those exercises, though, you should witness one more aspect of the English noun phrase—an aspect related to those we've just been looking at. We have seen that noun phrases are very hospitable to other sentence elements: they will take in just about anything that offers itself. As these bits and pieces are accommodated in the noun phrase, other elements are left behind. When parts get left behind, ambiguity can result. Sometimes the effort required from the reader to resolve the ambiguity is so negligible it's scarcely measurable. The underlined noun phrases in (13), which appeared in a sentence in a daily newspaper, make demands on the reader that he meets virtually automatically.

(13) The body, discovered in the basement of <u>a concrete building</u>, was identified as the remains of <u>a newspaper woman</u> who had lived in the neighbourhood in the late 1960s.

"A concrete building" means that the building was made of concrete. But "a newspaper woman" doesn't mean that the woman was made of newspaper. It means that the woman wrote articles for a newspaper. The noun phrases don't make these distinctions (the distinctions are lost when the noun phrase absorbs other elements). The reader makes the distinctions by consulting his knowledge of the word (no women are made of newspaper). And the reader makes the distinctions easily, without significant processing demands.

But other noun phrases can be slightly more distracting. Example (14) comes from a news report on social conditions in the United States.

(14) <u>Homeless experts</u> say that the problem will only get worse as the summer goes on.

What is a "homeless expert"?

A more likely interpretation soon supersedes the less likely one.

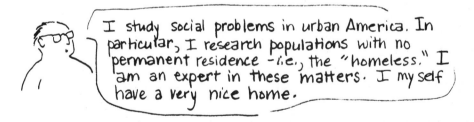

The reader resolves the ambiguity in the noun phrase by consulting his knowledge of the world. This doesn't take long—but it does take up mental resources that would be put to better use under better working conditions.

Other noun phrases can be much more stubbornly ambiguous. The following example cannot be resolved simply by consulting our knowledge of the world:

(15) <u>police arrest</u> **information**

Does this refer to information police use when they arrest people? Or does it refer to information about police arresting people? The underlined noun phrase in the next example (16), repeated from a student essay, could sit for a long time on the reader's mental desktop, while he tried to decode it:

(16) The protagonist suffers from <u>externally imposed reference</u> **systems**.

What are "externally imposed reference systems"? Consulting his knowledge of the world, the reader is liable to come up empty- handed. If it turns out that (16) is an important claim in the writer's argument, the reader is going to be at a disadvantage when he tries to construct the writer's meaning. When the writer revised, and unpacked the noun phrase to improve the reader's working conditions, "reference system" was abandoned. It turned out that, while this term was simple and meaningful for the *writer*, there were other ways of stating the point that made it more accessible to the *reader*.

(17) The protagonist finds her identity imposed on her from outside. She is the person others see her to be, and their vision of her is formed by the values and attitudes of the community.

The exercises that follow ask you to manipulate noun phrases in the interests of improving your reader's working conditions, choosing between the economics of, on the one hand, fewer words and, on the other hand, ease of processing.

Exercise

The passage below contains a lot of heavy noun phrases. Screen the passage's style, detecting those segments that impose unnecessary burdens on the reader. Rewrite by unpacking noun phrases, spreading their elements out into other parts of the sentence and other sentences.

The Australian basic-wage Royal Commission of 1920, seeking working-class standard-of-living criteria, was chaired by a widely-read and respected living-wage champion, husband of a controversial family-planning advocate. Despite the liberal- reform inclinations of the Commission's chair and its nearly 40% recommended basic-wage increase, one of the main legacies of the Commission was the unquestioned equation of the "family" wage with the male-provider wage.

Adapted from Kerreen M. Reiger (1989), 'Clean and comfortable and respectable': Working-class aspirations and the Australian 1920 Royal Commission on the Basic Wage. *History Workshop,* 27, 86-105.

7.4 Nouns and verbs

When a noun phrase loads up with other sentence parts, some parts go missing. Although the expression is more compact, it is also less complete. Sometimes completeness is over-completeness, and only wordiness. Then the grammatical options that permit a writer to pack a noun phrase are useful to both writer and reader. Other times, however, the missing parts leave a gap behind. When the writer revises to fill the gap, she improves the reader's efficiency.

Another feature of noun phrases, besides their capacity to load themselves up, can also leave gaps behind. Many nouns live other lives as verbs. The noun "attendance," for example, has another life as the verb "attend." When the verb "attend" turns into the noun "attendance," the transformation can leave items behind. In the following example (18), you will see that both the subject of the verb (the *doer* of the action) and the object of the verb (the thing that is *done-to*) can be eliminated.

(18) a) Many members <u>attended</u> the plenary session.
　　　　　 subject 　　　　　　　　 *object*
　　 b)Attendance was high.

Sometimes the more compact version is best. Other times its omissions leave the reader with too many inferences to make. In the following Sample (19), the underlined noun is a converted verb that has lost both its subject and its object.

(19) In the 1919, the Prime Minister, W.G. Higgins, proposed a Royal Commission into the Basic Wage. Because of soaring prices of living and waves of strikes, there was widespread <u>acceptance</u>.

What exactly was accepted? The proposal? The Royal Commission? The basic wage? And who accepted? The rewrite in (20) changes the noun "acceptance" back into the verb "accept" and provides both subject and object.

(20) In 1919, the Prime Minister, W.G. Higgins, proposed a Royal Commission into the Basic Wage. Because of soaring prices and waves of strikes, both trade unionists and employers <u>accepted</u> the government's initiative.

When verbs turn into nouns, they don't always lose their subjects and objects. But if they do carry them along, they often do so awkwardly. Some readers might consider the leftover subjects and objects in the (21) and (22) clumsy baggage.

(21) <u>Advocacy</u> of family planning by liberal reformers was prevalent.

(22) There was the <u>implication</u> by the Commissioners' report that a basic wage would ward off class conflict.

In each case, the writer can fix awkward sentence structure by changing the underlined noun back into a verb. Then subject and object settle comfortably around their verb.

(23) Many liberal reformers <u>advocated</u> family planning.

(24) The Commissioners' report <u>implied</u> that a basic wage would ward off class conflict.

When passage (20) revised (19) by reconverting the noun "acceptance" to the verb "accept," it filled in gaps with precise information. Presumably, the change would improve the reader's working conditions by eliminating uncertainties. But the changes that (23) and (24) make to (21) and (22) don't add any information, don't fill in any gaps, don't increase the expression's specificity. You could argue that these changes are a matter of style as only "taste," not as "reader's working conditions."

This might be a valid argument. So far, there is no overwhelming body of empirical evidence that readers do perform better with sentences like (23) and (24) than they do with sentences like (21) and (22). But, intuitively, we can sense that the sentences which install information around the

subject + verb + object
doer + action + done-to

pattern are simpler, and easier to process. Chances are, empirical evidence will soon catch up with our intuitions. Moreover, these *doer + action + done-to* sentences help writers avoid over-using forms of "be": "is," "are," "was," "were," and so on. "Advocacy of family planning by liberal reformers was prevalent" becomes "Many liberal reformers advocated family planning."

Many writing handbooks recommend that writers avoid "be" forms wherever possible and use "action verbs" instead—for colour or liveliness or all-round appeal. Most writers are probably willing to follow this advice—whether they see it as a matter of "taste" or of creating productive working conditions for the reader. But they can't think of any of those desirable "action verbs." So they're stuck with "is" and a handful of general verbs that are exhausted from over-use, and not very lively at all: "have," "go," "occur," "make," "do," "happen," "take place," "exist."

But it's possible that the lively verbs that writers are looking for are hiding in what they've already written—lurking there disguised as nouns. As we have seen, many English nouns enjoy life as verbs as well. Finding those verbs that have converted themselves into nouns, and changing them back into verbs, you may come up with the lively, direct style that not only satisfies standards of taste but also helps the reader process text efficiently and productively.

The exercise which follows gives you a chance to practise detecting nouns that can profitably be changed back into verbs. Many verbs-in-noun-form, of course, should be left just as they are: some of them may be performing a high-profile role by providing interpretive names for data. In the Chapter Six examples of defined abstraction, for instance, "supervision" in "therapeutic supervision" was a noun form of the verb "supervise," but it was also a crucial operator in the text's coherence, constructing meaning and guiding the reader's interpretation of data. But other noun versions of verbs are eligible targets for style monitors that assess and adjust the reader's working conditions.

Exercise

Each of these sentences contains a noun that was once a verb, and each sentence relies on a "general verb." Rewrite each sentence to change that noun back into a verb and to get rid of the "general verb." Where the doer or doers of the action, or the objects of the actions are missing, supply them. Make them up, inferring them from the context and from your knowledge of the world.

SAMPLE

Conviction occurs at different stages in the judicial processes of different countries.

Re-write:

Courts of different countries convict criminals at different stages in the judicial process.

---

(1) Satisfaction of employees' demands did not take place.

(2) An assumption exists that marginally profitable enterprises should not be subject to union principles.

(3) There is an appreciation of the fact that the research is still conclusive.

(4) Scholl's work has numerous references to the connections between crime and employment rates.

(5) Information was available to applicants seeking visas.

(6) Silent reading of library books occurs after these interactive sessions.

(7) A comparison of day-care facilities was done between communities with minimum-wage legislation and those without.

(8) The expression of this opinion by Koltz is at the end of his report of his fieldwork.

(9) There was an argument by employers that family should be defined as a man and wife and one child.

(10) There was the definite belief after consideration that the basic wage should provide for the children's as well as the parents' clothing.

7.5 Verbs and voice

Sometimes you will find passages in your writing that are semantically dense or grammatically awkward (though not necessarily *un*grammatical). If you suspect that these passages will consume too much of your reader's processing resources, you can zero in on its nouns, unpacking heavy noun phrases or converting nouns back to verbs. You can also check the verbs. One feature in particular of English verbs offers writers a chance to monitor and adjust style.

Verbs which take an object can assume either of two forms. Inspect the following examples to see these two options at work.

(25) a) *A dog bit Hap.*
   b) *Hap was bitten by a dog.*
   c) *Hap was bitten.*

(26) a) *Courts convict criminals* at different stages in the judicial process in different countries.
   b) *Criminals are convicted by courts* at different stages in the judicial process in different countries.
   c) *Criminals are convicted* at different stages in the judicial process in different countries.

(27) a) In the struggle for higher wages, *the unions quoted the Commission's findings,* but *employers rejected that evidence.*

b) In the struggle for higher wages, *the Commission's findings were quoted by the unions*, but *that evidence was rejected by employers*.

c) In the struggle for higher wages, *the Commission's findings were quoted*, but *that evidence was rejected*.

All the (a) entries in (25)-(27) take the form we looked at above when we thought about revising nouns back into verbs:

subject + verb + object
doer + action + done-to

(Check this for yourself by identifying *doer*, *action*, and *thing done-to* in (25a), (26a) and (27a).) In Section 7.4, looking at the benefits of converting nouns to verbs, we entertained the idea that this pattern provided the reader with good working conditions. This set of arrangements between a verb and its subject and object is called active voice. None of the (b) and (c) examples in (25)-(27) is in the active voice. They are all in the passive voice. The passive voice overturns the pattern by locating the *done-to* entry in subject position.

subject + verb (+ "by" + object of "by")
done-to + action (+ doer)

Passive voice also shifts the doer to a position after the verb—where it is vulnerable to disappearing altogether.

Hap was bitten.
Criminals are convicted.
The Commissioner's findings were quoted.
That evidence was rejected.

Now there's no sign of the agents who did the biting, convicting, quoting, or rejecting of evidence. Just as the noun forms of verbs rearrange the appearance of *doer* and *done-to* in the sentence, and permit the disappearance of some information, so does the passive voice.

When an instructor identifies your style as "passive," he doesn't mean to say that your writing is limp or unassertive. He means that it tends to select the passive voice over the active voice. This is a techncial matter, and not a matter of opinion. Either a sentence is passive or it's not. Less technical and more a matter of opinion are teachers' policies on passive voice. In recent years, many writing teachers who have diagnosed student writing have found it to be suffering from an overdose of the passive. They have sought to cure this affliction by urging students to revise for the active voice: *doer+action+done-to*. Often, these revisions can simplify expression at the same time as they fill in gaps left by information that drifted away in the passive version. The following passage, which is not only heavily passive but also relies on noun forms of verbs, is a candidate for revision to the *doer+action+done-to* pattern.

(28) In this class, a Whole Language approach has been taken. Books have been read to the class by the teachers or enjoyed individually during silent reading or centres time. Nursery rhymes have been studied. Extra marks were awarded for initiatives taken, such as preparation and presentation of an introduction to a rhyme.

Who takes a "Whole Language approach"? Who enjoys books individually— teachers? students? Who takes initiatives, prepares, presents, introduces? What is "centres time" (an ambiguous noun phrase)? Readers *could* answer all these questions by consulting their knowledge of the world and making inferences, but these consultations and inferences consume processing resources. The style of (28) creates poor working conditions for the reader. The revision (29) improves working conditions by selecting active voice and verb forms of nouns.

(29) In this class, teachers have taken a Whole Language approach. They read books to the class, or, during silent reading period and periods devoted to individual activity, students enjoy books by themselves. As a group, the class has studied nursery rhymes. When students initiate special projects—such as preparing and presenting an introduction to a rhyme—teachers award them extra marks.

The passage still presents some coherence problems: what is "Whole Language" about silent reading, for example, and how does silent reading relate to special projects? But the revision for style has constructed a picture of doers and actions and objects of action that is much more immediate than that in (28).

Pleased with the results of the kind of revision that transforms (28) into (29), composition specialists have explained the effect of the transformation in several ways. For one thing, they have suggested that the active voice is good because it gets rid of some prepositional material.

(30) Books have been read to the class <u>by the teachers</u>.
                                 Prepositional phrase
The teachers have read books to the class.

Prepositional phrases have a dim reputation among writing specialists, who claim that a build-up of such phrases ("of—," "by—," "with—") can have a rhythmic, sedating effect on the reader, putting him to sleep. Active voice is valued for its ability to eliminate at least one occurrence of the prepositional phrase.

Active voice is also valued for its specificity: it names the doer of the action. Whereas passive voice can be used to conceal information—

(31) The location of the aerospace plant has been decided.
(32) Refugees' claims will be assessed.

—active voice exposes information:

(33) The Prime Minister has decided on the location of the aerospace plant.
(34) Ministry bureaucrats will assess refugees' claims.

In these contexts, passive voice implies political underhandedness and routine manipulations of readers. Both implications are unattractive. In contrast, active voice suggests greater openness and honesty.

Finally, active voice has acquired a reputation as being more fundamental in readers' language competence. Some people argue that, as language learners, we master active voice much earlier, and that, in fact, passive voice is a relatively late acquisition in our language repertoires. We used the "early-learned" criterion Section 7.3 to identify "easy" words and distinguish them from "hard" words. The same criterion could apply in selecting verb voice, and it could explain any intuitive preference for "Teachers read books to the class" over "Books are read to the class by teachers."

These arguments in favour of the active voice add up to a large incentive to cleanse our writing of the passive voice: the passive puts readers to sleep; it is politically devious; it's harder for readers to process than the more basic active voice. If these arguments were conclusive, you would expect to see no instances of the passive in good writing. But take a look at celebrated prose: you will often find the passive. In E.B. White's admired essay "Once More to the Lake," for example, the passive shows up. White writes

(35) Some of the cottages were owned by nearby farmers....

He doesn't write

(36) Nearby farmers owned some of the cottages....

In "Politics and the English Language," George Orwell advises writers against the passive voice, but, in his famous essay "Shooting an Elephant," he begins with a passive construction:

(37) In Moulmein, in Lower Burma, I was hated by large numbers of people....

If he had revised for the active voice, he would have written

(38) In Moulmein, in Lower Burma, large numbers of people hated me....

But he didn't.

Since both White and Orwell provide readers with excellent working conditions—and these conditions include the passive voice—we should qualify our commitment to the active voice. Passive voice has its uses, and one of these is maintaining sentence focus. Roughly speaking, sentence focus is the natural emphasis that the first parts of a sentence receive. In (39a) below, "courts" gets the benefit of sentence focus; in (39b), "criminals" gets the benefit of sentence focus.

(39) a) Courts convict criminals at different stages in the judicial process in different countries.
b) Criminals are convicted by courts at different stages in the judicial process in different countries.

Over stretches of text, as the writer develops a subject, sentence focus can contribute to coherence. It can keep some items consistently in focus; it can show shifts to sub-topics by introducing new items to the sentence-focus slot. (Another name for this phenomenon is thematization: some items are thematized by their positions at the beginning of sentences; they become the screen through which the rest of the information in the sentence is viewed.) Sentence focus, then, contributes to *topic*—directing the reader's attention to some issues, and holding it there on those issues. Since the passive transformation affects the content of the sentence-focus slot, withdrawing doer and installing done-to, it is a major operator in thematizing information to contribute to topic emphasis. In (39) above, for example, (39a) would focus "courts," contributing to a passage which expanded on the working of the courts in the justice system; (39b) would thematize "criminals," contributing to a passage which developed information about criminals' participation in the justice system.

Sample (40) below shows thematization focussing the reader's attention in a consistent direction. "Pinnipeds" are first thematized; then they give way to "an English naturalist," only to be reinstated in the focus slot of the third sentence: the topic is "pinnipeds" and their divided classification, not the "English naturalist." But particularly interesting to us right now is the way the passive voice enables the writer to shift from a focus on ideas of divided origin to notions of common origin. Look at the operation of the passive in the last two sentences of the passage.

(40) Pinnipeds seem to fit comfortably into two categories: "wrigglers" — seals — and "walkers" — sea lions and walruses. In 1885, an English naturalist, Saint George Jackson Mivart, speculated that the two groups of ancient pinnipeds had taken to the sea independently, giving rise to the three modern families of seals, sea lions, and walruses. Recently, however, pinnipeds' relationship to one another and to other mammals has become a matter of intense dispute. Indeed, the widely held view that seals, sea lions, and walruses shared two lines of descent is opposed by the view that they evolved from one common ancestor. The notion that all pinnipeds evolved from a single ancestor is supported by new fossil evidence, by reinterpretations of earlier evidence, and by biochemical analysis.

Adapted from André R. Wyss (1989), Thicker than water. *The Sciences*, July/August, 34-37.

If the writer had followed the advice of handbooks and English teachers, he would have revised the last two sentences to the active voice:

(41) Indeed, the view that seals, sea lions, and walruses evolved from a common ancestor opposes the widely held view that they shared two lines of descent. New fossil evidence, reinterpretations of earlier evidence, and biochemical analysis support the notion that all pinnipeds evolved from a single ancestor.

But would this revision actually improve the reader's working conditions? I don't think so. In (40), the original, the reader enjoys a smooth transition from the "two-line-ancestry" idea to the "single-line-ancestry" idea:

	FOCUS			FOCUS		
[two groups, taking independantly to the sea]	**two-line descent**	+	one common ancestor	**single ancestor**	+	fossil evidence & analysis

The single-ancestor idea first appears as an argument screened through the well established two-lines-of-descent idea. The reader experiences no distracting milli-second when he thinks "What's this, then, this 'common ancestor'?" And then the common-ancestor idea is confirmed as having high status in the topic by immediately appearing in the focus slot of the next sentence. Passive voice accomplishes these seamless transitions.

The research of linguists who study sentence focus and thematization explains why writers like Orwell and White, or writers like you and me, use the passive voice, despite arguments in favor of the active voice. Sometimes the passive offers the best means of focussing the reader's attention and preventing him from being briefly disoriented as new information arrives for processing. And the research of linguists who study language acquisition has recently modified the claim that learners acquire the passive very late. Like everyone else who is trying to get a point across, even little children will use the passive to get the sentence focussed in the right place and get the listener thinking along the right lines.

The active voice is not always better than the passive voice. But revising for the active voice can help you deal with passages like (28) above, which tried to account for the goings-on in a "Whole Language" classroom. Just as you will sometimes find that the noun form of a verb is essential to delivering your topic compactly to the reader's desktop, you will also discover that the passive voice is sometimes essential to maintaining focus. But, other times, you will find that revising for verbs and for the active voice can help you clear up tangles and smooth the way for your reader.

Detecting the passive

Looking at simple pairs like—
The dog bit Hap.
Hap was bitten by the dog.

—most students find it easy enough to identify the passive version. It's the one where the doer of the action—the dog who bit—occurs at the end of the sentence, and the done-to—the one who suffered the bite—appears at the beginning. But most real-world instances of the passive don't display themselves so clearly. When you look at your own writing, you may have trouble detecting the passive voice.

If you can't find the passive, you won't be able to take advantage of the revision opportunities offered by the passive/active alternative.

So the following exercise asks you to practise identifying the passive and active voice. As you approach each sentence in the exercise, ask yourself

- what ACTION does the sentence refer to?

(Sometimes you will identify more than one action.) The answer to this question should point to a verb. Then ask yourself

- does the DOER appear before the action?

If the answer is "yes," the sentence is probably in active voice. If the answer is "no," it's probably in the passive voice.

The exercise asks you as well to *rewrite* passive constructions as active, and active constructions as passive. If you find a case of the active voice

(42a) An analysis of the skeleton of *Enaliarctos* has turned up a number of traits shared by all three pinnipeds.

you identify the action as "turn up," and the doer as "analysis." Then you up-root the doer from its position in front of the verb and replace it with what was done-to—"a number of traits":

(42b) A number of traits shared by all three pinnipeds have been turned up by analysis of the skeleton of *Enaliarctos*.

If, on the other hand, you come across a passive construction, you reverse the operation:

(43a) In the early 1970s, this view was reinforced by the discovery of the oldest known fossil pinniped, *Enaliarctos*.

(43b) In the early 1970s, the discovery of the oldest known fossil pinniped, *Enaliarctos*, reinforced this view.

However, some instances of the passive—in the exercise and in your own writing—will not be converted so easily. These are cases where the passive has obliterated the doer. When you go to convert the sentence to the active voice, you have no entry for the subject slot.

(44a) It is now thought that the three groups of pinnipeds descend from a common ancestor.

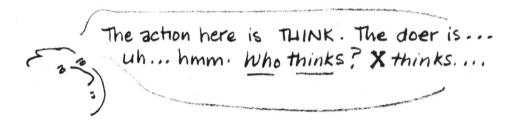

The action here is THINK. The doer is... uh... hmm. Who thinks? X thinks....

In your own writing, you can consult your research and reasoning to supply the answer. (In the process, you may find that you don't know the answer. Then you will have to reflect on the significance of this deficit.) In the exercise which follows, you will have to consult your knowledge of the world to construct or invent an answer. (In the process, you will replicate the reader's experience when she has to make inferences to specify what is not supplied in the text.)

(44b) Some paleontologists now think that the three groups of pinnipeds descend from a common ancestor.

In the exercise, you will also find cases that are neither active nor passive. Some of these present a verb that has no object—an action but no *done-to*.

(45) Pinnipeds descend from a common ancestor.

(46) Three thousand kinds of plants, thirty thousand types of insects, two hundred reptiles and amphibians, five hundred birds, and a hundred and forty mammals flourish in the dry forests of Cacao and Orosí.

In these sentences, there are no active/passive alternatives to choose between. In other sentences, you will find not only no object, but no action either. Some of these look very much like the passive, but they won't respond to your attempts to revise to the active voice.

(47) Even under the best of conditions, the road to absolute **zero will be** neither short nor smooth.

(48) In stark contrast are grim reports from city streets.

As you rewrite the active and passive constructions in the exercise below, you will come up with mixed results.

And you will come up with sets of choices that, in real life, could be resolved only by consulting the context of the sentences: the focus of preceding stretches of text; the essay's topic and argument. This exercise will not show you hard-and-fast rules that apply to every verb on every occasion. There are no such rules. But it will give you experience spotting the core of agent and action at the heart of some sentences, and it will give you practice manipulating those sentences until they settle down into satisfactory structures.

Exercise

Rewrite each passive as active, and each active as passive. Where passive constructions omit the doer of the action, supply that item in your revision to the active.

1. This project was funded by SSHRC.
2. Most Americans associate narcotics with addiction.

3. Drug addiction has been reclassified as a medical condition rather than a passion or vice.
4. The distinction between social convention and moral principle has been erased by social constructivism.
5. Columbus notes three geographic features on Ferninanda: a village, an unusual harbor, and an east-west coast on the northern end.
6. It will be shown by my research that miles and leagues were sometimes confused by the friar who transcribed Columbus' log in the sixteenth century.
7. Proponents of moral indoctrination confuse idea and practice.
8. This lapse in logic is celebrated by politicians and education reformers throughout the country.
9. Groups are successful only to the extent that their members share information and coordinate efforts.
10. The principle of respectful engagement is drawn from three decades of research on adult-child relationships.
11. Pulled inward by its own gravity, the cloud eventually collapses, and atoms collide with increasing violence, creating vast amounts of heat.
12. The parent-child relationship in these families is characterized by mutual respect and reciprocity.
13. The first law of thermodynamics was formulated in the 1840s by the German physicist Hermann von Helmholtz. It is the easiest to understand.
14. Thermodynamic principles are commonly stated in terms of restrictions, which are, for all intents and purposes, ironclad.
15. It was intended that this apparatus would cool a piece of copper to a millionth of a kelvin above absolute zero. A kelvin is the scientific unit of temperature equal to five-ninths of a degree Fahrenheit.
16. When a quantity of air is kept at the same pressure and cooled from 100°C to 0°C, it loses about a quarter of its volume.
17. Evidence corroborating the Watling track has been provided by archeological research conducted since 1982.
18. Upon Columbus' departure from San Salvador, an archipelago was encountered that does not exist on the Watling track.
19. The fate of these beleaguered woodlands has been largely ignored by the conservation community. Janzen realized that if, in the future, any Mesoamerican dry forest was to be available for study, a stand would have to be taken by him and other biologists.
20. A crested cedar waxwing homed in on the reflection of a holly tree in a window pane and crashed into the glass, breaking its neck. The waxwing's instincts, developed in the natural world, were rendered useless by the wall of glass, which lay well beyond the bird's range of experience.

Exercise

Read the report you wrote on documentation (Chapter 5). Identify all instances of the passive voice in that report. Try rewriting these. Which ones resist transformation to the active? Which rewrites improve the text, in your view?

Exercise

The following passage awaits revision. It lacks high-level guides to interpretation: supply these, telling your reader the significance of the facts presented. Add logical connectives to emphasize the argument you develop. The passage also lacks paragraph divisions: break it into paragraphs to signal to the reader that new material should be taking over the mental desktop. It uses the passive voice and noun forms of verbs: where these constructions interfere with focus, or create awkwardness, replace them with the active voice and verb forms.

It has been noted that, before the second quarter of the nineteenth century, the American city was a small, highly compact cluster. People got about by foot, and goods were conveyed by horse and cart. In the early 1830s and 1840s, early factories were built along waterways and near railheads at the edge of cities. In time, the factories were surrounded by proliferating mill towns of tenements and row houses. The older main cities were abutted by these new towns. Eventually, these industrial neighbours of the original cities were taken over by the cities: the enlargement of tax bases was desired. All of Philadelphia County was taken over by the city of Philadelphia. The city's instant growth from two to 129 square miles thereby took place. In 1889, most of the South Side was taken over by Chicago. In 1898, political amalgamation with Brooklyn, Queens, Richmond, and the Bronx was arranged by Manhattan. This kind of growth was the means by which all of America's great cities got big. With the acceleration of industrial growth, there was also the acceleration of urban crowding and accompanying stress. In 1888, transportation technologies appeared which led to horse-drawn trolleys and electric streetcars. All major urban centres were connected by these means of transportation, and the first wave of suburbanization was fostered. This suburbanization was promoted by the desires of the urban middle class. Home-ownership away from the ageing city core was desired by the middle-class, and single-family housing tracts were provided by developers. After World War II, the mass production of the automobile made possible the movement of city-dwellers to the empty spaces between densely-populated urban areas. Lower density was permitted by the automobile in these newly developed areas. Between the two World Wars, non-residential development occurred in the suburbs. Factories began to appear, and so did sizeable retail stores. In 1922, the first precursor of the modern regional shopping centre was built near Kansas City, being followed by other urban retail centres, as well as large department stores, in California and Texas. But suburban commercial development remained sluggish because it was still relatively easy to get to shopping and work in the downtown core, and there were only inefficient highway connections between suburbs. After World War II, hundreds of miles of urban freeways were constructed and there occurred the movement of population to areas reached by freeways. Between 1950 and 1980, the number of people living in suburbia went from 37 million to just fewer than 100 million. This can be seen to be an increase from 25 to 44 percent of the overall United States population. (There was a rough division of the other 56 percent between rural areas and central cities.) Then it was shown by Americans that they had a preference not only for living in the suburbs but also for working there. As early as 1973, the central cities were surpassed by the suburbs in total employment. Since then, there has been a steady widening of the gap.

Adapted from Peter O. Muller (1986), Are cities obsolete, *The Sciences*, March/April, 43-47.

7.6 Punctuation

If you have not so far considered punctuation a feature of style—that is, an aspect of the reader's working conditions—you will consider it such after you have read the following passage:

(49) Given that there is no evidence for a purely physiological explanation of addiction the whole process of labelling a drug addictive is arbitrary at best one of the more telling examples of this is the evolution of American public policy concerning cocaine as difficult as it may be to fathom today cocaine once was an active ingredient in soda-pop Coca-cola contained a dose of the drug until 1903 though narcotics researchers have explored the addictive potential of cocaine for the past fifty years in the laboratory only upon a sudden rise in recreational cocaine consumption as well as a proportional rise in compulsive cocaine use during the early eighties did government agencies ordain that the drug be regarded as

addictive in fact that judgement directly contradicted the most comprehensive experimental findings available.

Adapted from Stanton Peele (1989), Ain't misbehaving': Addiction has become an all-purpose excuse. *The Sciences* July/August, 14-21.

Sample (49) provides the reader a strong topic statement: Coca-cola in 1903 and government moves in the 1980s should be interpreted as evidence of "arbitrariness." The passage doesn't burden the reader with strange words, stupefying noun phrases, or awkward passives. But it's hard to read anyway. We can feel our minds stumble when words we've taken to belong to one sentence are pulled out from under us by the next sentence; we can nearly measure the time and resources it takes to recover our footing. Of course, nobody ever writes a passage like (49). But it does illustrate how important punctuation is in managing the reader's working conditions.

Most mature writers know how to handle most punctuation. They wouldn't think twice about putting periods at the ends of sentences, capitals at the beginnings, and so on. Yet some punctuation marks are harder to master. Even some relatively experienced writers don't feel confident using semi-colons /;/, colons /:/, and dashes /—/.

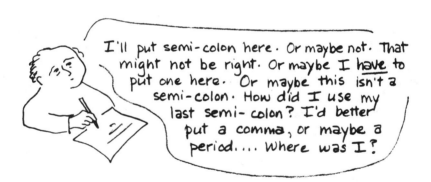

Because lack of confidence can disturb the composing process, and because punctuation is an important instrument for managing the reading process, the following sections will explore the uses of these three punctuation marks: semi-colons, colons, dashes.

7.6.1 Semi-colons

Over time, the semi-colon has changed its uses. Even as recently as the end of the last century, the semi-colon often showed up in sentence positions where it rarely appears today. When a feature of language trails behind it a record of recent change, its occurrence in contemporary usage will still show some signs of those changes. In other words, in any sample of prose from different writers and different publications, you will find some departures from the normal use of the semi-colon. Such variations—and similar variations in the use of the colon and dash—may account for people's nervousness in using these punctuation marks.

For the purposes of academic writing, we will consider two uses of the semi-colon. We will consider these the best uses of the semi-colon. The first is easy, and doesn't require a lot of investigation.

Semi-colon in elaborate lists

In lists that join complex items, the semi-colon can function as a sort of double comma. If I want to join parallel items that themselves contain commas, I can use the semi-colon to separate the items.

(50) **The studies were conducted in three cities: Palo Alto, California; Baltimore, Maryland; Minneapolis, Minnesota.**

(51) **Several forms of evidence suggest that pinnipeds descend from a common ancestor: new fossil evidence, the discovery of *Enaliarctos* in particular; new interpretation of old evidence, shifting emphasis from differences to similarities; biochemical analysis, revealing few significant differences between the genes of seals and those of walruses and sea lions.**

Without the semi-colons, the reader would have to determine the boundaries between list items, for the commas by themselves would not be sufficient evidence that one item is finished and another is beginning: they might be marking boundaries inside the item itself. Without the semi-colons, both (50) and (51) would impose unnecessary processing burdens on the reader.

Semi-colon and independent clauses

Roughly speaking, independent clauses are grammatical entities that could be sentences. Sometimes they are sentences, standing by themselves:

(52) <u>The bottom turn of the inner ear passage is greatly enlarged in</u>
                     INDEPENDENT CLAUSE
   <u>both width and diameter</u>. <u>Its back opening is expanded and set</u>
                     INDEPENDENT CLAUSE
   <u>in a deep pocket of bone</u>.

Sometimes they don't stand alone but, instead, join together to make a sentence:

(53) <u>The bottom turn of the inner ear passage is greatly enlarged in</u>
                     INDEPENDENT CLAUSE
   <u>both width and diameter, and its back opening is expanded and</u>
                            INDEPENDENT CLAUSE
   <u>set in a deep pocket of bone</u>.

One of the mechanisms available for joining independent clauses is the semi-colon.

(54) <u>The bottom turn of the inner ear passage is greatly enlarged in</u>
                     INDEPENDENT CLAUSE
   <u>both width and diameter; its back opening is expanded and set</u>
                     INDEPENDENT CLAUSE
   <u>in a deep pocket of bone</u>.

Consider this joining capacity of the semi-colon its best use. Unlike the comma, the semi-colon is grammatically powerful enough to hold independent clauses together in a sentence. North American readers generally frown upon sentences made up of independent clauses held together by a comma:

(55) Mechanisms of inspection and regulation increased state control of Britain's prisons, financial support furthered this state control of corrections.

Instructors call these joinings "comma splices," and consider them errors. But the same readers accept sentences comprised of independent clauses held together by a semi-colon:

(56) Mechanisms of inspection and regulation increased state control of Britain's prisons; financial support furthered this state control of corrections.

The semi-colon suggests to readers that they see the two assertions as closely related—more closely related than if the clauses were separated by a period.

If you're not sure it's really independent clauses you are joining with the semi-colon, you can test your usage by trying to replace the semi-colon with "and". Try this test in the sentences which follow. You will find one valid and two invalid uses of the semi-colon.

(57) By 1865, the organization of Britain's prisons had been subjected to a process of centralization; brought about by the mechanisms of state inspection, regulation, and financial subvention.

(58) The main objectives of the Prison Commission were rationalization and uniformity; because the process of centralization had put the Commission in charge of an exceedingly disparate and heterogeneous set of penal establishments throughout the country, with enormous variation of regime from prison to prison.

(59) The appointment and training of officers was transformed to ensure a uniformed, disciplined staff; the payment of officers was similarly standardized.

If the "and" test doesn't yield conclusive evidence, try the "independence" test. Look at the element on the left of each of the semi-colons below. Can it stand alone as a sentence? Look at the element on the right? Can it stand alone? If the answer is "no" to either question, you have discovered an invalid use of the semi- colon.

(60) The doctrine that an inmate's standard of life must be lower than that of "free labourers" was reiterated through the system, as a costing principle; and as a proper penological goal.

(61) These changes also affected the conditions endured by the prisoners themselves; who were, after all, the ultimate objects of administration.

(Notice that this test shouldn't be applied to semi-colons working in elaborate lists like (50) and (51).)

Properly used, the semi-colon is a subtle device for managing the reader's comprehension. Unobtrusively, causing scarcely a ripple on the surface of the text, the semi-colon signals to the reader that he should keep certain ideas grouped together as closely related.

Exercise

Correct the invalid uses of the semi-colon you discovered in Samples (57)-(61).

7.6.2 Colons

The colon is a near-relative of the semi-colon. It, too, can join independent clauses, but it prefers independent clauses that have a particular kind of logical relationship to one another. And, unlike the semi-colon, it can join an independent clause to certain kinds of phrases.

Colon and independent clauses

When the colon joins independent clauses, it implies something like "to paraphrase what I have just said," or "in other words."

(62) An independent clause is a construction that can stand on its own: it is a potential sentence.

The clause which follows the colon in (62) doesn't add to the first part of the sentence the way the clauses following semi-colons do. Instead, it says the same thing again, in different words. In (62), the element following the colon repeats to clarify and enforce the saying that precedes the colon. Sample (63) is another instance of the colon implying "in other words."

(63) The medieval suburb was extra-mural: it developed outside the town walls.

The element to the right of the colon—"outside the town walls"—is another way of saying "extra-mural." The colon enables the writer to enrich the first version of this fact about suburbs by emphasizing and clarifying it through repetition.

Each of the elements in (62) and (63) are in a sense equivalent in value: the elements on each side of the colon are expressed at the same level of generalization. Besides being able to pair such equivalent elements, the colon can also negotiate between different levels of generality. In (64) and (65), the colon still signals repetition of the same idea, but this time at a lower level of generality.

(64) New material is abundant: a single paper announces and locates no fewer than 370 new sites in the desert of Cholistan.

(65) The prison command structure was centralized and decidedly vertical, and this steep hierarchy was continued throughout the lower tiers of authority: prison warders were organized on a military ranking system and a large number of the prison staff — from ranking officers to members of the Commission — were selected on the basis of their previous military training and experience.

In (64), the element to the right of the colon says again that "new material is abundant," but says so by giving an example of abundant new material. In (65), the mention of "warders" and "officers" and "members of the Commission" and military systems and background says again that the prison command structure was hierarchical from top to bottom. In both (64) and (65), the colon says, in effect, "the next part of the sentence will repeat and prove what has just been said by saying it in a more specific way." In both cases, the colon makes the relation between the two clauses more explicit than it would be if they occurred as separate sentences.

In (64) and (65), the colon is like a step enabling the reader to descend comfortably from a general statement to its less general illustration.

Colons and phrases

In the capacity illustrated above, as a device for "stepping down" the levels of generality, the colon can also be used to connect an independent clause with phrases—that is, with strings of words that are not clauses and could not stand on their own as sentences. In this capacity, the colon appears in its rather well known role as an introducer of lists.

(66) **In a democratic society, the education system should pursue three goals: excellence, equality of access, and community involvement in decision-making.**

Notice that the elements to the right of the colon could not stand on their own: they are only noun phrases. (Here the colon is showing how it is more versatile than the semi-colon, which is supposed to stick to joining independent clauses together.) Notice as well that the colon is signalling a descent from general elements—"goals"—to more specific elements—"excellence," "equality," "community involvement in decision-making." Now the colon is saying not only "in other words," but "namely."

The colon's ability to say "namely" does not depend on a list following it. In (67) the colon says "namely," but only one element—not a list—follows it.

(67) **State intervention in broadcasting had some real and some plausible technical grounds: the distribution of air waves.**

The element to the right of the colon *re-states* an element from the other side: "the distribution of air waves" re-states, in more specific terms, "some real and some plausible technical grounds."

The colon's wide reputation as introducer of lists can lead writers to put colons where they have no place. As the writer sees a list appearing on the horizon of the sentence, he can be tempted to deposit a colon at the beginning of a series of items.

(68) **The official representation of penology included: the state, the offender, and the relationship of censure between them.**

From the criteria established above, we can see the (68) presents an invalid use of the colon. For one thing, the element on the left is not a finished sentence: "The official representation of penology included... "—what? And, for another thing, the material on the right of the colon doesn't re-state an element from the left. The writer can correct (68) in either of two ways. He can eliminate the colon:

(69) The official representation of penology included the state, the offender, and the relationship of censure between them.

Or he can keep the colon and reconstruct the sentence to conform to the structure that permits the colon to say "namely":

(70) The official representation of penology included three terms: the state, the offender, and the relationship between them.

It's not the list itself that activates the colon, but the grammatical and semantic relationship between the elements on each side of the colon. Don't drop a colon into the middle of a sentence whenever you feel a list coming on.

7.6.3 Dashes

Dashes can be useful devices in prose. They can do some of the work normally assigned to colons. And they can—in some cases—take over from commas. But dashes can also be rather unreliable characters. Sometimes dashes behave as very respectable members of the punctuation community. Other times they behave too informally to be admitted to that community.

The informal dash

The slightly disreputable character of the dash can be traced to its background: the dash can show up in informal and casual writing, where the writer's haste to express himself prevails over the need to be precise.

(71) Had a pizza—too much pepperoni—went to Margaret's—no news.

The relationships between these elements are ambiguous. Excess pepperoni caused the visit to Margaret? News about what was heard where? The meaningfulness of casual expressions like this normally depends on an intimate relationship between reader and writer: knowing the writer and his circumstances well, the reader can make reliable inferences about what the writer had in mind. (The diary-like quality of (71) suggests that this kind of expression is especially likely to turn up where the relationship between writer and reader is absolutely intimate: the writer *is* the reader.)

In your academic writing, you can't assume this intimacy with your reader. So the kind of ambiguity associated with the dashes (71) is unacceptable. Yet still you may find dashes showing up in your drafts as catch-all mechanisms that help you get from one idea to another without a lot of tricky grammatical manoeuvring.

(72) The medieval suburbs were ragged settlements outside the town walls — they housed the poorest labourers — this source of labour was dependent on the town's commerce.

The dashes that connect these three independent clauses do nothing to reveal the writer's view of the logical relationships between the facts expressed. Although the dashes may make things easy for the writer, they drive the reader to strenuous effort after meaning. The next version (73) is grammatically more complex: the dashes have been replaced by a more elaborate sentence structure which delivers to the reader the writer's idea of the suburban labourer's simultaneous exclusion from and dependency on the town.

(73) Although the poorest labourers were housed in ragged suburbs that were separated from the town by the town walls, these workers nevertheless depended on the commerce that went on within the walls.

The new version (73) gets rid of the ambiguities generated by the list-like sequence that came about with the dashes in (72).

Sometimes, however, dashes can play more legitimate roles in formal writing. One of those roles is the connecting function performed by semi-colons and colons; the other is the role of marking interpolations.

Dashes as connectors

Dashes can function in any of the slots we have assigned to colons. Saying "in other words," the dash can join independent clauses.

(74) Addiction is still most commonly associated with narcotics use — drug and addiction seem almost synonymous.

(75) The independent clause can stand on its own — it is a potential sentence.

Saying "the next part of the sentence will repeat and prove what has just been said by putting it more specifically," the dash can enable the reader to "step down" from one level of generality to a lower one.

(76) The more psychologists and lawyers dismiss forms of misbehavior as uncontrollable compulsions, the less people will be held accountable for their actions — often, the only penalty for even criminal misconduct is undergoing counselling in a treatment centre.

Saying "namely," the dash can introduce *re-statements* of elements just the way the colon can.

(77) The drugs most often thought of as addictive are the opiates — heroin, morphine, codeine.

In each of these instances, the dash is emphatic punctuation: it calls attention to the subsequent element, insisting that the reader pay attention to what's coming. This kind of emphasis can help the writer manage the reader's attention resources—if it's used sparingly. An essay abounding in emphatic dashes will become too exclamatory, calling attention to too many items. "Look at this!" shouts the essay. "And this ! And this !" Pretty soon the reader will have too many emphatic entries on her mental desktop; she will be left on her own to make decisions about what really has priority and what can safely be filed or put aside.

Dashes as markers of interpolation

The emphatic dash can also call attention to some elements normally enclosed in commas. We will call these elements interpolations, and we will say that an interpolation is anything that can be *inserted into a sequence*; conversely, it is anything that can be taken out without impairing the host sentence's structure and functioning. Writers normally use commas to introduce interpolations.

(78) The new policy, an obvious response to constituency pressures, was criticized by the opposition.
(79) These syntactic features, common to most bureaucratic utterances, are rarely discussed.

(80) European nations, including France, where much of America's heroin supply is processed, have had negligible addiction problems.

In each of (78)-(80), the commas surround an interpolation: the elements marked by the commas could be removed from the sentences without damaging their grammatical viability. Samples (78)-(80) would still be sentences if the interpolated elements were taken away. And each of the pairs of commas could be replaced by pairs of dashes.

(81) The new policy—an obvious response to constituency pressures—was criticized by the opposition.
(82) These syntactic phenomena—common to many bureaucratic utterances—are rarely discussed.
(83) European nations—including France, where much of America's heroin supply is processed—have had negligible addiction problems.

In (81)-(83), the dashes emphatically mark the interpolations, drawing the reader's attention to them in ways that the commas do not. But you have to pay close attention to the commitment you make when you choose either comma or dash at the beginning of an interpolated element. If you put a dash at the beginning of the element, you must use a dash—not a comma—at the end, too. In your first drafts, you may find sentences like this:

(84) At one end of the spectrum are tales of high-powered celebrities—entertainers, athletes, political figures, and at the other end of the spectrum are stories of neighborhoods infected by drug-related violence.

The writer chooses the dash to introduce the interpolation "entertainers, athletes, political figures," but closes the interpolation with a comma. The reader waiting for a dash to mark the end of the interpolated element will wait a long time. Revision for the final draft corrects this potentially disorienting inconsistency.

(85) At one end of the spectrum are tales of high-powered celebrities—entertainers, athletes, political figures—and at the other end of the spectrum are stories of neighborhoods infected by drug-related violence.

The risks and benefits in this use of the dash are the same as those arising from using the dash in place of colons: if you use too many dashes, the dash loses its power to emphasize select items for the reader's particular attention. If everything is emphasized, nothing is emphasized. On the other hand, well placed dashes can arrest the reader at important points that would otherwise be muffled or concealed by commonplace punctuation.

Exercise

This exercise will give you practice in choosing appropriate punctuation to mark boundaries between phrases and clauses. Be aware that your choice of punctuation can help you emphasize certain elements of information.

*At each * introduce a dash, comma, semi-colon, colon, period, or nothing. Some of your choices will be rule-governed. But other choices will be a matter of judgement. Choosing a dash over a comma or a period over a semi-colon will reflect your goals in managing your reader's attention.*

1. "Senator"

The senator * a long-time party supporter * was appointed ambassador to Ecuador * he was rewarded for his loyalty * however * the press began to attack the appointment * and investigate Senator Big * learning of his involvement in a series of U.S. real-estate deals * members of the press * eager for headlines * began to question his political independence from American interests * they went on to associate Senator Big with major supporters of right-wing governments in Latin America * governments whose actions habitually * and shamelessly * violated civil liberties * one industrious reporter * a journalist from the Southam chain* even found a copy of an old luncheon speech of Senator Big's * in which he questioned the authority of government to intervene in the private sector to enforce certain civil liberties * freedom of speech and freedom of association * public attention was aroused * letters to the editor complained about the appointment * civil libertarians petitioned the government * the Minister asked the Senator to reconsider his acceptance of the appointment * then the Prime Minister asked for a meeting with Senator Big * the senator decided not to go to Ecuador *

2. "Addiction"

The fundamental tenet of Alcoholics Anonymous * that alcoholism is never cured * has been imposed on every bad habit imaginable * criminal misconduct * excessive jogging * extra-marital sex * the use of narcotics * as a result * a thriving * and growing * addiction-treatment industry has developed in the United States * from 1942 to 1976 * the number of people being treated for alcoholism in America increased twentyfold * since 1976 these numbers have continued to grow * yet Americans over twenty-one drink less today than a decade ago * while people are drinking less alcohol * more are being treated for alcoholism * one explanation for this paradox is that the threshold for labeling a person chemically dependent has been lowered * Kitty Dukakis referred herself to a treatment centre because she had got drunk a few times after years of moderate drinking * meanwhile * new addiction-treatment groups modeled on Alcoholics Anonymous have proliferated * the National Council on Compulsive Gambling has grown even more rapidly during the eighties than the AA-inspired National Council on Alcoholism * sometimes compulsive gamblers are admitted to hospitals * frequently they are treated in the same inpatient wards as alcoholics * and there is also a National Association on Sexual Addiction Problems * as well as a national network of Sex Addicts Anonymous * both these groups support hospital treatment for "victims" of compulsive copulation.

Adapted from Stanton Peele (1989), Ain't misbehavin': Addiction has become an all-purpose excuse. *The Sciences*. July/August, 14-21.

7.7 Statements about the argument

We have looked at a number of ways of improving the reader's working conditions. These measures have focussed on sentence-level *style:*

- replacing hard words with simple ones when the simple ones will do as well
- unpacking heavy noun phrases
- converting nouns back into verbs
- choosing between active and passive voice to manage sentence focus
- looking for the subject + verb + object core of sentences
- punctuating to signal logical relationships and to emphasize important items.

All these measures are designed to reduce the processing burden imposed on the reader. Free of unnecessary complications or uncertainties at the level of words and sentence structure, the reader can give her whole attention to content.

The last strategy that we will look at for improving the reader's working conditions is the *statement about the argument*. Statements about the argument don't entirely qualify as elements of sentence style: they move beyond the sentence by pointing to whole sections of text, managing the reader's outlook on content. At the same time, however, statements about the argument do qualify as features of style in that they diminish the obstacles between the reader and the essay's content. Like other aspects of style we have considered, statements about the argument direct the reader's attention to important locations in the essay's topic.

Statements about the argument comment on the writing and reading processes themselves. They expose the workings of the discussion, helping the reader keep her mental desktop well organized, and well prepared to receive up-coming material. There are three types of statement about the argument: forecasts, summaries, evaluations.

7.7.1 Forecasts

Forecasts point forward, telling the reader explicitly what is coming. Topic statements, of course, do this too, by anticipating the content of the paragraph or section the reader is embarking on, and by providing a guide for interpreting that content. Forecasts differ from topic statements in that they anticipate the *form* rather than the *content* of what's coming. They tell *how* the subject will be presented.

The most common type of forecast is the *enumerated list*. If readers encounter "first," or "(a)," they know that sooner or later they will come across "second," or "(b)," and possibly "third," or "(c)." This kind of numbering helps readers organize the way they absorb information; it helps them get ready for new items, keeping space open on the mental desktop. In Passage (86) below, the writer prepares the reader to receive a series of "constitutional arguments" (six in all, although the excerpt here presents only three).

(86) Lawyers will recognize that these moral positions, if we accept them, provide the basis for the following constitutional arguments: (a) The constitution makes treaties part of the law of the land, and the United States is a party to international conventions and covenants that make illegal the acts of war the dissenters charged the nation with committing. (b) The constitution provides that Congress must declare war; the legal of issue of whether our action in Vietnam was a "war" and whether the Tonkin Bay Resolution was a "declaration" is the heart of the moral issue of whether the government had made a deliberate and open decision. (c) Both the due process clause of the Fifth and Fourteenth Amendments and the equal protection clause of the Fourteenth Amendment condemn special burdens placed on a selected class of citizens when the burden or the classification is not reasonable; the burden is unreasonable when it patently does not serve the public interest, or when it is vastly disproportionate to the interest served.
Ronald Dworkin (1977), Civil disobedience. *Taking Rights Seriously*. Cambridge, Mass.: Harvard UP. 206-222, 208-209.

I think you will agree that this writer's argument is complicated. In the face of such complexity, readers are glad to see any device that helps them manage the flow of information across the desktop. Forecasts are such management devices.

The writer can further strengthen the enumerated list by telling how many points he will make.

There are four points to consider here. First,....

As long as the list is not complete, readers know they are still in the stage of argument named at the beginning of the series.

Not all forecasts are numbered. Some refer to stages in the discussion.

My starting point in this analysis....

The next point is the one most closely associated with the behavioralist outlook....

Before going on the describe the results of our inquiry, I will describe....

Whereas topic statements answer the "why-are-you-telling- me-this?" question, forecasts answer the "what-are-you-doing?" question.

Forecasts say explicitly how the parts of the essay fit together. If you have a complex and interesting topic, forecasts will help your reader see how the parts of the argument fit together, and be aware of the moment when one part gives way to another.

7.7.2 Summaries

Summaries point backwards, reminding readers of what has gone before. The reader uses these reminders to keep his mental desktop tidy. The summary prompts him to retrieve important material that has been set aside and to keep it handy. The summary packages this material compactly, so it can be accommodated in the reader's attention span.

Sometimes writers will actually say that they are offering summary. Two-thirds of the way through an article about "Negotiating ethnicity in an uncertain environment" (*Ethnic and Racial Studies* 7 (1984), 360-373), Susan J. Smith writes:

(87) To summarize the position so far: strong theoretical arguments support a suggestion that the labelling of criminals and crimes constitutes a means of wielding social power, to which both labellers and the labelled respond; empirical evidence intimates that the images underlying such labels vary according to race.

Often, however, we don't get the explicit "summary" cue, but only the "so far" or its equivalent:

so far we have seen that....
having established the reliability of....
now that we understand the sources of this confusion....
the account of ethnicity given in the preceding paragraphs....

Unless they appear at the end of an article or chapter, strategic summaries are very often accompanied by forecasts of some sort. Smith, for example, in "Negotiating ethnicity," follows her strategic summary with this sentence:

(88) A question remains about the extent to which the distribution and manipulation of power within an inner city community is realized by virtue of race or ethnicity, relatively independently of underlying economic and political structures.

Readers would rightly anticipate that this "remaining question" is the next issue that will be addressed in the article.

Strategic summaries answer the "what-are-you-doing?" question by saying to the reader, "I've brought you to this point; this is where we stand." And by briefly restating the gist of the preceding discussion, they help the reader carry forward important material.

Here — let me help you with that.

GETTING HELP
WITH CARRYING
FORWARD
IMPORTANT
MATERIAL

7.7.3 Evaluations

Evaluations comment on the quality and function of the argument at that point. Whereas summaries and forecasts direct readers' attention to what has been said or what *will be said*, evaluations direct attention to what is *being said*.

In the following passage (89), from "Civil disobedience," Ronald Dworkin uses strategic evaluation to help readers focus on the long and intricate reasoning by which he demonstrates his claims. Having explained that prosecutors, in deciding whether to press charges, must distinguish between laws that protect fundamental moral rights and laws that are based on technical and political assumptions, Dworkin doesn't just state the conclusion that follows from that explanation. Rather, he tells the reader explicitly that his next assertion is the "main point" of this sequence of the argument.

(89) The point of the discussion here is this: if a particular rule of law represents an official decision that individuals have a moral right to be free from harm, then that is a powerful argument against tolerating violations that inflict those injuries.

In (90), excerpted from "Market, culture, and authority: A comparative analysis of management and organization in the Far East," Hamilton and Biggart set out the rather complicated objects of their research, sketching differences, similarities, patterns of interdependence. To make sure the reader is finding her way through these complexities, they insist on one point in particular.

(90) Despite these similarities, Japan, South Korea, and Taiwan have substantially different forms of enterprise or firm organization, particularly in the export sectors of their economies. Moreover, in each country the firm is embedded in a network of institutional relationships that gives each economy a distinctive character. The important point here is that, if one looks only at individual firms, one misses the crucial set of social and political institutions that serves to integrate the economy.

By insisting on the "point," these writers emphasize the connections between parts of the discussion: what is now being said is the high-level outcome of the preceding discussion. Moreover, it is important, and must be remembered. The reader has to reserve a prominent place on the desktop for this material.

Evaluations help readers distinguish between lower-level, supporting material and high-level material that they must notice and retain to understand the argument as a whole. Such evaluations can be bold:

This is a crucial principle...
From this we discover an important point...
The most significant conclusion that can be drawn....

Evaluations can also explain the working relationships of parts to one another. "Let me explain..." tells the reader that this part of the discussion does explaining work, clarifying what has gone before. "This case shows..." tells the reader that this part of the discussion interprets at a higher level details that have just been presented.

In all, statements about the argument openly signal how the parts of the discussion are related to one another. Forecasts point forward, connecting current material with what is up-coming; summaries point back, connecting what has been said with current material; evaluations focus on the current saying, explaining its status or function in the argument as a whole.

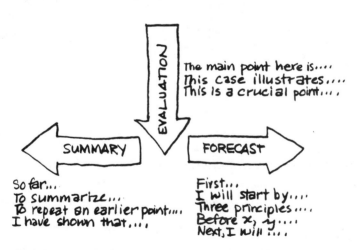

EVALUATION

The main point here is.....
This case illustrates.....
This is a crucial point.....

SUMMARY

So far...
To summarize....
To repeat an earlier point....
I have shown that....,

FORECAST

First...,
I will start by....,
Three principles....,
Before x, y....,
Next, I will ....,

As a reader, you will find such statements helpful in getting the gist of an argument and preparing to use it in your own thinking and writing. Notice that these statements often appear at the beginnings or endings of paragraphs or sections. Be on the lookout for them.

As a writer, you can help your own readers make their way through your argument by offering these kinds of statements. They can help you maintain close contact with your reader, for they suggest that the discussion is an event you are experiencing together. Since you are the one most familiar with the event, you are in a position to point out its noteworthy aspects. Your statements about the argument offer direct, unmistakable instructions to the reader's information-management device.

Readers welcome statements about the argument when reasoning is complex and proof and explanation are extensive. However, if the argument is thin or obvious, and proof is meagre, readers will not need any help in understanding what's going on. In such cases, statements about the argument will only draw attention to the argument's barrenness.

Exercise

Review your report on documentation (Chapter Five) and your essay on glue-sniffing (Chapter Six). Introduce statements about the argument in those places were they will usefully instruct the reader in how to manage the information you are presenting.

Rescuing the reader

Early in this chapter, in Section 7.2, we saw a reader stunned by a passage he had read:

> If in an epistemological figure characteristics of objectivity and systematicity are present then it may be defined as a science, on the other hand where these criteria are absent, as is the case in Foucault's view in respect of the human sciences, we may only speak of a positive configuration of knowledge being present.

(This is a real passage from a real book, the identity of which I will conceal.) We are now in a good position to identify the features of style that make the reader's working conditions nearly impossible here. First, the reader has to find for himself the boundary between two back-to-back noun phrases: "an epistemological figure characteristics of objectivity and systematicity.") Then the reader has to search back for the referent of "it." All the while "epistemological figure" is sitting on the desktop, difficult to digest. Then the reader goes on to find that "on the other hand" doesn't belong to the first sentence, but to the second. The desktop is a mess, and further disordered by the unnecessary filler "in respect."

This reader and his predicament may seem to be a lost cause. But, in fact, we can rescue him, by rewriting the passage according to some of the principles discussed in this chapter. We can sort out the tangles in sentence structure which force the reader to concentrate on syntax: the re-write below uses short, simple sentences. We can ease the burden of "epistemological configuration" by first mentioning "ways of arriving at knowledge." We can repeat important elements to save the reader the trouble of retrieving items himself. The resulting passage is still not easy reading, but its difficulty now is attributable to content, not style. In the passage's original version, content and style conspired to defeat the reader. In the revision, style obstacles are removed from the desktop, leaving the reader room to concentrate on complicated content.

> In Foucault's view, there are two ways of arriving at "scientific" knowledge. One way is truly a science; the other is not. An epistemological configuration which is characterized by objective and systematic methods is a science. But an epistemological configuration which is not characterized by these methods is only a positive configuration of knowledge, and not a science. Foucault maintains that the human sciences belong to this second category.

CHAPTER EIGHT

scholarly styles and scholarly arguments

8.1 Styles and arguments

Chapter Seven concentrated on those features of word choice and sentence structure that can relieve congestion on the reader's mental desktop, clearing space for the essentials of content. These features of style will help your readers concentrate on what's important in your essays. Because scholarly writing typically presents complicated content, reader-friendly style is very important to the academic writer. But it's not only academic writers who benefit from these strategies to improve the reader's working conditions. Any writer who addresses his reader efficiently tries to estimate the processing burdens the reader will face, and tries to relieve those burdens wherever possible.

Chapter Seven's reader was the Everyman Reader. His portrait was a composite of the general characteristics of people's reading behavior, their ways of remembering and understanding. In this chapter, we further refine that portrait, adding characteristics peculiar to the Academic Reader. You may already have detected some mysterious inclinations in the Academic Reader—unaccountable

and unpredictable preferences for certain forms of expression and modes of presentation.

While the Academic Reader shares with the Everyman Reader the same cognitive limits and resources, he also has some special features of his own. We've already looked at one area where these special features operate: documentation. As we saw in Chapter Five, academic writers document their sources according to rules which few people outside the scholarly community know anything about. In turn, these documentation practices reflect the nature of activities in that community. But we also saw that there are several competing sets of rules to which writers adhere.

The first part of this chapter will look into some practices which resemble documentation in that they are *conventional* in the academic community. We will look at word choice again, this time taking into account the Academic Reader's preferences. We will also look at titles, divisions and headings, introductions and conclusions. In each case, we will be able to identify general tendencies to which academic writers conform. But we will also discover a range of variation in some cases. Some members of the scholarly community express conservative views on the rules of proper expression (you have probably already found this out). But, alongside these blanket expressions of conservatism, diverse practices flourish, emerging from differences between disciplines, and differences between generations of scholars. When you face contradictions and disagreements among your instructors as to the *one-and-only* way to document your papers, you serve yourself best by maintaining a polite scepticism, and doing your best to replicate the methods current in the discipline in which you are writing. Similarly, when you are confronted with competing evidence as to, for example, the *one-and-only* way to put headings and divisions in your essay—be calm.

You are merely witnessing a natural feature of human communities to make claims about the proper use of language. Sometimes these claims are not unanimous.

In the second part of this chapter, we will look at the Academic Reader's predispositions at another level—the level of argument itself. Although here, too, we could discover a range of variation, we will also be able to identify a strong tendency towards what we will call a "challenge to established knowledge." The Academic Reader values discussions which oppose an element of established knowledge with new information or new interpretation. The Academic Reader is used to these kinds of argument: he likes them. In the second part of this chapter, you will have a chance to observe the characteristics of this kind of writing, and to practise it for yourself.

8.2 Words

In Chapter Seven, we saw that word choice can affect the reader's working conditions: unfamiliar words take up a lot of space on the desktop; easy words take up little space. Yet academic writers—students and professional scholars alike—are prone to select hard words. Why do they do this?

Part of the answer we have already considered. In Chapter Seven's Section 7.3., we conceded that the academic writer is working in highly specific domains, where the broad, loose concepts of everyday life are analyzed into small pieces, labelled and manipulated. So the academic writer is liable to say "nonspecific goal strategy in problem solving" where other people would say "thinking."

But other influences also push the academic writer towards "hard" words. These influences are traditional, and we can locate them in a long-standing idea in our culture that writing should be fancier than spoken language, that it should be more elevated and dignified. Historians of the language suggest that the first showings of this idea coincided with the growth of literacy among the middle classes. Having gone to the trouble and expense of getting educated, and getting used to reading, members of the middle class wanted something to show for their efforts. One of the ways they could display their education was to write elaborate prose, full of words found only in books. The "right" way to write, they felt, was with language as distinct as possible from that of everyday speech.

We still use language as a way of displaying our education. And, if there is one place where signs of education are most often displayed and paraded, it is the academic community. So it's natural, perhaps, that academic writers feel some pressure to select, for example, "ascertain" instead of "make sure of." Any pre-schooler could use and understand "make sure." "Ascertain," on the other hand, is a word we are likely to get hold of only after some education. It's a high-priced word, taking some time and effort to acquire. Finding a place for it in an essay, writers hope for some pay-off for their investment in education. But you should resist these pressures to select the fancy, elevated word and reject the simple, humble one—for two reasons.

First, as a student writer, you may find yourself using words you've glimpsed in your reading, but of which you have no extensive personal experience as a writer and speaker. Your lack of experience with the word can lead to trouble. Sample (1) comes from a student paper on an essay by E. M. Forster. Having consulted his thesaurus, the writer decided to use "evince" instead of "show."

(1) The image evinces that the desire to own property can make a person think too much about material things.

"Evince"—a word rarely heard in conversation—was so unfamiliar to this writer that he was unable to supply the proper syntactic environment for it. Sample (1) is not a good sentence: "evince" doesn't like to be followed by a "that" clause.

Second, our culture's commitment to displays of high-priced vocabulary is dwindling. Accordingly, academic style is abandoning fancy word choice in favor of simpler selections. Vestiges of eighteenth- and nineteenth-century notions do persist: you may have been rewarded for precocious showings of vocabulary in Grade Eight. But, on the whole, this way of signaling the difference between speech and writing is withdrawing from the academic scene.

Other distinctions do remain, however. One of these is the ban on *contractions* in academic writing. Contractions are typical of speech, helping speakers achieve the emphasis and intonation that get their point across to their listeners. For a while I thought that contractions were beginning to infiltrate academic writing. But I've reconsidered: as far as I can tell, the Academic Reader is still touchy about contractions. (You may have noticed that I use lots of contractions in this book. I like them, and I can justify their use by noting that this book is not addressed to the Academic Reader the way a scholarly article is. However, your instructor, who will also read this book, may identify herself as an Adademic Reader and may not approve of these contractions.)

Another distinction between speech and formal writing is the presence of "slang" expressions in the former and their absence in the latter. While the move away from fancy words has introduced many everyday words into academic writing, it has not gone so far as to admit slang expressions. So deep is this resistance to slang, and so well known, that you will have no trouble selecting from (2) and (3) the form of expression which would satisfy the Academic Reader and the one which would disturb him.

(2) This weirdo freaked out.
(3) One member of the community who occupied a socially and economically marginal position showed signs of anxiety.

All academic writers, even relatively inexperienced ones, know that sentences like (2) are unacceptable in university or college writing.

One other feature of academic style, however, is open to some uncertainty: the use of the pronouns "I," "you," and "he." The following sections will address the uncertainties.

8.2.1 "You" and "I" in the academic essay

The eighteenth- and nineteenth-century ideas about prose that I mentioned above were largely based on the idea that writing should be as distinct as possible from conversation. If you think about this idea for a minute, you will see that this distinction is one that *separates* the reader from the writer—puts as much distance as possible between the two participants in the communicative event.

Conversation, with its particular features, is face-to-face and intimate.

Reading and writing, on the other hand, are long-distance rather than face-to-face.

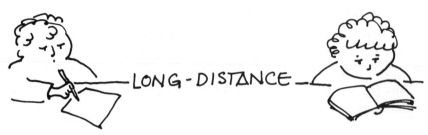

And reading and writing, except in the case of letters and similar "special delivery" situations, are public rather than intimate. Once the text is composed and published (even if publication is only submitting an essay), it goes out into the world on its own: its readers may be utter strangers to the writer, just as the writer may be personally unknown to the readers.

Now, what should writers do about this big, silent space between reader and writer? The typical eighteenth- and nineteenth- century answer to this question was to emphasize the difference between conversation and writing: to use the kind of words rarely heard in face-to-face conversation; to use the kind of elaborate sentence structure impossible to plan in the midst of talk. And one final step in this separation of reader from writer was to banish "I" and "you" from the text. After all, these pronouns signalled intimacy and connection. They were tokens of real, particular participants in the communicative event, and sounded altogether too conversational.

Nowadays, we have a slightly different response to the big space between readers and writers. We value directness now, and we try to overcome the distance and make closer connections. The trend towards conversational word choice is one sign of this changed attitude towards the relationship between reader and writer. Another sign is the reappearance of "I."

"I" makes an appearance
Not very long ago, "I" was Number One on the list of forbidden words in academic-essay style. And even now many students—maybe the majority—arrive at university or college convinced that they must not use "I" in their essays.

Yet "I" is surely a natural pronoun to use in the writing situation. Obviously, a specific, identifiable person has produced the essay, and "I" is the most appropriate way for this person to represent himself or herself. Why write

The controversy will be examined....

or

It was noticed that....

when the truth of the matter is that

I will examine the controversy....

or

I noticed that....?

Unfortunately, the case is not always as clear as these alternatives suggest. Although academic style is moving towards making closer connections between reader and writer, it is moving slowly in the "I" area. Some of your instructors will still shudder at the mere glimpse of an "I" in an essay. And they can rationalize their aversion. They will say that the academic essay is supposed to be objective and impersonal: "I" is a sign, to them, of a subjective, personal stance. (Test this argument for yourself: is "I will examine the controversy" in fact more subjective or personal than the passive version "The controversy will be examined"?) Moreover, many academics argue that, when student writers use "I", they tend to make sweeping claims ("I think that...," "I feel that...") unsupported by evidence. The "I" seems to sanction otherwise unfounded or unexamined assertions.

Yet, in the midst of this conservatism, or right under its nose, you will find many, many instances of "I" showing up in published scholarly articles. After listing the questions his paper will address, a writer comments on the focus these questions construct.

(4) Note that I consider only entry-level jobs here. Although technological change may have consequences for the skill composition of entry-level jobs that mirror those for the occupational structure as a whole, it may affect entry and later-level jobs very differently. Consequently, I do not address issues of changes in skill levels for the occupational structure generally. The emphasis on entry to the labor market is due mainly to the assumption that the importance of formal education as a criterion for occupational access is greatest and most transparent at the point of initial involvement in the labor force. Later, such factors as the length and nature of an individual's job experience and actual performance on the job assume increasing importance for occupational allocation, whereas formal education becomes less critical.

I also focus on the length of formal education, not denying that the content of one's educational program or the particular degree, diploma, or other certificate held are very important for occupational entry or that a more thoroughgoing test would incorporate indicators of other aspects of education. I only assert that 'years of schooling' is read by employers as an indicator of either skills acquired or trainability (the technical-functional view) or as a signal of occupationally relevant attitudes and values (the credential perspective). To the extent that years of schooling provides access to high-skill jobs, this is evidence in favor of technical functionalism; insofar as it gives entry to jobs with requirements other than skill, this indicates credentialism.

   Alfred A. Hunter (1988), Formal education and initial employment: Unravelling the relationships between schooling and skills over time. *American Sociological Review 53*, 753-765. p. 755.

   In an article that reports findings on human reasoning, the writer combines a forecast with an expression of his main claim:

(5) There are also theoretical reasons which will be discussed in the next section for supposing that conventional problem-solving is an inefficient way of acquiring schemas. In the last few years, my collaborators and I have obtained experimental evidence supporting the same conclusion. These results are summarized below.

   John Sweller (1988), Cognitive load during problem solving: Effects on learning. *Cognitive Science 12*, 257-285, p. 260.

   And maybe you will remember these sentences from a definition quoted in Chapter Six:

(6) As I shall demonstrate, ethnostatus distinctions rarely produce "ethnic groups" in this sense, since, according to my conception, the identities formulated tend to govern behavior only in certain contexts and can be readily set aside or altered as the situation dictates.

*   *   *

As I shall demonstrate, ethnostatus distinctions by-and-large do not reflect groups organized by a leader to achieve a political goal, and certainly there is no active recruitment.

James B. Walram (1987), Ethnostatus distinctions in the western Canadian subarctic: Implications for inter-ethnic and inter-personal relations. *Culture* 7, 1, 29-37, p. 31.

Passages (4)-(6) above are only examples of "I" appearing in academic prose: they can't provide statistically conclusive evidence of its frequency. But they do show that "I" can be a legitimate actor in scholarly communication. And they show that "I" often appears in episodes that represent the writer's scholarly action—his discoveries, his reasoning, his intentions in his address to the reader.

Exercise

From the periodical section of your university or college library, and/or from readings you are using in your coursework, collect instances of the uses of "I" in scholarly prose. Following the format set out in the exercise at the end of Chapter Five, report your findings on the appearance of "I."

"You" makes an appearance, and then withdraws

"You" refers to the other side of the communicative event: the listener or reader. So its use in writing goes towards bridging the gap between reader and writer, and making closer connections. Just as "I" naturally acknowledges the fact that an essay has a writer, "you" seems to acknowledge the existence of the reader.

However, despite the naturalness of "you," I do not recommend its use in essays because it does seem to antagonize readers. When the student writes

(7) You notice an increase in productivity among unionized farm labourers.

the Academic Reader is liable to react unfavourably.

This reaction may be a little unfair: the writer didn't really mean that her instructor in particular notices this increase. She meant something like "reasonable, alert people with access to the relevant data." (Generously, she included her reader in this group.) But the reader takes the reference personally, and finds it presumptuous. He takes offence.

On the whole, in academic writing, it is better to avoid offending your reader unnecessarily. So don't write "you." Instead, figure out *who* it is who notices this increase: other researchers? you ? If you want to suggest "reasonable, alert people," you might try "we":

(8)   We notice an increase in productivity.

8.2.2 Can "he" mean "she"?

Our ways of speaking and writing reflect our social experience. Sometimes these reflections are very direct: documentation practices in general, for example, directly reflect the nature of scholarly work, its system of beliefs and practices. Sometimes these connections are not so obvious: the exact positioning of punctuation in documentation, for example, does not so directly reflect social experience.

When social experience and our ways of interpreting it change, our ways of speaking and writing change, too. For example, a child in Grade Two in the 1990s will address her teacher in ways different from those adopted by the Grade Two child in the 1890s. The change in speech—less formality, freer exchange—reflects changes in the child's status in our culture, and changes in our interpretation of childhood. Similarly, changes in women's social experience and in our interpretation of that experience have exerted some pressure on ways of speaking and writing. Here we will consider the significance of some of those changes for the academic writer, focussing on pronoun usage.

Traditionally, the pronoun "he" has stood in for the general type. In (9)-(11) below, "teacher," "user," and "reader" do not name individually identifiable persons, but instead name general types.

(9) The teacher encourages initiative. He rewards students who undertake special projects.
(10) The software user gets confused at this point. He has too many choices.
(11) The reader can concentrate on only a few items at a time. His attention span is limited and inelastic.

When a singular antecedent names a class of persons that includes both males and females—as in "teacher," "user," "reader"—traditional usage has called for the singular masculine pronoun "he." "He" is considered to mean "she" as well.

But traditional pronoun usage has been the object of reformist criticism. Like many other standard practices in our everyday lives, it has been analyzed and condemned for its failure to reflect women's participation in the life of the community. Traditional pronoun usage in (9)-(11) appears to suggest that males rather than females use computers, teach, and read.

To eliminate apparent sex bias in writing, individuals and organizations have adopted personal or corporate style policies. Here are some of the measures they have adopted.

Writers add alternative "she" to singular pronoun "he":

(12) The software user gets confused at this point. He or she has too many choices.

This may seem a little awkward to you. But its increasing occurrence even in speech seems to be smoothing out its clumsy sound. And, besides, academic writing often goes to lengths to measure up to the standards of expression characteristic of formal written English. So the "he or she" policy is a useful one. But some sentence situations make excessive demands on this policy.

(13) The software user gets confused at this point. He or she has too many choices, and, once he or she has selected from the menu to suit his or her purposes, the screen is entirely redrawn, leaving him or her no trace of the preceding step.

The "he or she"/"his or her"/"him or her" policy isn't working very well in (13), even though its application is grammatically and ideologically acceptable. In these situations, writers resort to other measures.

Writers eliminate some pronouns by re-introducing the antecedent:

(14) The user gets confused at this point. He or she has too many choices, and, once the user has selected from the menu to suit his or her purposes, the screen is entirely redrawn, leaving the user with no trace of the preceding step.

Writers change the antecedent to a plural noun, permitting the plural pronoun "they," which is unspecific as to gender:

(15) Users get confused at this point. They have too many choices, and, once they have selected from the menu to suit their purposes, the screen is entirely redrawn, leaving them no trace of the preceding step.

Writers select "one" as pronoun to singular antecedents, "one" being unspecific as to gender:

(16) The user gets confused at this point. One has too many choices, and, once one has selected from the menu to suit one's purposes, the screen is entirely drawn, leaving the user no trace of the preceding step.

Although (16) is grammatically tolerable, and seems to be ideologically moderate, it doesn't sound very good. English, even formal, written English, doesn't find "one" easily digestible in large doses. When "one" begins to build up, it becomes quite unpalatable. Even for demonstration purposes, I couldn't bring myself to use the final "one": I went back to the antecedent in "leaving the user no trace...."

Some writers make a new pronoun to serve the "he or she" function: "s/he":

(17) The user gets confused at this point. S/he has too many choices, and, once s/he has selected from the menu to suit his/her purposes, the screen is entirely redrawn, leaving him/her no trace of the preceding step.

The "s/he" usage, along with its slashed partners "his/her" and "him/her," has some logic to it: if English doesn't supply a singular pronoun indicating both genders, then we'll make our own. But other, more powerful logics overcome this practice, and suggest that it may not take deep root in the field of acceptable grammatical choices. For one thing, while English is very hospitable to new words with new meanings (lexical items), it is very *inhospitable* to new function words. "S/he" is a function word, not a lexical item. For example, in the last decade or so, English has gladly accepted the word "punk" to refer to young people who express their frustration by means of certain forms of clothing, personal ornament, and posture. "Punk" is a lexical item, and it is welcome in the language. But new function words—words like conjunctions "and" and "but" or pronouns "you" and "they"—are not welcome. (Imagine a new word doing the work of "the" or "but." You can't.) And there's another reason for thinking this new pronoun isn't going to go far: "s/he" has no counterpart in speech. How would you read (17) aloud? Even very formal occasions would leave the speaker tongue-tied.

As long as there is no parallel for "s/he" in spoken English, it doesn't stand a very good chance of being widely used in written English.

Evaluating the policies

The "one" solution in (16) sounds too stiff and pompous for the English we use at the end of the twentieth century (although a "one" here and there in your writing will sound all right to most readers). The "s/he" solution is probably too artificial to become your regular practice. So, to solve The Pronoun Gender Problem, I suggest you adopt a policy which combines these strategies:

- using the "he or she" system [(12)] unless it gets too awkward [(13)];
- replacing, where convenient, the pronoun with its antecedent [(14)];
- using plural antecedents where convenient, to permit plural pronouns [(15)].

There's also a fourth policy you might be interested in. Some writers and speakers go straight for "she" and "her" in some situations where pronouns serve singular antecedents with unspecific gender; they leave the "he" and "him" and "his" set for other situations. As far as I can tell, there's no rule for deciding when to use "she" and when to use "he," as long as the two usages don't appear too close to each other. For example, (18) seems just fine.

(18) The user gets confused at this point. She has too many choices, and once she has selected from the menu to suit her purposes, the screen is entirely redrawn, leaving her with no trace of the preceding stage.

But (19) is confusing and strange, for it suggests that the writer conceives of "the user" as two different and distinct people.

(19) The user gets confused at this point. She has too many choices, and, once he has selected from the menu to suit his purposes, the screen is entirely redrawn, leaving him no trace of the previous step.

Sample (19) shows that, if you alternate between "she" and "he" as pronouns capable of standing for nouns naming general classes, you have to be consistent over stretches of text.

In this book, I have followed this last policy. Through some passages, I have made the reader "she" and the writer "he." Through other passages, I have reversed this assignment of gender—to avoid suggesting that women always read and men always write. I hope this practice has not confused or distracted you.

What would the Academic Reader think of this practice? To answer this question, we will have to dismantle him (or her), and reveal that the Academic Reader is not one person but many different people. While these readers share many predispositions, their preferences are not entirely unanimous. You will still find readers who insist that "he" does mean "she," and that any efforts to adjust usage to new social realities are trivial and even improper. But I think you will find that most academic readers are hospitable to writers' attempts to work through this period of change, adjusting their style to reflect social and political ideals of equality.

Exercise

Introduce pronouns where appropriate to replace the underlined forms of the noun applicant *in the following passage. (Sometimes the noun* applicant *will resist being replaced by a pronoun. In those cases, just leave it.) In doing so, develop a policy—for this passage, at least—of pronoun use which avoids sex bias.*

The applicant submits the applicant's passport or equivalent document to the commission. To submit along with the applicant's passport, the applicant prepares a file which includes testimony of other parties as to the risk to the applicant's life and well-being as well as the applicant's own testimony on such risks. If other documents as to the applicant's fugitive status are available – arrest warrants, indictments, medical reports – the applicant gathers them and includes them in the applicant's file. Within a statutory period, the applicant will appear before the commission for an informal interview. Because the applicant may have only slight competence in English, an interpreter or consultant may accompany the applicant to the interview. The consultant not only translates commissioners' questions and the applicant's answers but also explains to the applicant the principles which determine the proceedings.

8.3 Titles

The titles of scholarly publications have their own special sound, and the Academic Reader (we've put him back together) has an ear for this sound. Here are some examples which you, too, will probably recognize as sounding academic:

Semantic priming with abstract and concrete words: Differential asymmetry may be postlexical

Appreciation of pragmatic interpretations of indirect commands: Comparison of right and left hemisphere brain-damaged patients

Suburban socioeconomic status change: A comparison of models, 1950-1980

Migration or depopulation of the metropolis: Regional restructuring or rural renaissance?

Social differentiation in criminal victimization: A test of routine activities/lifestyle theories

"The place is the asylum": Women and nature in Robert Frost's poetry

The free trade diplomacy debate and the Victorian European common market initiative

While titles like these may please the Academic Reader,

they can offend the ear of the non-specialist reader:

But it's more than taste that dictates the style of the scholarly title. Its features reflect academic values and academic activities. We'll look at these features now, and infer from them principles you can follow in composing titles for your work.

One of the first things an observer might notice about the titles in the sample presented above is that they are all quite long and complex: none of them matches the short, snappy titles of best-sellers displayed at the supermarket check-out. This length and complexity suits the academic community's practices—one of which is to publish articles on similar topics in the same journal. Now, if articles in say, the *Journal of Social Issues* were allowed to have titles like "An Important Social Issue," these titles would provide readers with no way of distinguishing one article from another. Another scholarly practice—one with which you are by now very familiar—is to document sources by listing references. If these references didn't have distinctive titles, the lists which named them would be very uninformative to the reader. The scholarly title says *a lot*, representing as fully as possible the document it stands for.

Since you are not publishing your essay in a scholarly journal, and you do not expect to be cited by other scholars, you might think that these features of style have nothing to do with you. Think again: think of your instructor receiving, all at the same time, 15 or 35 essays on Margaret Atwood's *Surfacing*, or on labor militancy on the frontier. If your English instructor comes across 14 or 33 or 35 essays all called

Surfacing
or
Essay #2
or
Essay for English 100

the titles will provide him with no means of distinguishing among these papers. Similarly, if your history instructor gets 14 or 33 or 35 essays called

Labor militancy on the frontier
or
Second Essay
or
Essay for History

the titles will provide her with no means of distinguishing among these essays. In fact, the titles are useless. The essays might as well have no titles at all.

Moreover, these no-title titles do nothing to prepare the reader's mental desktop for the kinds of arguments and the main categories of thought that will be exercised in the following discussion. And that is one of the main functions of the scholarly title: preparing the desktop to receive in an orderly way the material that's coming up. A reader approaching an article called, for example, "Migration and depopulation of the metropolis: Regional restructuring or rural renaissance?" will be ready to construct material which has to do with cities depleting themselves, and ready to give priority to the competition between the two interpretations of this depletion named in the title.

In composing a title, make sure you differentiate your essay from the others your instructor will be receiving. Make your title represent the focus you have developed, and the interpretation of data you will offer. And use your title to prepare your reader to concentrate exactly on the core of your evidence and argument.

Exercise

Devise titles for your interpretations of baboons and Brian's case (Chapters Two and Six). Devise titles for your report on documentation (Chapter Five) and your essay on glue-sniffing (Chapter Six). Show your titles to your classmates; ask them what they think. Compare your titles to theirs.

8.4 Divisions and headings

A good title can do a lot for the reader. It can focus her attention on the high-level issues that dominate the discussion; it can prepare her to receive information in an orderly way. But a title can only do so much. For one thing, there's a limit to how long and complex even a scholarly title can be: the title can represent only a few main elements of the whole argument. And, for another thing, the title can't stay on the reader's desktop indefinitely. While it can provide very important information-management instructions, the title itself will soon give way to other material that arrives for processing.

So, to take advantage of the power of titles to guide the reader's work, and to compensate for the title's relatively short life on the desktop, writers often resort to a system of *headings*—little titles distributed throughout the document. Writers *divide* their text into parts and give each part a title of its own.

There are two types of headings: functional and content-related.

8.4.1 Functional headings

Some scholarly writers use conventional systems of headings which present titles something like the ones below (but with wide variations between disciplines and publications):

Introduction
Method
Results
Discussion
Conclusion

These headings name the *function* of each section: the section labelled "Introduction" provides an overview of the issue and its parts, and describes relevant research by others; the section labelled "Method" explains how the writer gathered data, and so on. Functional headings do not forecast the *content* of each section: we can't tell from the heading "Discussion," for example, what is actually discussed. But functional headings are nevertheless useful to the reader in that they signal relationships between parts of the document. Working through the section called "Introduction," the reader knows how that material relates to the whole argument: it's an overview of the subject which establishes a broad context for the details that are going to follow. Encountering the division or space that follows the section called "Introduction," the reader knows that the introduction is over: the next part is not introductory, and the discussion will now become more detailed and specific. Functional headings help readers orient themselves.

8.4.2 Content-related divisions and headings

Other writers use content-related rather than functional systems of headings. Whereas the system of functional divisions and headings can remain relatively constant from writer to writer and article to article—no matter what the subject— content-related headings are custom-made for each occasion. The system of headings below comes from an article about compensation for victims of crime. After an introduction that is not labelled (it's obviously the introduction because it is at the beginning and it makes claims that are more general than the information which follows), the writer divides and labels her material according to the content of each section.

The victim in Anglo-Saxon and Early Norman England
The victim in the 12th and 13th centuries
The reforms of Henry II
The effects of Henry II's reforms on victims
The appeal procedure
Motivations of appellors
Royal pardons
The decline of appeal
Summary and conclusions

From Janelle Greenberg (1984), The victim in historical perspective: Some aspects of the English experience. *Journal of Social Issues* 40, 1, 77-102.

Unlike the "Introduction/Method/Results/Discussion/Conclusion" system, this writer's system of headings is one that will never appear anywhere else: she has devised it to manage the content of this particular argument. And it is certainly helpful to the reader. Each heading tells what the focus of the subsequent section will be, and relates it to the topic of the whole paper. Although the last heading— "Summary and conclusions"—is functional rather than content-related, it does forewarn the reader that the writer is now climbing back up to higher-level claims, and that her detailed inquiry is done.

8.4.3 Using divisions and headings

There is no question that divisions and headings are useful. Everything we have learned about the reader so far suggests that headings—especially content-related headings—can help manage the mental desktop by preparing the reader to interpret incoming material as contributing to the high-level concepts named in the heading. Moreover, in the process of composing headings, the writer himself may come up with a clearer picture of his argument, and may find new and better names for things; in turn, these names can lead him to revise for more meaningfulness. But headings aren't always a welcome addition to the package you deliver to your reader. Under certain conditions, you are better off not using headings.

The essay is short

Headings and divisions help your readers orient themselves in long, complex arguments supported by extensive detail. When the discussion is short—less than, say, four pages—the reader doesn't need this kind of help. If strong topic statements effectively reinstate your main claims, your reader will have little trouble keeping important material in mind. Headings could be only an unnecessary ornament.

The essay is not coherent

Sometimes the draft of an essay will show a tendency to leave the reader at the gap: in Chapter Three, we saw a reader at the gap, trying to gather courage to leap from "letters about children" to "Church concern about superstition." A writer who senses this dangerous space between the elements of the essay might resort to headings to try to encourage his reader to risk the leap.

Family correspondence

The Church and superstition

But these headings do nothing to actually bridge the gap: it's still there, and it's still a dangerous passage through with the writer might lose his reader.

Headings can make writers think they have repaired the gaps in their essay when, in fact, they haven't. Headings can make writers feel they are presenting an argument when all they are really offering is a list of mentions.

The reader doesn't like headings

In some of his manifestations, the Academic Reader likes headings very much: he is accustomed to seeing them in his reading; he uses them himself in his own writing. But in some of this other forms, the Academic Reader doesn't like headings at all. He never uses them himself, and, moreover, he blames headings for list-like incoherence. He thinks headings tempt writers to neglect the necessary repairs to their argument that would close the gaps.

Because headings and sub-headings are so common in published scholarly prose, I think you can consider the first manifestation of the Academic Reader the more common one. But, if you do run across him in the second form, which condemns headings, offer him essays without headings.

Exercise

1. Change the functional headings you used in your report on documentation to content-related headings.

2. Introduce content-related headings to your essay on glue-sniffing.

8.5 Introductions and conclusions

Student writers are often very concerned about introductions and conclusions. These elements of their essay-writing practice weigh heavily on their minds.

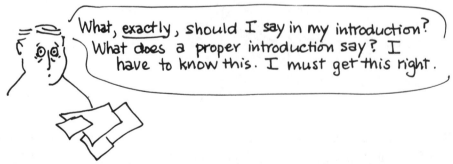

What, **exactly**, should I say in my introduction? What does a proper introduction say? I have to know this. I must get this right.

Their concern reflects the high degree of formality associated with beginnings and endings generally. Greetings and farewells, anthems and applause, registration and graduation—the rituals which begin and end social events in our lives—are often the most conspicuously formal elements of the occasion. As part of our acculturation as social beings, we learn how to conduct ourselves properly at these openings and closings of events and encounters.

A BEGINNING and AN ENDING

Most of us are at least unconsciously aware of the formality of beginnings and endings (introducing ourselves to one another; parading past the audience at convocation). And we sometimes feel especially anxious about those beginnings and endings when the type of occasion is relatively unfamiliar to us, or we are interested in having it go well. Student writers at university or college are certainly interested in having things go well. And, as well, the academic writing situation may be, for them, one of the relatively unfamiliar social situations whose formalities arouse anxiety in the newcomer.

There's no denying that scholarly introductions and conclusions are as formal as student writers think they are. Approaching the beginnings and endings of essays, the Academic Reader exercises some marked preferences and expectations. But, once you catch a glimpse of these preferences and expectations, and once you incorporate this insight with what you already know about every reader's needs, you will find yourself writing good introductions and good conclusions. These important passages will not necessarily come easily, but they will satisfy the situation.

First, we will rid ourselves of a common and debilitating misconception about introductions; then we will go on to examine the features of scholarly introductions and conclusions.

8.5.1 Getting rid of a misconception

Many student writers spend long, tortured hours composing their introductions. And these long hours are all the more painful because these writers know that, even after the introduction gets done, they still have all the rest of the essay to write. This situation can make writers feel desperate and miserable.

These writers assume that they can't embark on the body of the essay until they have composed a perfect introduction with a big "thesis statement."

This is not so. Although the introduction is the first thing the *reader* encounters in the essay, it is by no means the first thing the *writer* must compose. It may very well be the last thing the writer composes. In fact, trying to compose a permanent introduction before you have drafted the body of your argument can cause you unnecessary pain. After all, if you haven't yet completed your first full exploration of your topic by writing a draft, how do you be sure what your argument really is? And if you don't know what your argument really is, how can you write your introduction? What are you introducing? The hardest writing of all faces *any* writer when he has to put words down on a page without knowing what he has to say. Don't put yourself through this ordeal. Don't force yourself to write a complete and permanent introduction before you get started on the body of your essay.

The all-purpose introduction

And don't put your reader through the product of this ordeal. An introduction composed out of nothing, or next-to-nothing, will mislead your reader, miscueing her information-management devices and loading her desktop with irrelevancies. Passage (20) below illustrates the kind of over-general, all-purpose introductions writers are liable to produce when they haven't fully explored their topic.

(20)

Land is all around us. We build houses on it, grow crops on it, build factories and shops on it, travel across it. Land is at the centre of many important issues in modern life. This essay will discuss some of these important issues.

There are different ways of viewing land. Land can be viewed as a form of property that can be traded at will. Market forces determine its possession. Land can also be viewed as having a sense of stewardship attached to it. Then it is a form of common property, which may be expressed in the succession of generations or in the wider community having an interest in how the property is used. Humans have a biological attachment to land, and this may explain their emotional attachment to it.

The writer of (20) has learned that introductions are "general" compared to the rest of the essay. So he starts with a general saying: "Land is all around us." No reader would dispute this claim, but the Academic Reader would question why it has to be made. (A generality like this one comes very close to the category of *platitudes*, which we considered in Chapter One.) If the writer makes such a general, uncontroversial claim, he has to follow right on its heels with some showing of its relevance. The writer of (20) follows the generality with claims at a slightly lower level of generality. Now the Academic Reader, overcoming his distaste for the first generalization, and searching for relevance, seizes these next generalities as indications of the main focus of the essay: will the essay be something about land's residential, agricultural, commercial, and transport capacities? The next two sentences do nothing to resolve the uncertainty: what are the "important issues" which may or may not involve buildings, crops, and travel?

As the introduction continues through a second paragraph, more generalities flow across the reader's desktop. The connections between these claims and those of the first paragraph are unclear, so the reader is left to figure out for herself how to handle these items: are *these* the "important issues"? What *are* the issues? What exactly does ownership have to do with the fact that land surrounds us? By the end of the second paragraph, most of what the writer intended as introductory will have fallen off the desktop, and what remains will be unorganized and crowded by the reader's attempts to guess at connections. The writer might just as well have composed no introduction at all. These polite generalities (which, in effect, say little more than "here comes an essay") only cause trouble.

The introduction which repeats the assignment

Sometimes, convinced that they have to have an introduction before they can proceed, and stuck for something to say, student writers will deposit a re-wording of the assignment at the start of their essay.

(21) *Assignment:* Discuss narrative point of view in *Annie John*, showing the ways point of view controls the reader's interpretation of events.

> *Introduction*
> Narrative point of view controls the reader's interpretation of events in several ways. This essay will discuss point of view in *Annie John*.

(22) *Assignment:* Compare the land-title claims of the Nishga to those of the Maori.

> *Introduction*
> Many aboriginal peoples have made land-title claims. To understand the nature of these situations, the claims of the Nishga and the Maori must be compared. Differences and similarities will be found.

Now, imagine a literature instructor or history instructor encountering these introductions: will these readers be enlightened by (21) and (22)? Will they leave these introductions feeling they have a clear picture of how the argument will be conducted and what main points it will lead to? Add to your image of the instructor the fact that she is receiving 15 or 35 essays all on the same topic: will introductions like those in (21) and (22) distinguish these essays from one another? To all these questions, the answer is "no."

As we will see in the examples which follow, the scholarly introduction precisely represents the argument which follows. Neither the all-purpose introduction nor the introduction which repeats the assignment accomplishes this.

8.5.2 The scholarly introduction

Below are two examples (23) and (24) of scholarly introductions. The first is compact, and we will examine its features in some detail. The second is longer;

you will see for yourself how the conventional features of the scholarly introduction arrange themselves over greater stretches of text.

(23)

> Introductory paragraph from Jane Hurwitz Nadel (1984), Stigma and separation: Pariah status and community persistence in a Scottish fishing village. *Ethnology*, 23, 2, 101-116.
>
> This paper addresses the problem of how and why a small, dependent, and stigmatized occupational community may maintain its social identity long after the material basis for its existence has disappeared. It examines the life history of Ferryden, an east coast Scottish "fishing village" which does not fish. It will argue that the ideology of the fisherfolk, who have historically been marked as a distinct and low-prestige occupational, residential, and kin-based group, has been used to redefine and preserve village unity in the face of drastic ecological change. It argues further that this means of cultural adaptation contains the seeds of its own destruction and will, in the long run, prove fatal for community identity. Studies of occupational communities in complex societies suggest a strong link between work, residence, and social image (Horobin 1957; Dennis, Henriques et al. 1969; Lummis 1977). The example of Ferryden suggests the possibility of a considerable lag between the ecological and the symbolic transformation of a community's status. The dynamics of boundary-marking between fisherfolk and nonfisherfolk will be placed within a context of economic and political dominance and dependency in eastern Scotland. The discussion is based upon data collected during a year of fieldwork and archival research in Ferryden and Montrose in 1975 and 1976.

This opening immediately establishes the topic of the article (no polite generalities here) and tells how the topic will be developed. Certain sequences call attention to the article as a working mechanism, and name its actions: "This paper addresses..."; "It examines..."; "It will argue..."; "It argues further...." These sequences present elements of the argument at a high level of generality:

- stigmatized (shameful or low-prestige) social identity of a community can last longer than the economic conditions that were the reason for the community coming about in the first place;
- shared ideology (values and beliefs) can hold a community together even in the face of changes that would fragment it;

- paradoxically, these ways of responding to change and resisting fragmentation can themselves mean, finally, the disappearance of the community.

They also introduce more specific elements of the topic at a lower level of generality:
- Ferryden, an east-coast Scottish fishing village which no longer fishes;
- the economic and political character of eastern Scotland.

Having read the introduction, readers know what the article is about: the behaviour of a stigmatized community in the face of change. Readers also know how the topic will be developed: they can expect to hear details about a fishing village called Ferryden and the part of Scotland in which it is situated. And they are given a guide for interpreting those details: facts about Ferryden are significant in light of the general concept of the endurance of low-status communities. Although the opening paragraph has fully prepared the reader for the discussion which will follow, it has not taken over the function of the discussion itself: we still have to read the article to know "how and why" a community "persists"; how "ideology" holds the members of the community together; and why the community's self-preserving response to change is actually self-defeating.

And notice that, although the introduction expresses some very high-level concepts—"social identity," "ideology," "unity," "ecological change," "cultural adaptation"—these are not mere politenesses. These abstractions are attached to the specific concerns of this article: fisherfolk in Ferryden. Although concepts like "social identity" and "ideology" could figure in arguments of any number of articles and essays and books, in this article they are anchored to lower-level data on the people who live in this village. The introduction makes this clear, and thereby prepares the reader to receive the particular information which is coming up.

As well, the introduction prepares the reader to manage up-coming information by supplying the high-level names that will interpret data in the body of the article. You remember that high-level, interpretive abstractions *condense* details, making them manageable and meaningful. These high-level names also contribute to the reader's efficiency, giving him categories that can incorporate lower-level information, and thereby save space on the mental desktop. In (23), the writer provides these useful names right at the start: "community identity," "ties of kinship," "village status," "survival as a distinct entity," "pariah status," "stigma," "fisherfolk unity," "solidarity." And then, in the body of the article, she repeatedly reinstates them to help the reader handle many details about Ferryden and the people who live there.

Passage (24) below shows other writers preparing their reader to receive a complicated argument supported by extensive data. Like the author of the article about stigma, they too use their introduction to make the main categories and logic of their argument visible to the reader.

(24)

> Introductory paragraphs from Gary G. Hamilton and Nicole Woolsey Biggart (1988), Market, culture, and authority: A comparative analysis of management and organization in the Far East. *American Journal of Sociology* 94, S52-S94, pp. S52-S54.
>
> Several social science disciplines have been interested in the structure and functioning of economic organizations. This widespread interest is largely grouped around three perspectives. Especially in economics (Chandler 1977, 1981; Teece 1980; Williamson 1981, 1985) but also in anthropology (Orlove 1986) and sociology (White 1981), scholars have studied economic decision making in regard to the conditions under which business firms arise and operate in relation to market- mediated transactions. We call this general perspective the "market approach." The second perspective on economic organization is the "cultural approach," which suggests that cultural patterns shape economic behavior. This perspective was formerly a preserve of anthropologists (e.g., Benedict 1946; Douglas 1979; see also Orlove 1986) but is now widespread among a large number of scholars from diverse backgrounds. Studies of corporate culture, (Deal and Kennedy 1982; Peters and Waterman 1982; Kanter 1983) and comparative culture studies of Japanese (Ouchi 1981, 1984; Pascale and Athos 1981; Vogel 1979), Swedish (Blumberg 1973; Foy and Gadon 1976), Yugoslavian (Adizes 1971), and other nationalities have increased manifold in the past 10 years. The third perspective is a political economy perspective, which we call the "authority approach." Scholars in all social science fields have worked on economic organization from this wideranging perspective, from the seminal work of Marx (1930) and Weber (1958, 1978) to such recent studies as Granovetter (1985), Perrow (1981, 1986), Portes and Walton (1981), Haggard and Cheng (1986), Reynolds (1983), and Mintz and Schwartz (1985).
>
> This paper assesses the relative efficacy of each of these three approaches in explaining the industrial arrangements and strategies of three rapidly

developing countries of the Pacific region — South Korea, Taiwan, and Japan. We argue that, while market and culture explanations make important contributions to understanding, neither is alone sufficient. A market explanation correctly draws our attention to state industrial policies and entrepreneurial responses. But a market explanation cannot account for the distinctive and substantially different organization arrangements that have appeared in the three countries. A cultural explanation, however, enables us to see, correctly, organizational practices in Japan, South Korea, and Taiwan as generalized expression of beliefs in the relative importance of such social factors as belongingness, loyalty, and submission to hierarchical authority. But looking at culture alone obscures the fact that business organizations, no matter how well they accord with cultural beliefs, are fundamentally responses to market opportunities and conditions. Enterprise may be culturally informed, but it remains enterprise. Moreover, cultural variables are insufficiently distinguishable in the region to have clear explanatory force.

In this paper we argue that the political economy approach with a Weberian emphasis produces the best explanation of the three. This approach incorporates elements of the market and culture explanations but does so from the point of view of the historically developed authority relations that exist among individuals and institutions in each society. We argue that market opportunities do indeed lead to innovations in organizational design but that these innovations are not simply a rational calculus of the most efficient way to organize. Organizational practices, instead, represent strategies of control that serve to legitimate structures of command and often employ cultural understandings in so doing. Such practices are not randomly developed but rather are fashioned out of preexisting interactional patterns, which in many cases date to preindustrial times. Hence, industrial enterprise is a complex modern adaptation of preexisting patterns of domination to economic situations in which profit, efficiency, and control usually form the very conditions of existence.

8.5.3 The scholarly conclusion

Conclusions cause almost as much concern among writers as introductions do. Like beginnings, conclusions suggest formality, and writers worry that they won't fulfill their reader's formal expectations.

Realizing that conclusions resemble introductions in that they are more general than the rest of the essay, some writers get the idea that conclusions repeat introductions.

(25) *Introduction*

Many aboriginal peoples have made land-title claims. To understand these situations, we must compare the claims of the Nishga with those of the Maori. Differences and similarities will be found.

Conclusion

In conclusion, many land-title claims are being made by aboriginal peoples in the world today. In this essay, the claims of the Nishga and the Maori were compared. Differences and similarities were found.

And, sensing the special status of the conclusion, some writers will make a flourish at the end, gesturing towards a Big Issue, and often referring to the future.

(26) In conclusion, many land-title claims are being made by aboriginal peoples in the world today. In this essay, the claims of the Nishga and the Maori were compared. Differences and similarities were found. Not until the importance of these claims is understood will peace and harmony between races be achieved.

The Academic Reader will not respond favourably to either of these conclusions (25) and (26), for reasons you can probably figure out. The writers themselves are usually not happy with conclusions like these, either.

Yet this way of going about things is not completely off track. The scholarly conclusion is closely related to the introduction. And the scholarly conclusion can invoke Big Issues, and it can, in a certain way, allude to the future.

The conclusion's relationship to the introduction

Both introduction and conclusion make claims at a high level of generality. And, in both cases, those high levels of generality interpret the data found in the body of the essay. So, if the introduction provides the reader with high-level, interpretive concepts which represent the argument which follows, then the conclusion is bound to repeat those concepts. While the introduction prepares the reader to receive the argument,

the conclusion confirms the reader's understanding of the argument.

The conclusion reassembles the parts of the argument, leaving the reader with a firm impression of the writer's meaning. If the conclusion surprises the reader, then something has gone wrong. Either the body of the essay has failed to get important points across, and left the reader shuffling amongst ambiguities, or the conclusion fails to accurately represent the argument.

The conclusion, then, is closely related to the introduction. But it does not exactly repeat the introduction. Conclusions which are repetitions of the introduction sound strange. The reason they sound strange is that the reader addressed at the end of an essay is not exactly the same reader who is addressed at the beginning. At the end, the reader is familiar with the details and course of the argument: he has been through it. To simply repeat the introduction suggests that the reader hasn't heard a word you said.

A strong conclusion takes advantage of the reader's new familiarity with the argument, risking complexities that would have been impossible at the beginning of the relationship between writer and reader. In the conclusion of the article on stigma, excerpted below, you will see a writer even going so far as to bring up details: she can be confident that her reader can handle these, that he will know what to do with them, having already experienced the whole argument.

Conclusions, Big Issues, and the future

Details are one form of complexity which conclusions can tolerate. Another is reference to adjacent topics: having fully disclosed her argument, the writer can claim its overall *significance* by showing how it relates to other matters, or how it refines our knowledge of important issues. The conclusion can tell the reader what he has gained by mastering this argument.

Moreover, the conclusion can develop claims about the significance of the argument by suggesting its impact on future reasoning and research. Samples (27) and (28) are final sentences from scholarly conclusions.

(27) Current theories and practice frequently assume problem solving is an effective means of learning and consequently may require modification.
John Sweller (1988), Cognitive load during problem solving: Effects on learning. *Cognitive Science* 12, 257-285, p. 284.

(28) Unravelling the development of the state and the character of property relations is a more promising starting point for analysis than a blind or even reserved acceptance of legal court data and definitions.
John L. McMullan (1987), Crime, law and order in early modern England. *British Journal of Criminology* 27, 3, 252-274, p. 270.

You may feel that you are not always in a position to suggest directions for future research and reasoning. But be assured that you can make claims about the significance of your argument, its intersection with larger issues. In effect, with these claims, you interpret your own argument, stating its meaning.

The passages (29) and (30) below are the conclusions to the articles whose introductions you read in Section 8.4.2. In (29), you will see the conclusion to the article about stigma reinstating and reassembling elements that have dominated sections of the preceding discussion: the persistence of community, "sets of values," castigation, identity, the disappearance of the economic basis for the village's existence. But you will also see the conclusion doing more than merely restating these conditions: it fully and finally explains their relationship to one another. It says what it means to have learned that the Ferryden community identity persists—despite it being a low-prestige identity and despite its economic justification having disappeared. Having read about Ferryden—so what? Well, now we know that members of a stigmatized, low-status community can—contrary to what we might expect—actually cherish their identity as a way of protecting themselves from their negative status outside the community.

(29)

The society in which this fisherfolk community has persisted is built upon sets of values by which the fisherfolk, despite their encapsulation, have also been conditioned. Respectability is one such value. Respectability is closely entwined with property and property relations. Traditionally, those groups and classes with little access to property – in particular fishers, miners, weavers and travellers (pejoratively called "tinks") – have been looked down upon, castigated for immorality, and regarded as dangerous and polluting. While the fisherfolk of Ferryden value their identity, they also have longed for respectability. Looked at in this way, True Ferrydenerhood takes on a new paradoxical dimension. From the outset, the fisherfolk's homes and livelihood were owned by the lairds, or mortgaged to the fishcurers. The only property the Ferrydeners ever owned free and clear was their community. To lose it would be to take away their source of dignity and respect, to render them less than fully human. It would reduce them merely to what Scottish novelist Lewis Grassic Gibbon called "coarse fisher brutes" (Gibbon 1971).

That is why community and village must be distinguished in Ferryden. The village is an artifact, a tool for production and profit-making which has outlived its original purpose, and which may or may not find another one. Its inhabitants pursue a variety of interests The community is another, smaller entity with an entirely different life and lifespan. For the True Ferrydeners, the fisherfolk community is a myth which tells them who and what they are. It is the product not merely of occupational and residential commonality, but of their need to defend themselves against the constant reminders of common oppression and evil reputation. Rather than internalizing the low opinion of outsiders, the Ferrydeners have reacted by forming a virtuous counterimage of themselves, a negation and a denial of stigma. This is their defense. They have embraced fisherfolk identity because it stands as the cornerstone of their collective self-esteem. As they sing in the Ferryden Anthem, "Don't let us be strangers, as long as we are together."

In (30) below, from the end of the article about organizational patterns in the Far East, you will also see the conclusion reassembling the topic—and doing something more. You will see it revealing the significance and implications of what has been learned, turning finally to look at an adjacent issue—the American firm—after its long argument about the Far East.

(30) CONCLUSION

The theoretical question underlying this paper is, What level of analysis best explains organizational structure? We argue that, on the one hand, profit and efficiency arguments are too specific and too narrow to account for different organizational forms. Economic models predict organizational structure only at the most superficial level (e.g., successful businesses seek profit). On the other hand, cultural arguments seize on such general, omnipresent value patterns as to make it difficult to account for historical and societal variations occurring within the same cultural area. Culture pervades everything and therefore explains nothing. The authority explanation provides the most successful explanation because it aims at a middle level, at explanations having historical and structural adequacy. We argue that enterprise structure represents situational adaptations of preexisting organizational forms to specific political and economic conditions. Organizational structure is not inevitable: it results from neither cultural predispositions nor specific economic tasks and technology. Instead, organizational structure is situationally determined, and, therefore, the most appropriate form of analysis is one that taps the historical dimension.

Given this conclusion, then, this analysis suggests that the key factors in explaining economic organization may not be economic, at least in economists' usual meaning of that term. Economic and cultural factors are clearly critical in understanding the growth of markets and economic enterprise, but the form or structure of enterprise is better understood by patterns of authority relations in the society. This suggests further that the economic theory of the firm may in fact be a theory based on, and only well suited to, the American firm as it has developed historically in American society. Chandler's analysis of firm formation in the United States concentrates on how firm development permitted the lowering of costs under changing market conditions. It is important to note, however, that firm development also allowed the concentration of economic interests and market control by private parties. The American state (in both the 19th and 20th centuries) exists to allow the market to function in the service of private interests; it intervenes only to prevent market breakdowns or overconcentration. This state role was not an inevitability dictated by the market, however, and emerged from a historically developed vision about the "correct" state/industry relation. The American vision has always been that of a weak state and powerful private institutions (Hamilton and Sutton 1982). Industrialists of the 19th century, unfettered by transportation and communications impediments, realized that vision with the aid of a laissez-faire government. But the American firm, like the firms in Japan, South Korea, and Taiwan, had no inevitable developmental sequence to traverse.

8.6 Styles of argument

You may have noticed in the two introductions above a feature we did not discuss—heavy clumps of documentation. The article on organizational patterns in the Far East was particularly heavily referenced. In this passage, for example, the citations nearly outweigh the text itself:

> This perspective was formerly the preserve of anthropologists (e.g., Benedict 1946; Douglas 1979; see also Orlove 1986) but is now widespread among a large number of scholars from diverse backgrounds. Studies of corporate culture (Deal and Kennedy 1982; Peters and Waterman 1982; Kanter 1983) and comparative culture studies of Japanese (Ouchi 1981, 1984; Pascale and Athos 1981; Vogel 1979), Swedish (Blumberg 1973; Foy and Fadon 1976), Yugoslavian (Adizes 1971), and other nations' industrial practices have increased manifold in the past 10 years.

These clumps of documentation situate the writers' contribution to research in relation to other knowledge on the subject. The situating citations legitimize the writers' claim to the reader's attention by showing their familiarity with the subject and their membership in a community of shared knowledge.

These citations also *locate the article on the map of established knowledge.* On this map, no spot can be occupied simultaneously by more than one article: that is, the publication must be original. Some disciplinary locations on the map are very heavily populated. In these locations, you will find the majority of scholars working. Competition for space is keen, and scholars vie for positions.

One way they can get title to a location on the map is by claiming to have *added* to existing knowledge: a space that has been recognized as unoccupied or only tentatively claimed gets filled up with new data and further reasoning. Sometimes the space has not yet been recognized: it has gone unnoticed by others. Then the scholar not only adds knowledge but also erects the structure to house it—an annex to existing structures. Another way scholars get title to a position on the map is to evict the current occupant. They show that previously established knowledge cannot claim that ground because it is faulty or undeserving in some way.

These ways of claiming territory all involve a challenge to existing patterns of knowledge. Sometimes the challenge is predictable—as is the case with additions that fill acknowledged spaces. (This is not to discount the work that contributes these additions: often, these locations have stood empty for years, waiting for the data and reasoning that only brilliant research can supply.) Sometimes the challenge is more daring and unexpected: when the writer not only adds new knowledge but also has to describe or construct the location which it will occupy, she has to make risky and difficult theoretical moves. Other times, the challenge is a bold confrontation which seeks to replace one item of existing knowledge with another: what has been assumed so far is *wrong*, and must be done away with. In each case, staking out a location means saying

what has been thought so far is inadequate to explain reality.

The Academic Reader is accustomed to this kind of argument. He expects scholars to make this claim about the inadequacy of existing knowledge. He makes this claim himself in his own writing.

Can the student writer find a place to stand on this map? Some people might argue that even graduate researchers have a hard time claiming a location, and that undergraduates have no chance in the competition. But I think this is not the best way to look at the situation. When the Academic Reader reads student essays, he isn't looking for the irresistible claim to a desirable position as much as he is looking for the style of argument and the mode of reasoning that typically makes such claims. Students can develop that style and practise that way of reasoning. The following sections will introduce you to its features.

8.6.1 The sound of a claim being staked

As we have seen, one of the functions of the scholarly introduction is to situate the document in relation to established knowledge. So, in these introductions, you will hear claims being staked; you will see writers positioning themselves on the map.

Sometimes you will hear them moving in on the targetted location aggressively. The following excerpt shows a writer taking an unusually combative stance.

(31)

> From introduction to Mike Brogden (1987), The emergence of the police — the colonial dimension. *British Journal of Criminology* 27, 1, 4-14, p. 4.

"Modern police history begins not in Britain itself but in Ireland, with the passing of the Irish Peach Preservation Force Act in 1814, when Peel was Irish Secretary." (Jeffries, 1952, p. 53)

Introduction

The Irish legislation is as arbitrary a debut of the professional police as the normative references to the Metropolitan Police Act 1829. Other organised forces had been in existence for many years prior to that date. Salaried state-appointed policing was hardly an invention of the Anglo-Saxon race. Ethnocentricity, inadequate comparative knowledge of policing, and a-historicism are the hallmarks of the Anglo-American sociology of the police. Chauvinism still prevails, among today's Reithian (Picke, 1985), as well as the Bunyanesque camp-followers (Scraton, 1985). The failure to consider the wider contours of the emergence of the professional police has been near-total.

* * *

The tunnel vision of students of British policing has frustrated an adequate account of police origins and functions. Explanations have been bound by context and by an insular historiography. One gap in that literature can be plugged. The imperial circumstances of professional policing in Britain need to be explored.

In most cases, however, the writer approaches his territory more politely. In the following excerpt (32), the writer doesn't simply claim that established views are seriously mistaken, but, instead, describes the conditions that have misled people into accepting them. He tells why people think this way: we have mistakenly assumed that the U.S. is more punitive than other nations because of the difficulties in measuring relative degrees of punitiveness among nations. (In the original, footnotes document the previous research which the writer questions; these footnotes are not included in the excerpt, but superscript numbers show the points to which they are attached.)

(32)

From the introduction to James P. Lynch (1988), A comparison of prison use in England, Canada, West Germany, and the United States: A limited test of the punitive hypothesis. *The Journal of Criminal Law and Criminology* 79, 1, 180-217, pp. 180-181.

Cross-national comparisons of crime and criminal justice practices have potential for defining limits of change in criminal justice systems. Unfortunately, the requisites for good cross-national comparisons are quite stringent. Too often such comparisons misrepresent differences in practices or account for observed differences in terms that are too general to serve as a guide for policy. At specific case in point is cross-national comparisons of incarceration rates. A number of studies have concluded that the United States is the most punitive of industrialized nations. Those studies have based their conclusions on the fact that the United States has the highest prison population per thousand.[1] In fact, although the United States has the largest per capita prison population, that statistic does not necessarily result from a more punitive policy on the part of its courts. Other factors may readily explain differences in prison populations.

One such factor is the greater extent to which the United States tends to legislate morality, as seen, for example, in its more comprehensive laws on the criminalization of prostitution, drug use, and other victimless crimes.[2] Also, the United States has a much higher crime rate than other countries.[3] Crimes in the United States are violent or otherwise serious in greater proportion than in other nations. The isolation of these and other competing explanations of observed differences in prison populations and the systematic examination of these alternatives present in other countries provide information specific enough to serve as a guide to policy-making.

The Article is intended to be a model for such specificity. It will reexamine the use of incarceration in several countries, including the United States, and, by introducing a more precise methodology than has been employed in the past, it will control for several of the most obvious competing explanations. The first section of this Article reviews earlier approaches and described the methodological modifications introduced. The second section presents the new data and the conclusions that they support.

Sometimes the writer makes only a brief gesture towards current assumptions, contradicting and overturning them swiftly.

(33)

From the introduction to Elizabeth Rapley (1987), Fénelon revisited: A review of girls' education in seventeenth century France. *Histoire sociale — Social history* 20. 40, 299-318, p. 299.

"Nothing is more neglected than the education of girls." With this critique, first published three hundred years ago, the famous educationist, Fénelon, passed a judgement on seventeenth century feminine education which has remained fixed from his time to our own. The opinion is still widely held, that there was no serious interest in feminine education in France until the end of the seventeenth century. But in fact, Fénelon's book was itself evidence of the progress which had already taken place in feminine pedagogy. A hundred years earlier few, if any, French churchmen would have concerned themselves with the schooling of girls. Interest in female instruction as a specialization was born in the seventeenth century.

Other times, the established position has to be more thoroughly contested: it is a location divided up and occupied by many productive, industrious scholars whose complex claims are not so easily overturned.

(34)

From the introduction to Bruce Curtis (1987), Preconditions of the Canadian state: Educational reform and the construction of a public in Upper Canada, 1837-1846. *The "Benevolent" State: The Growth of Welfare in Canada*. Ed. A. Moscovitch and J. Albert. Toronto: Garamond. 47-67, p. 47-48.

Recent work in the social history and political economy of North American educational reform has been situated to a large extent in a "social control" paradigm. In this paradigm educational reform is treated as a response on the part of élite groups or ruling classes to the social unrest associated with industrial capitalist development. Depending upon the particular version of the "social control" thesis one encounters, educational reform is seen as an attempt to control urban poverty and crime, an attempt to repress the menace of class struggle on the part of the working class, or both.

"Revisionism" in social history and "reproduction" theory in neo-Marxist political economy — the two main versions of the social control thesis — have produced major advances over earlier models of the nature of educational development and the role of educational institutions in capitalist societies. Revisionism opened enormous new fields of investigation for educational history, including the study of literacy and rates of school attendance, and the investigation of reform ideologies.[1] Neo-Marxist reproduction theory, which in North America was very much affected by revisionism in social history, produced thorough refutations of many propositions and conceptions derived from liberal educational theory.[2]

Yet the social control thesis has tended to mystify educational development. In explaining the transformation of capitalist societies, the social control approach has tended to abstract in a misleading manner from the concrete political context in which actual educational reforms were made. The assumption — sometimes quite valid — that key social groups agitated for educational reform in an effort to control or repress workers has led to a failure to investigate historically the educational activities of workers themselves.[3] The view of educational reform as an essentially repressive process aimed at the control of the "poor" or the working class by an "élite" or bourgeoisie has directed attention away from both the political conflict and struggle over education, and from an analysis of the content of educational reform. In fact, as I will argue, far from simply aiming to repress or neutralize the political activities of certain classes in society, educational reform in mid-nineteenth-century Upper Canada sought to reconstruct political rule in society by reconstructing the political subjectivity of the population.

Examples (31)-(34) show different ways of approaching target locations on the map of established knowledge. Recognizing this variation, we can nevertheless construct a pattern which sketches the general style of moves a writer makes as she claims territory for her research and reasoning. She

- states the currently held view;
- describes the extent of that view, saying who holds it;
- explains the sources of that view, the reasons why people think that way;
- explains why that view is an inadequate explanation of reality;
- contradicts the view, replacing it with her main claim.

The following exercise asks you to practise staking a claim by following this pattern.

Exercise

1. In Chapter Two, you read a two-page excerpt from Fiske and Hartley's Reading Television *in which the authors examined the meaning of violence on television. Stake a claim for the knowledge you acquired from that discussion by following the pattern suggested above. Begin by identifying the common assumption which Fiske and Hartley's work overturns. (You shouldn't have to look too far for this assumption: many people condemn violence on television. Reflect for a minute on their reasoning to discover the assumptions that appear to support their view.) Go on to describe the extent and origins of this assumption, and its inadequacy. Then replace this assumption with a claim derived from Fiske and Hartley's argument.*

2. At the end of Chapter Three, you made a plan for writing about stress, designing a topic which would arrange and interpret the data provided in the exercise. Now perform on these data the same operation that you performed on the Fiske and Hartley analysis of televised violence: what common assumption do the data contradict, in part or in whole? Having identified this assumption, go on to follow the pattern described above and in (1) of this exercise.

3. Apply this style of argument to other work you have done in this course. For example, does your essay on glue-sniffing actually overturn common assumptions about such practices or their treatment? You could even try applying this style of argument to your report on documentation: do your findings in fact contradict what many people would expect to be true?

8.6.2 Justifying the claim

Obviously, your contradiction of a widely-held assumption cannot stand its ground all by itself: it needs proof and development to help it hold the territory it has claimed. While the introduction will represent the main features of the argument that supports the claim, the body of the essay fully justifies the claim.

The articles which follow the claim-stakings (31)-(34) excerpted above present the writers' extensive and original research. Sometimes this research has occupied years of their lives. The undergraduate writer is not likely to have this kind of research at hand to back up her claim. Where does she find the means to hold onto the position she has taken?

She uses her reading to justify her claim: she summarizes, evaluates, interprets, compares, defines. The body of the essay calls in her sources to back her up. Having contradicted the assumption that, for example, televised violence is harmful—

> Televised violence is not necessarily the damaging and brutalizing influence on modern consciousness that many claim it to be.

—she anchors the contradiction by referring to the research which justifies it:

> As Fiske and Hartley (1982) have suggested, viewers' interpretations of violence on television differ from their interpretations of violence in real life. Viewers "read" televised images of violence as messages not about violence but about conflict between social classes and about the triumph of socially esteemed characteristics over their opposite.

In the discussion which follows the contradiction, the writer uses the strategies you have practised in this course: she summarizes and evaluates Fiske and Hartley's argument; she might compare their research to the research of other scholars; she might define an important term to promote her argument. If the writer does have original research at hand—data gathered, for example, from particular television broadcasts she has analyzed—she incorporates those data into her argument, interpreting them to show how they support this new way of looking at television violence.

8.6.3 Securing the claim

Justifying the claim takes up by far the largest part of the essay. In presenting the full version of the argument, the writer uses all the techniques you have learned to keep the reader working efficiently: reminding him of the main parts of the argument; positioning logical connectives emphatically; making statements about the argument itself, keeping the desktop clear of the muddle that disproportionate detail can create. But, finally, the reader still needs a strong conclusion to confirm his grasp of the writer's points. In this style of argument which challenges established knowledge, the conclusion reassembles the parts of the argument and explains its significance. But it often does more: it can also accommodate the overturned assumption in its confirmation of the new way of looking at things. Here, for example, the conclusion of the article on organizational patterns in the Far East finds a place for the concepts it has shown to be inadequate to explain reality.

(35) Given this conclusion, then, this analysis suggests that the key factors in explaining economic organization may not be economic, at least in economists' usual meaning of that term. Economic and cultural factors are clearly critical in understanding the *growth* of markets and economic enterprise, but the form or structure of enterprise is better understood by patterns of authority relations in the society.

Similarly, the student writer can also accommodate the old idea in her conclusions to the new argument:

(36) Common assumptions about the harmfulness of televised violence are based on our perceptions of television as a populist medium. Television often shows ordinary people using commonplace products in familiar situations — situations like adoles-

cent dating or doing household chores. This atmosphere of ordinariness and familiarity is bound to make us think that viewers witness TV violence as to some degree plausible and "realistic." But within this generally familiar realm, viewers do know how to evaluate those elements that are out-of-the-ordinary and not part of daily life—elements like high-speed car chases and shoot-outs. Viewers know how to interpret these as mythic versions of life rather than replicas of life.

You may be wondering why writers would bother to accommodate the overturned assumption after going to all the trouble of discrediting it. Admittedly, many writers don't bother calling in the rival view. They only stand their ground.

But many other writers do invite the discredited notion back into the picture, finding a place for it.

NEW IDEA   IDEA WHICH HAS BEEN
SHOWN TO BE INADEQUATE

By doing so, they show their reasonableness. After all, if the overturned assumption has held a conspicuous position on the map of established knowledge, then it must have had *something* to recommend it. And, moreover, if it was a widely held idea, many researchers and scholars counted on it, incorporating it into their own reasoning. When the writer avoids completely repudiating the widely held assumption, and invites it back into the picture, he pays his respects to established reasoning, and shows himself so familiar with that reasoning as to have earned the right to challenge it. As well, he pays his respects to fellow thinkers, who may have been counting on this idea, and will be upset to see it evicted from its established position. By positioning the idea nearby, leaving it diminished in its holdings but not entirely destitute, the writer shows himself a responsible member of the discipline.

If professional scholars are careful and respectful in their treatment of the discredited idea, student writers should probably also be careful and respectful. After all, they have fewer credentials and less status, and, consequently, may seem to have less right to challenge established knowledge. By accommodating the overturned idea, they can legitimize their position.

Exercise

In the preceding exercise, at the end of Section 8.6.1, you identified an assumption which the data on stress showed to be inadequate. Now compose a conclusion which confirms what you argue about the phenomenon of stress, but also finds a place for the common assumption you have shown to be inadequate.

Exercise

The data below are abstracted from Stanton Peele (1989), Ain't misbehavin': Addiction has become an all-purpose excuse. The Sciences *July-August, 14-21. Use them to argue against a common assumption about addiction. In your introduction, identify the common assumption, sketching its extent and origins. In your conclusion, accommodate the discredited assumption. Provide your discussion with a scholarly title.*

"Addiction"
- opiates used commonly through most of recorded history
- since 18th century, addictive effects noted
  —symptoms on withdrawal
  —symptoms of overuse

- 19th century, growing use of opiates in Europe and U.S. (physicians dispense narcotics indiscriminately; patent medicines, available over the counter, contain opium)

  _____

- U.S. goes on to lead the world in narcotics addiction
- control of drug uses shifts from physicians to government & law-enforcement officials
- during the 19th century, leading consumers of opium: white, middle-class women
- by 1920, users: poor immigrants and minority males

  _____

- 1925, Philadelphia General Hospital: first effort to study experimentally addiction in human drug users
  —addicts given placebo, or forced to exert themselves physically —> their symptoms of withdrawal disappear

  _____

- Research into narcotics use by U.S. soldiers who served in Vietnam
  —subjects of study: 500 men who had used narcotics in Vietnam
  —75% of those who reported using narcotics 5 or more times reported being addicted and suffering withdrawal symptoms when they hadn't been able to get narcotics in Vietnam
  —half of those who reported being addicted used narcotics again on their return home
  —one-eighth became readdicted

  _____

- many contemporary experiments in which rats and monkeys self-administer drugs in the laboratory
  —study at Rutgers University found it necessary to change diet of rats to get them to drink significant amounts of alcohol
  —other studies: rats have to press a bar to get narcotic injection; number of required presses is slightly increased —> rats don't press bar and don't get narcotics
  —study at Simon Fraser University: rats housed together in large cage would not choose opiate solution over water; rats isolated in small cages drank

significantly more opiate; when rats which had been isolated and forced to drink opiate liquid were placed in the large cage with other rats, they chose water

---

- observation of pharmacologist at Addiction Research Foundation, Toronto: drug user or alcoholic often continues to seek intoxicated state even after completing the period of withdrawal.

8.7 The student as scholar

The activities described and assigned in the first part of this book were activities characteristic of the student's work at university or college: summary, critical summary, and comparison are operations typically called for in writing assignments. At the same time, they are activities undertaken by professional scholars as well, as parts of larger projects of research and reasoning. By the time we got to the report on documentation, we were more fully located in the domain of scholarship itself: you gathered data first hand, devised a method for analyzing and interpreting them, presented your findings. The descriptive-definition assignment also called on you to work decisively and independently, managing data to come up with new formations and original definitions. The style of argument described in this chapter especially asks you to assume a scholarly stance and handle knowledge and argument the way scholars tend to.

But all along, we were accompanied by a sneaking suspicion: that students can't write as scholars do because they don't know enough. Scholars are supposed to know *everything* that can be known about a subject before they write *anything* about it. (We've seen the signs of this know-it-all posture in the heavy clumps of citation in introductions, and in the huge lists of references that trail from the end of scholarly articles.) If a student writer pays attention to the sneaking suspicion, and takes the know-it-all rule to heart, he can find himself in an uncomfortable position. Even after extensive research, he may find that he can't get himself to complete the assignment. (If you think you have problems with the know-it-all rule, you should see the predicaments that some graduate students get themselves in, researching and researching until the end of time, and never finishing their master's or doctoral theses.)

How can the student get out of this uncomfortable position? How can he write in a scholarly way when he doesn't know everything? Mainly, he can be realistic. The Academic Reader is realistic about what he can expect from student writing, so the student might as well be realistic, too. He can realistically identify the limits of his knowledge, and then work within those limits. He can say to himself, "I have read x, y and z. From reading these articles, which probably don't tell the whole story, but which do tell a lot, and are relatively up-to-date, I am in a position to attempt a definition of early-childhood education." When he addresses his reader, he reveals these limits:

(37) Several educationists (Hart 1982; Zolt 1918; Winter 1979) have provided developmental accounts of learning in the preschool years. From these accounts, which focus on cognitive rather than cultural or social features of learning and instruction, we can define early-childhood education as....

The reader may know of 11 or 17 or 65 "accounts of learning in the preschool years" that the writer has never heard of. So be it. The student writer can't know everything, and reasonable readers don't expect him to. What reasonable readers do expect—and respect—is a clear statement of sources and scholarly reasoning within the limits of those sources.

CHAPTER NINE

making presentations and writing examinations

During your university or college career, you will certainly have to write examinations and you will probably have to make oral presentations. These activities are like essay-writing in that they too are processes by which you turn your reading into writing. But they differ in some important ways from essay-writing. And they can cause students a lot of worry and upset. In this chapter, we will look at these writing situations in such a way as to give you means of coping with the special circumstances of making oral presentations and writing examinations.

9.1 Oral presentations

Few students seem to enjoy making oral presentations to their classmates and instructors. Even normally confident and optimistic students can feel dread or alarm at the prospect of having to be solely responsible for a block of public time during which they must command the attention of their listeners.

Their anxiety is understandable. We all know that, when we stand up in front of people and speak out at length, we draw attention to ourselves and make a long-lasting impression. The things we do during that time are remembered by our audience, and get attributed to our personalities. And, if we are overcome by the situation and do uncharacteristic things like trembling, or speaking inaudibly or incomprehensibly, or becoming confused or forgetful, we can feel that we have not conveyed our true selves.

I can't eliminate the pressure you will feel to perform well when you speak formally. It's a natural response to the reality of the situation: the setting for making an oral presentation can expose—or even create—weaknesses in ourselves we would rather not think about.

However, if you understand the communicative context in which you will have to perform, you will stand a better chance of coping with this pressure, and not letting it get you down. The following sections aim to help you acquire that understanding. In particular, they focus on a crucial and revealing fact: *written English and spoken English differ*. This difference can account for some of the difficulties that face presenters.

We have all had the experience of listening to someone read aloud a paper he or she has written:

AN ESSAY IS READ
ALOUD

Despite our best efforts to pay attention, by the time the speaker is through with his presentation, we would be hard-pressed to summarize the paper as a whole, although we may have grasped one or two points. And it's not only in the classroom that this situation arises. At scholarly meetings, academics read their papers to one another, and the periods following the presentations are reserved for discussion. But these discussion periods are sometimes sadly silent. Members of the audience don't know what to say because they are not sure that they know what was said.

As language-users, we have well developed capacities for receiving and understanding *speech*. But our capacities for understanding spoken writing are not well developed. If you write out an essay which you plan to read aloud in order to fulfill your obligation to make an oral presentation, you may save yourself from the embarrassment of being at a loss for words, but you will not succeed in engaging and convincing your listeners, because they have few strategies for understanding spoken writing.

So what *do* you do to engage and convince your audience? We will approach this question by looking at the differences between *writing* and *conversation*, and then establishing the middle ground between these two kinds of expression: formal speaking. This is a genre of communication that has its own features; once you know about them, you will be better prepared to take on formal speaking assignments with confidence rather than panic.

9.1.1 The situation: you and your reader

In conversation, your audience is in front of you and participates actively in the communicative event. Except on those unhappy occasions when one speaker dominates, conversation is a dialogue, and, as users of language, we learn the rules of turn-taking and interruption. Moreover, we respond to one another's utterances alternately and immediately, and the course of conversation is determined or negotiated by this spontaneous alternation.

TURN-TAKING IN FACE-TO-FACE COMMUNICATION

In essay writing, your audience is remote. The reader can even be unknown to you (as, for example, you and I are completely unknown to the authors of the articles excerpted throughout this book). And, whereas conversation is a dialogue, writing is a monologue. The writer necessarily dominates the event, and the reader's response to the writer's utterance is postponed—sometimes for centuries.

The formal speaking situation is like conversation in that it is *face-to-face*, but like writing in that it is a *monologue*. If you ignore the face-to-face element of the situation and conduct yourself as if you were all by yourself in this enterprise—as you are when you write—your speech will seem more unnatural than it has to.

You can overcome part of the unnaturalness of a face-to-face monologue by directly acknowledging the social situation—the physical presence of your audience.

- Look at your audience instead of your papers.
- Use "I" and "you" frequently, as signs that your are properly aware—and respectful—of your listeners' presence.

Even though the nature of the occasion denies the audience the normal rights of turn-taking and response, you don't need to add insult to injury by behaving as if your listeners weren't there.

9.1.2 Structure: planning, repetition, and proof

Conversation is unplanned. Although we may have in mind general goals for our talk, and before important situations we may figure out what we want to say, we are unlikely to set out into conversations with an exact notion of the course we will make them take.

A SPEAKER ENCOUNTERS RESISTANCE WHEN HE TRIES TO PLAN OVERTLY THE COURSE OF THE CONVERSATION

The structure of conversation is associative: one thing leads to another, with each participant contributing to the direction of the talk according to what comes to mind on the spot. Partly because of this associative structure, and partly because of there being more than one contributor to the discussion, conversations can end up in surprising, unexpected, or unforeseeable places.

Academic writing, on the other hand, is planned: the writer has a specific destination in sight, and announces and enforces his intentions in various ways: titles, headings, topic sentences, paragraph organization. The structure of the essay is logical rather than associative: instead of one thing haphazardly reminding speakers of something else they could say, claims are organized according to principles of generality and detail, statement and proof.

Your listeners, who are experienced readers of academic prose and experienced conversationalists, will not be so skilled in *hearing* discourse that is organized logically rather than associatively. At the same time, the oral situation will deprive them of many of the clues that they ordinarily depend on in understanding *planned* discourse: titles, headings, paragraphs, and so on. Even the physical dimensions of the written text can help readers orient themselves. For example, readers can know when they're nearing the end of an article because they can glance ahead and see the list of references appearing on the next page. Knowing that they are so close to the end, they can interpret that part of the article as "conclusion" and pay special attention to the kinds of things the writer is saying by way of confirming his argument. But *listeners* can't glance ahead to find out how much text is left. This absence of clues as to length can explain listeners' restlessness as an oral presentation draws on: is the end near? Is this conclusive material that deserves special attention?

When you speak formally, you will have a specific destination in mind, and your oral presentation will be planned discourse. But your audience will be hearing it rather than reading it. Clearly, you can't replicate in speech the devices that normally make readers' understanding of planned discourse easier.

But you can help your listeners by supplying some of the kinds of statements about the argument that we looked at in Chapter Seven. Let your listeners know what you are up to.

"I will begin by giving some background...."
"Later I will...."

"To show you what this means, I will describe...."
"In the last part of this discussion, I will be...."
"To conclude, I am going to...."

Just as you can't glance ahead in conversations to find out how much is left to go, you also can't glance back to confirm your interpretation of what has gone before. This may account for the frequency of repetition in conversation. Participants repeat earlier parts of the conversation not only to get the facts straight but also to establish mutually agreed-upon topics.

When we get to Honolulu, I'm going to do a lot of shopping. My thongs are worn out. Do you have thongs?

I have nice thongs. So, you're going to Honolulu?

Yes. Honolulu.

CONVERSATIONALISTS USE REPETITION TO CONFIRM WHAT HAS GONE BEFORE

A coherent essay will use repetition, too, to confirm the reader's interpretation of detail. But, in an essay, readers have further means of confirming their understanding of the material that's being presented: they can *slow* the pace of their reading, dwelling on important points to get them firmly positioned on their mental desktop.

The material you offer in an oral presentation will always be more complicated than that which shows up in informal conversation. So the need which conversationalists normally feel for confirmation will be even more acute among your listeners—as pressing as the needs of readers of complex arguments. Yet, unlike readers, your listeners won't have the chance to slow the pace and dwell on complexities. Nor will they be able to interrupt you to ask for confirmation the way of the owner of the nice thongs did.

- *Anticipate* those areas where your listeners would ask for or look for confirmation if they could: transitions from one sub-topic to another, for example; the middle of long stretches of detail, for another example.

- *Repeat yourself* more often than you think you should, to help your listeners keep important material in mind. Use strategic summaries often.

In conversation, unsupported opinions are plentiful. Unproven notions and stubborn attitudes abound, and rarely are conversationalists asked to support their claims. When a participant asks for substantiating evidence, the request can seem rude.

A CONVERSATIONALIST'S REQUEST FOR PROOF SEEMS RUDE.

Academic essays, on the other hand, must provide full proof for their major assertions: scholarly writing depends on the complicated systems of development and evidence we have examined in this book.

The claims you make in your oral presentations must also be capable of proof. Your audience will not expect to hear you express unfounded notions or commonplace ideas with little basis in fact. At the same time, however, because the situation makes your audience listeners rather than readers, they will have a hard time following the rather complex evidence that usually supports claims in scholarly writing. Thorough scholarly proof, as we have seen, is usually lengthy—and listeners' short-term memory is limited. You need to develop strategies for dealing with these conditions.

- Present your evidence selectively. Don't exert yourself to load your listeners with all available evidence—most of it will be lost to them as it slides off the mental desktop randomly. Put your efforts instead into picking a manageable handful of especially striking evidence.

- If examples are appropriate to your subject, choose two or three to present thoroughly. A listener's need for illustrative examples is even more acute than the reader's because the listener can't stop to dwell on complicated, high-level generalization and abstractions until they sink in.

- Try a narrative technique, telling the story of how the evidence led you to the ideas you are offering. Listeners seem better able to absorb stories than any other form of discourse. Even very young children can pay attention to and remember information presented in narrative form, and you may be able to use this liking for stories to make the proof for your claims more accessible to your listeners.

- If they are compatible with your subject, use visual aids—handouts, overhead projections, blackboard drawings—to express important elements of your evidence. This way, you make your listeners temporarily into readers. (Numbers are especially eligible for visual presentation because lists of figures are extremely difficult for listeners to grasp.) But remember that the members of your audience can't pay attention to you at the same time as they read, so don't put too much reading on the visual aid, and don't announce crucial points while your audience is having its first look at graphic material.

9.1.3 Style: the grammars of speech and writing

The English that we are used to hearing differs from the English we are used to reading and writing. While most writing is composed of observable sentences made from identifiable clauses, linguists have trouble identifying the same kinds of sentences and clauses in speech because speech contains so many bit and pieces—sentence fragments and false-starts and trailing-off endings. And conversation relies on "fillers" that stop up the pauses which speakers of English seem to find intolerable: "yes, well...," "so-o-o...," "hm-m...," "well then...." And noun phrases are much lighter in speech: whereas writers have time to plan heavy noun phrases, speakers are more likely to scatter attributes across several clauses. Below, passage (1) presents a heavy noun phrase more characteristic of writing, while (2)'s lighter noun phrases resemble those of speech.

(1) <u>Extensive longitudinal and cross-cultural research including interviews with and observations of hundreds of children</u> led Kohlberg to conclude that moral development moves through three levels.

(2) <u>Extensive research</u> led Kohlberg to conclude that moral development moves through three levels. <u>This research</u> was both longitudinal and cross-cultural. <u>It</u> included interviews with hundreds of children, and observations of them too.

Although your listeners may have got used to coping with heavy noun phrases in their reading, they won't be used to hearing them. Likewise, they will not be accustomed to hearing the long, complicated and impeccable sentence structures of written English, relentlessly proceeding without fragments and false-starts.

At the same time, however, your oral presentation will not have the air of authority you want to give it if it's full of false-starts and sayings that dwindle into nothing.

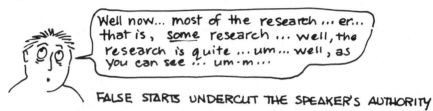

Well now... most of the research ... er... that is, some research ... well, the research is quite ...um... well, as you can see ... um·m ...

FALSE STARTS UNDERCUT THE SPEAKER'S AUTHORITY

Yet your audience won't be prepared to hear and understand an essay read out loud, because listeners aren't used to hearing the complicated sentence structures of writing. So your formal speaking must have a style halfway between conversation and essay. How do you arrive at that style?

Don't try to achieve that style by writing out "natural" speech—with fragments, fillers, false starts, and so on—and then reading it. Composing "natural" speech is a task so difficult that even gifted dramatists sometimes fail to overcome its inherent problems, and certainly it takes an experienced actor to then deliver even a skilfully composed script. Instead, rely on you own capacities as a speaker.

- Compose your presentation in *note form*—phrases and key words rather than complete sentences. This will force you to express yourself in a readily understandable conversational style.

- Make your notes exceptionally *legible*. This will prevent you from losing your place and having to resort to fillers and false starts or having to peer at your notes to pick up where you left off.

Let me see...hm-m..., where was I?... mumble, mumble, mumble...

A SPEAKER LOSES HER PLACE

To be sure, there are obstacles in the way of making a successful oral presentation. The situation overturns the normal conditions of turn-taking, response, and requests for confirmation people are used to when they get information in a face-to-face situation. At the same time, they are deprived of the means they normally use for absorbing complicated information from a written text: they can't go at their own pace, pausing and reflecting in order to refine their understanding. And there are no paragraphs or headings and divisions to help them orient themselves.

But you can overcome these obstacles if you keep your listeners' needs in mind. Besides, there are also advantages to this kind of face-to-face situation. Voice inflection, physical gestures, facial expression—all these means for emphasis and encouragement that are missing from the page are available to you when you have the chance to get your message across face-to-face. Whereas the essay-writing situation can isolate writers from readers in an atmosphere of somewhat arid neutrality and impersonality, the oral presentation, despite its relative formality, can put the speaker in touch with his audience in a way that's stimulating for both listener and speaker.

9.2 Examinations

In this book, we have identified certain standards of coherence and clarity appropriate to university or college essays. And we've looked at the means by which these standards are met: planning that generates complex rather than simple topics; orderly movements through the levels of generality; repeating important points to secure them in a prominent place on the reader's desktop; screening word choice and sentence structure to remove unnecessary demands on the reader's resources; composing introductions that make the argument visible to the reader and conclusions that confirm her interpretation of detail. These activities are time-consuming. They take a lot of planning, revision, and deliberation.

Exam-writing situations seem almost by definition to deny you the opportunity to meet academic writing standards that are achieved in the ways I've just mentioned. There's no time to plan, deliberate, revise—no time to coax a complex topic out of hiding and then devise effective ways of communicating it to the reader. Having to take an examination that calls for essay writing can make students feel just as desperate as they do when they have to make an oral presentation. University writing has to be clear and coherent; clarity and coherence take time to achieve; examinations deny writers time. It seems a pretty discouraging situation.

Fortunately, it's not as discouraging as it looks. For one thing, standards of expression are somewhat relaxed in examination situations. For another thing, there are ways to prepare yourself.

9.2.1 Guessing

Sometimes students prepare for examinations by trying to guess what topics will come up.

Their guesses are not likely to be too far off the mark, if they've been paying attention in class, and they've noticed the instructor's inclinations. Exam questions are rarely a complete surprise.

However, the guessing approach can lead you to put all your eggs in one basket. When you get to the exam, and you don't find the questions you predicted, you may feel desperately unprepared for the questions that are asked.

Prediction has some virtues as a way of preparing to write exam essays: it forces you to review the course in an analytical way, looking for main issues. But prediction is not as good a method of preparation as one which makes you more flexible—ready to write about anything.

9.2.2 Ready for anything

Compare examinations to job interviews. Well-prepared candidates can't possibly predict all the questions interviewers will ask. Every recruitment situation is in some ways unique and has unforeseeable qualities. The candidate who tries to force his pre-packaged answers on the interviewer will not make a good impression. Interviewers want to see a candidate respond to the situation as it is, not as the candidate imagined it.

But well-prepared candidates will go into the interview having organized their ideas about their own experience and qualifications, and having concise and convincing ways of describing them. And well-prepared candidates will have something to say, too, about the institution or firm that is hiring—ideas and questions based on good information. Successful candidates go into interviews *ready to talk:* they have ways of expressing what they know about themselves and what they have discovered about the employment situation. Either they have a lot of experience talking about these things, or they find ways—in advance—of expressing their knowledge and ideas.

You want to go into the examination situation in the same way—ready to write about what you know, having organized your knowledge beforehand. You can do this in several ways.

- *Write summaries of important material.* Summarizing will force you to identify the gist of readings and lectures, and to find efficient ways of expressing that gist. The time you spend devising these efficient ways of expression beforehand will be time saved for thinking and writing during the exam session. Moreover, writing out coherent summaries beforehand will force you to form clear logical connections between parts of the material you are studying. These connections are bound to be useful in composing coherent arguments during the exam session.

- *Find the high-level abstractions which name the crucial issues addressed by the course.* Actually, this can be part of the summarizing activity, but it deserves special mention because of the role abstract categories have in helping you manage information and retrieve details from your memory. (Do you remember the party-game tray of random, untitled items that defied recall? You don't want to find yourself in an exam trying to remember a party-game tray of unmanaged details.) Preparing to write an exam on 19th century European history, for example, you can gather otherwise scattered details about workers in England under "labour militancy and industrialization." This will help you not only in recalling specifics, but also in planning your essay in direct response to the exam question: you have a ready-made topic element that you can manipulate with other topic elements to develop an answer to the question at hand.

- *Write down your ideas about the material covered in the course.* Don't wait until the exam session to articulate what you've learned: go into the examination having something you want to say. Your exam answer must always relate to the exam questions, but these questions can still be vehicles by which you express broadly and emphatically what you've learned.

All these preparatory activities involve writing, and that's the best way to approach essay-type examinations: get ready to write by writing. Then you won't be struck dumb by the examination page, and the examination will only be the last step in a writing process that began under hospitable conditions—at home, with your books and notes around you, with the opportunity to review and speculate, and the time to discover and articulate the meaning of what you know.

If you make examinations the final step in your own writing process, you won't be at their mercy, humbly praying for a question you can answer. Instead, you will use the special conditions of exam writing—the somewhat relaxed standards of expression—as your opportunity to express yourself as fully as possible.

Printed in Canada